THE BEST I RECALL

Charles N. Prothro Texana Series

THE BEST
I RECALL

A Memoir

GARY CARTWRIGHT

University of Texas Press

Austin

Requests for permission to reproduce material
from this work should be sent to:
Permissions
University of Texas Press
P.O. Box 7819
Austin, TX 78713-7819
http://utpress.utexas.edu/index.php/rp-form

∞ The paper used in this book meets the minimum requirements of
ANSI/NISO Z39.48-1992 (R1997) (Permanence of Paper).

LIBRARY OF CONGRESS CATALOGING-IN-PUBLICATION DATA
Cartwright, Gary, 1934–, author.
The best I recall : a memoir / Gary Cartwright. — First edition.
pages   cm — (Charles N. Prothro Texana series)
Includes index.
ISBN 978-0-292-74907-8 (cloth : alk. paper)
ISBN 978-1-4773-0745-8 (library e-book)
ISBN 978-1-4773-0539-3 (nonlibrary e-book)
1. Cartwright, Gary, 1934–   2. Sportswriters—Texas—Biography.
3. Authors, American—Texas—20th century—Biography.
I. Title.   II. Series: Charles N. Prothro Texana series.
F391.4.C37A3   2015
976.4′0630973—dc23
[B]
2014047159

doi:10.7560/749078

The only things important are what you remember.
JEAN RENOIR

PREFACE

I F YOU ARE WONDERING HOW I CHOSE THE book's title, *The Best I Recall*, it's because during its writing I used that term repeatedly while trying to dredge up scraps of autobiographical detail. Some of what you are about to read, then, is drawn, sometimes word for word, sometimes in fragments, from things I wrote years ago—which in turn sometimes depended on remembering things that happened even longer back in my fifty-year career. It's been a jagged, uneven journey and now that I'm attempting to recall the details, I'm finding that my memory is so badly flawed that I can't tell you what I had for breakfast.

Everyone who makes it into their seventies has trouble remembering, but the problems are particularly acute when you are trying to assemble a coherent recollection of events and people and make clear what is fact and what is fiction. I have always had trouble along these lines and have concluded that fact is often indistinguishable from fiction, especially given the gravity of the human condition. This is particularly true for people like me, who have spent a fair amount of time rebelling against sobriety. Therefore, each reader must decide if the stories have a ring of truth. Try to think of it as a game where there are no losers.

THE BEST I RECALL

1

P EOPLE ASK HOW I GOT TO BE A WRITER AND
I tell them I can't remember. That's not entirely true. The
how part is a little foggy but I remember the why, and I
believe the how and the why might be connected. In high school,
I loved writing wild, disconnected passages in my notebook, plea-
suring in the freedom of expression without the burden of too
much thinking or the nasty exactitude of passing or failing grades.
I did most of my writing in study hall, an adjunct of the library at
Arlington High School, enjoying the solitude and the musty smell
of old volumes, secretly pleased at the sense of order and permanence they represented. Writing in my notebook was an effortless
pursuit, and I thrilled as the words came flying off my pen like
sweat off a wild pony.

I never dreamed that anyone would actually read the gibber-
ish in those notebooks, but to my great surprise Miss Emma Ous-
ley, who taught English and journalism at AHS, not only read
what I'd done but was impressed. She called me aside one day and
said, "You know what, Gary? You have a talent for writing." Well,
bless me, until that moment nobody had ever connected me with
that word—"talent." I was momentarily thunderstruck. So off I
stumbled, on a slow and haphazard journey searching for something I couldn't understand but instinctively loved—reporting the

happenings of my surroundings and writing about them in short, coherent sentences. You know, like Hemingway and those guys.

Journalism, English, and history were my favorite classes. I still love to read history and struggle with its meaning, which seems to change as I age. It's not history itself that changes, of course; it's our perception of history. I attribute my awareness of this phenomenon not to my own progress as a deep thinker but to some inbred skepticism that causes me to doubt and double-check what I hear and see. This doubt, I've come to believe, is partly a by-product of the mediocre quality of my primary education in the Arlington school system. I've been obliged to learn and unlearn at the same time. I'll give you an example. I had a history teacher in the seventh grade, Miss Peggy Bayless, who taught us that the WPA—a social services agency that provided jobs for the unemployed—stood for "We Piddle Around." Though I was fairly sure she was joking, I sensed that she was attempting to shape us with caustic ideology—that her core message was a warning that the only people who succeed in life are those who don't give a damn about the weak and helpless. I wasn't nearly bright enough to express such thoughts back then, so I concentrated on something simple—sports. I wasn't talented enough to be very good at sports, but I had a gift for writing about them and hence took the path of least resistance into the study of journalism.

I OWE MY CAREER TO A LOT OF PEOPLE, FIRST of all to my dad, Roy Cartwright. Daddy grew up in Denton, not far from the campus of what was then North Texas State. He hungered for a college education, but his own father thought college was a waste of time and refused to put up the money. Daddy never forgot that slight and blamed his limited education for his inability to get a top management job at the defense plant where he worked during World War II. I stayed in college mainly to please him—and to spite that awful old man who was my grandfather—and eventually got a degree, a BA in journalism.

I still think about Daddy quite often, and about Mama and

Granny. Granny Hawk, everyone called her—even when she was a young woman, because she was always nagging young'uns to wash their hands and change their underwear. Her family name was Izora Shaw. She was an orphan who grew up somewhere around Denton and married three times. Her first husband was Eugene Hufford, who died of blood poisoning at an early age after cutting his finger on a piece of rusty tin. Had she only known about the curative powers of zinc oxide, Granny believed, she might have saved him. There was always a tube of zinc oxide near her bedroom table, and I keep some on hand to this very day. The Huffords had one child, my uncle Gene. Uncle Gene and his wife, my aunt Dot (short for Dorothy), had three children, my cousins Paul, Larry, and Daisy, my playmates growing up. Granny's second husband was my grandfather, Will Cartwright, who I never got to like, much less love. The marriage to Will Cartwright didn't last long. Then she married a mechanic named Bill Hawk, who used to race motorcycles and midget autos. Bill Hawk was the grandfather I got to know and love, a remarkable man that I'll always hold close to my heart.

Granny and Bill more or less raised me, in the tiny oil town of Royalty, just south of Monahans and some distance north of Fort Stockton. They had moved there about 1938–39, when Bill secured a franchise to operate a Texaco station. The station became a sort of community center. We followed them to Royalty, because the oil field was the only place my dad could find work during the Depression. We lived in a pair of wood-frame houses, next door to each other. This model of house was called a shotgun house, because it was claimed you could fire a shotgun in the front door and the shot would zoom all the way to the back door without touching anything. The houses were enclosed in a fenced compound, to keep us safe from the riffraff that collected around oil fields. Bill's Texaco station was next door to our compound, just beyond the fence, and it quickly became my refuge. Bill and his gang, especially the amiable Punk Weaver, watched over me, as did the two pit bulls that they maintained, Old Jack and his pup, Boss. I had my own dog for a time, a little Boston terrier named Zipper, but he got out of the fence one day and got killed by a car. The pit bulls were much smarter than Zipper, and of much sturdier stock.

Granny and Bill Hawk made it their job to spoil me at every opportunity. One of my earliest memories is going with them to see *Gone With the Wind*, at a movie house in Fort Stockton. I slept through the entire film, snuggled against Bill, inhaling the wonderful aromas of tobacco and aftershave lotion. He was a stubby, muscular man with soft white hair and a scruffy beard. He usually wore a green Texaco uniform, except when we went out; then he put on a suit and tie. When we were at home, I took a nap every afternoon next to Granny, in her big bed, under her large fan, a habit I continued until I was nearly grown. But I loved hanging out with Bill and the guys at the service station. Somehow Bill and his friends always had time for me. He was also chief of the town's volunteer fire department and maintained the fire truck in a shed next to the Texaco station. How many kids have their own fire truck as a plaything? Bill had someone make me a little fireman's uniform—a raincoat, boots, and fireman's hat. I also had a baseball uniform, symbolizing that I was the batboy (actually, the mascot) of the Atlantic Oil Company team. Bill managed the team, Daddy played second base, and Punk Weaver was the star pitcher. Punk was everyone's best friend, a tough but gentle man who could play the harmonica and the guitar and whistle through his teeth. One day he mysteriously disappeared and they discovered his body a few days later, under a bridge on the Pecos River. He had been robbed and murdered by a villain named Hugo White. I don't know if I ever saw Hugo White, but for many years that name haunted me and conjured up dark images of evil. On rare occasions, the images are still with me.

When World War II started, suddenly there were jobs in the defense plants all over Dallas and Fort Worth. That's when we moved to Arlington. At the same time, Bill and Granny bought a farm near Keller, north of Fort Worth, and for a couple of years the farm became my favorite place to be. There were some cows that I learned to milk, some piglets that needed chasing, and a yard full of chickens and turkeys, some of which I named. Granny and Bill lived in a small farmhouse, heated by a potbellied stove, while they built a much larger and grander house next door. A creek ran through the property, in spots deep enough to swim. Then one Sunday while my mom and my younger sister, Gail, were at church, there was a phone call, telling us that Bill had dropped dead of a heart attack. That's the last time I remember crying. I guess that's when I began to grow up, when I learned that the people you love won't always be there. It's a hard lesson, but it's one that requires mastering. Bill Hawk: I loved to say his name. I've always intended to write about him, and I think I just did.

THE TEXAS WHERE I GREW UP WAS STILL RIGIDLY segregated. There were two Hispanics in my class all through grade school and high school, and no blacks. With one memorable exception, the only blacks I saw were those on the street, or the maids or handymen who worked for my parents or neighbors, or the customers in the drugstore where I worked.

The clerks in the drugstore made a private joke of this one old black man who showed up nearly every morning to buy chewing tobacco. "I wants a plug of Brown Mule," he'd say, placing a dime on the counter. We didn't laugh in his face, of course, but when one of us said in dialect, "I wants a plug of Brown Mule," it always got a laugh.

The exception was a stunner, a real eye-opener. It involved my paper route, delivering the *Fort Worth Press*, a newspaper that I would later work for. My route included a section northwest of the railroad tracks that divided Arlington, a section I didn't know existed until I got my paper route. It was a treeless ghetto of unpaved streets, falling-down shacks, abandoned cars, and run-down businesses—known locally, of course, as Niggertown. Though I never felt threatened, I was shocked to discover this world so nearby and yet so startlingly different from my own. Pedaling my bike through those forlorn streets made me feel uneasy, but more than that it made me feel sad, seeing people so helpless, so abandoned. There was always the smell of frying meat, the sights of skinny dogs sleeping in mud puddles and women hanging out wash. A feeling of hopelessness hung over the neighborhood like a black curtain.

MY TIMING, OR MAYBE IT'S JUST LUCK, HAS always been above average—right place, right time, right group of friends. After five semesters of college—two at Arlington State, three at the University of Texas—I began to review just what it was I thought I was doing. I was getting an education, of course, as my parents wanted me to do, but the financial strain of keeping me in school was taking a toll on them. My dad was working six and sometimes seven days a week at General Dynamics in Fort Worth, helping produce the B-36 bomber for the Air Force, an occupation in which he took considerable pride and much pleasure. But I suspected (rightly, as it turned out) that the pressure was killing him. Mama worked in a fancy women's dress shop in Arlington and took occasional buying trips to New York to stock up on the latest fashions, a job that made her happy but sometimes caused friction in their marriage: I think my dad felt a sense of shame that his wife had to help support us. We enjoyed a comfortable family life, with our share of luxuries—including a vacation trip to Mexico City the month after I graduated from high school—but I felt some sense of guilt for taking far more than I was contributing to the general weal. My grades were barely passing, and I had no idea what the future would bring or how to handle it.

I thought seriously about dropping out of school and joining the navy. Fortunately, an older friend named George Mills convinced me that this was a very bad idea. A graduate of an Arlington High class several years ahead of mine, George had spent four years in the navy and understood the sacrifice that many years in the service could extract from a young man. "If you really want a break from your education," he advised me, "volunteer for the draft. You'll spend two years instead of four, and that way you can finish college on the GI Bill." The Korean War had ended by this time, but the government was still drafting men for the army and the GI Bill was still helping support our generation. Some years later I used it to finance a house as well as to pay for an education and was (and still am) grateful, and proud to have served. Compulsory military service is an ancient tradition, dating back to Athenian democracy, and I was sorry to see our country do away with it. A conscription army is good for the nation, and it is good for young people, both men and women. Military service gives us an appreciation of a larger world. It teaches us to live and work with compatriots from all parts of the country, from all linguistic groups and social strata, contributing greatly to national cohesion. Inspired by George Mills's advice, I volunteered to be drafted in the late fall of 1953, and a few months later, when I received a notice to report for induction, I felt a curious sense of liberation. Whatever was about to happen, it would be an adventure.

On the bus to Fort Bliss in El Paso, where I would do basic training, I met a new friend, H. G. Wells, from Tulia. H.G. was no relation to the famous writer whose name he shared, but he was a talented, innovative, very likable young man. I learned that he had been president of his class at North Texas State—or maybe president of the student body, I forget which—and he had an upbeat attitude about life, the army included. "We ought to use the army for our own good," he told me. "Don't let it use us." I stuck close to H.G. all through basic training. One afternoon as we were mopping the orderly room, we realized that our mops and buckets gave us the chance to move freely about the base. The army had furnished us with ideal props to disguise nefarious intentions. Who would think to stop and question two buck privates with mops and buckets? So we mopped our way to the PX, where we drank beer for a couple of hours before mopping back to the company compound, completely undetected. In the weeks that followed, we repeated this ruse several times.

I gradually realized that I was making peace with the army, and vowed to guard that peace with care. One very hot afternoon as we were returning from a twenty-five-mile march, I noticed with some disdain that a lot of the men were dropping out. Some of them were understandably exhausted, but I suspected that most were habitual slugs, naturally lazy creatures whose talents should be limited to nothing more demanding than scrubbing pots and pans or pulling all-night guard duty. While contemplating such unworthy thoughts, I missed a step, tripped, and fell on my butt.

Deeply embarrassed, I was scrambling to my feet when Corporal Roberto Gonzales came running in my direction. Gonzales was a popular member of the cadre charged with training our company, Dog 8. Recently returned from the war in Korea, he was a veteran of combat and had earned a Purple Heart, a Silver Star, and other decorations. Gonzales was a good guy, worthy of respect.

"Cartwright!" he shouted. "You okay?"

"Yeah, I'm fine," I told him. "I just tripped."

"You need to sit down," he decided.

"No, really, I'm okay. I need to get back to my men." I don't know where that came from—*get back to my men*—a line from some movie, I imagine. I just blurted it out, but it seemed to touch Corporal Gonzales's sense of honor.

He took my arm and led me to a bench, across the road from a Dairy Queen.

"Stay here," he told me. "I'll get you something cold to drink." Before I could protest, he was off on his mission of mercy, and I was sitting with my M1 rifle across my lap, watching my column of men disappear down the road, rifles at right shoulder arms, wondering, What should I do now?

When Corporal Gonzales returned, he had not only a cold drink, but a jeep to transport me the final few miles to our company area. The other slugs who had fallen out were hurried into the back of a two-ton truck, which would transport them in shared disgrace, but I had my own private jeep. As I started to crawl into the back of it, however, I accidentally banged my knee against the side of the vehicle, hard enough that for a couple of days I walked with a genuine limp. By the time we got back to the company compound, I was half convinced that I was a casualty of some heroic action, whose details I couldn't exactly remember.

My heroics were rewarded a few days later when the company commander informed me that I had been chosen Soldier of the

Month for Dog 8. One of the benefits of the honor was a three-day pass, a luxury almost unheard of for guys in basic training. Once I had enjoyed three days of freedom (most of it in Juárez, Mexico, just across the border) I would begin preparing to compete against soldiers from other companies for the title of Brigade Soldier of the Month. Should I prevail at brigade level, I would advance to the big show—competing for Soldier of the Month for all of Fort Bliss. Aware that my company commander regarded this as a feather in his own cap, I suggested that I might better prepare for the task ahead if I could work with my pal, H. G. Wells. He agreed. So while our Dog 8 comrades were marching and drilling, H.G. and I sat in the cool of our hut, sipping lemonade and memorizing army manuals.

Brigade competition turned out to be ridiculously easy, especially for anyone with ROTC training—a few questions about the M1 rifle and the military chain of command. I passed with flying colors. I would have gone all the way except for a trick question at base level. They asked me to identify what I took to be a drawing of an American eagle. Only in this case it wasn't an American eagle—it was the insignia of a full colonel. Who would have guessed?

MY TIME IN THE ARMY ALSO PROVIDED MY FIRST up-close encounter with black people. President Truman had ordered the army integrated a few years earlier, and I enjoyed being in a company with black soldiers, most of whom were friendly and good-natured. There was, however, one memorable exception—a particularly obnoxious, thickly muscled guy named Prather, who wore a permanent scowl and shouted out vile oaths as we marched in formation. His favorite phrase was "motherfucker," a term I had never heard before. Prather apparently saw it as his mission to indoctrinate us in the language of his culture. Today the term is fairly common, but at the time I was shocked and deeply offended by the words, as were most of the others in our company. Prather was universally hated, and we all tried our best to avoid him.

One day, however, I found myself alone with Prather, the two of us assigned to dig a foxhole. I realized at once that he didn't intend to do any of the work, so I took my entrenching tool and began digging while he sat to one side, mouthing obscenities and making occasional threats against me and against the world in general. At that moment I actually feared for my life, something I had never felt before or since. Some device of defensive mentality seized control of my brain, and without realizing what I was doing I began formulating a strategy to save my life. I waited until Prather was looking away and then I hit him against the side of the head with the shovel. I hit him as hard as I could. He dropped to his knees, then collapsed facedown in the dirt. For a moment I thought he was dead. Then I heard him moan.

He tried to stand, but fell back down, rolled over, and covered his battered head with his hands. Finally, he managed to get on his hands and knees and crawl a short way. A drill sergeant who heard the confrontation ran in our direction just as Prather was again attempting to stand. "What happened over here?" he shouted. I didn't say anything, but Prather brushed sand out of his eyes and said, "I fell down, motherfucker! Mind you own business."

That was the end of Prather, at least for me. He disappeared from our company later that day, and we never heard of him again. Far as I know, he recovered. I still can't believe that I hit a man with a shovel, that I tried to kill him, but unless you have felt your life threatened, you don't know what you might do. I've thought about this many times, and I know that the fact that Prather was black somehow intensified my sense of danger. Would the same thing have happened if he had been white? I don't know.

A FEW MONTHS LATER, DURING THE SECOND HALF of basic training at Fort Belvoir, Virginia, I made friends with a black guy from Baltimore named Francis. The friendship began by happenstance. We were marching in formation, Francis on my right flank, when we passed a barracks where a bunch of GIs were playing with a pet raccoon. We looked at each other and I saw on his face a grin of bemused irony. "Did you see what I saw?" he said.

"Looked like a coon," I told him.

"It did," he admitted. "A damn coon!"

We both started laughing, at what, I've never been sure. But we became friends at that moment. Francis lived in Baltimore, and a week or so after the coon sighting he invited me to come home with him for the weekend. I accepted, grateful for the invitation; I'd never had a black friend or visited a black home. The next day, however, he came to me in great distress. He had apparently talked to his family and they had decided my visit was not a good idea. Nobody said it was because I was white, but it didn't need saying. Francis and I remained friends, but after that there was always a distance between us, a coolness that neither of us could overcome. After basic training, I never saw him again. I have never forgotten him, however.

Over the years I've had a few other black friends, but none of the friendships went anywhere or lasted long, which I deeply regret. I have come to accept it as the way of the world for people of my age and background.

AT FORT BELVOIR, I WAS IN ARMY SUPPLY SCHOOL, where I finished first in my class and got to spend my weekends in Washington, D.C. Though I hated the idea of wasting my army career in some musty supply room, I knew that new opportunities would soon present themselves. At this point in my life I was desperate to explore the world, and I applied for permanent assignment to bases in either France or Germany. I thought my odds of seeing Europe were good because a friend from high school, Kenneth "Light Dry" Latham—so called because he once exclaimed, "I prefer a light dry wine"—was in charge of brigade personnel where duty assignments were issued. By this time my parents had moved from Arlington to Fort Worth so my dad would be closer to his work at General Dynamics. Light Dry thought he was doing me a favor by assigning me to permanent duty at Wolters Air Force Base in Mineral Wells, a one-hour drive west of Fort Worth. With a sinking heart, I read my orders: instead of spending the next year and a half drinking wine in Paris, Prague, or Berlin, I could drink mineral water in a tumbledown resort on the edge of the Texas desert.

As things worked out, Wolters AFB wasn't half bad. Because I could type, I was assigned to the orderly room of an engineering company. The mission of our company was building landing strips for a nonexistent fleet of military aircraft, but like most everything else in the peacetime army, thousands of people spent thousands of hours doing almost nothing—at least nothing that contributed to national defense. Go along and get along, that was the ticket. I knew a good thing when I saw one. As a company clerk, I was exempt from KP, guard duty, and other unpleasant tasks. Instead, I was assigned to write letters for the first sergeant and the company commander, draw fire-prevention posters, and once a month strap on a .45 pistol and guard the company payroll. I also got to preview bulletins from base headquarters, and that's how I discovered that the base swimming pool was looking for Red Cross–certified lifeguards. I had just such credentials, thanks to a Red Cross course I had taken after my first year of college. Moreover, I was a certified Red Cross swimming instructor, which gave me authority to train other swimmers as lifeguards. On the basis of these qualifications, I was reassigned to temporary duty as chief lifeguard of Wolters AFB.

I spent my final summer in the army working on my tan and teaching the wives and daughters of base personnel how to swim. I also struck up a romance with the smart and attractive daughter of a master sergeant. Kay Smith was still in high school and three or four years my junior. Her father, the hard-boiled master sergeant, did all he could to break up our romance, which of course only made it more exotic and attractive. He knew, however, that time was on his side: in five or six months my hitch would end, I would be discharged, and Kay would become just one more thing I had to leave behind. Though what happened next was far more complex than me getting discharged and forgetting Kay, I have to admit he was essentially correct.

Approaching my twenty-third birthday, I was caught up in a

vortex of competing forces, none of which I fully understood. Several of us in my company decided to take night courses at Texas Christian University, whose campus was about an hour away, in Fort Worth. The army encouraged soldiers who had been drafted out of college to continue their education and paid for the classes. We were all short-timers, meaning we were counting the days until we were civilians again. I was thinking of returning to the University of Texas and maybe seeking a law degree, but TCU was an easy and attractive alternative. So was studying journalism. I was writing a weekly column for my base newspaper and enjoying the freedom to speak my mind, however limited that was. I had entered a short story in a base contest and won second place, which pleased and thrilled me and made me look again at what I might accomplish as a civilian.

My future seemed to be falling into place. I have thought many times that college degrees don't matter in my line of work—writing—but without the time and effort it took to graduate I wouldn't have ended up where I did. Two years in the army helped me grow up and convinced me I needed to finish college. Thanks to the very generous GI Bill, I was able to afford my final year and a half at TCU, where I met Dan Jenkins and Edwin "Bud" Shrake and some others who helped shape my future. The night course that I took at TCU was in public speaking, which attracted me only as an easy and probably fun subject. But one of my classmates turned out to be Flem Hall, a popular columnist and sports editor of the *Fort Worth Star-Telegram*. As the incoming president of the Football Writers Association of America, Flem was expected to give a talk on national television during halftime of the College All-Star Football Game the next summer, a thought that terrified him. During a coffee break I introduced myself and told him that I'd been reading him for years and had decided to be a sportswriter—a small but well-placed lie. Flem took an interest in me, suggesting that once my hitch was up he might help me find a newspaper job.

A few days after my discharge, Flem invited me to his office and introduced me to the city editor, who was looking for a warm body to cover the night police beat. The job had dreadful hours—6 p.m.

until 2 a.m.—and paid only $55 a week, but it was exciting and a chance to work for a real newspaper, in a real city with a gritty history of crime and corruption. My first year on the crime beat, Sigma Delta Chi (a society of professional journalists) gave me an award for best feature story, a tale about this funny old man who had reported the theft of all four wheels on his wagon. The award came with a fake-gold plaque and $100, which was a small fortune back then.

COVERING THE NIGHT POLICE BEAT WAS WHERE I learned to use fear as a battle-ax. It is cold and relentless out there, and fear is your primary weapon. Fear can induce paralysis, and will if you allow it, but it can also inspire accomplishments that at times seem unlimited. A reporter's great fear is failure to get the story, get it right, get it first. Whatever it takes, the story is what counts. In later years, after I started writing sports, asking tough questions of a ballplayer who had just lost a game was nothing compared to facing a mother who had watched her child be crushed by a passing automobile. Every reporter needs to start on the police beat. It teaches you to be smart and tough and to make peace with your demons when they present themselves.

I remember walking into the press room of the Fort Worth police station that first morning in the winter of 1956 and looking around at the hard faces of the competition. *Fort Worth Press* staff writer Bud Shrake loomed over his small desk, tufts of straw-colored hair leaking under the rim of a hat pushed to the back of his head, tie askew, a cigarette in his mouth, typing with one finger. A radio reporter named Bob Schieffer was talking on two phones at once. Shrake, of course, would eventually be recognized as one of our state's best writers ever, and Schieffer would become a network star at CBS News, but at the moment they were just struggling young reporters who represented competition—i.e., the enemy. In time I realized that competitors faced the same primal fear I experienced, that cooperation is not only possible but necessary in this cutthroat business. For this reason alone, enemies usually become friends.

The police radio crackled in the background, codes that were at the time unintelligible but that quickly became second nature. As I recall, Code Fourteen meant somebody had probably been shot dead. So you were off like a bullet. The *Star-Telegram*'s desk was nearest the door, so its occupant got a head start anytime something big happened. How would a reporter know what was big? Well, if you saw two homicide detectives racing for the stairs, the first rule was, Chase after them and ask questions later. Another rule was, Dress like a detective. That way, when you get to a crime scene and start asking questions, people will assume you have a right to be there. During my years on the police beat, I wore a snap-brim hat and a trench coat, kept a Lucky Strike smoldering at the corner of my mouth, and tried to remember to call all women "sister." Except for Saturday, when all the reporters worked past midnight, I was alone in the press room after about 10 p.m. That meant I had the whole city to myself. If there was a major fire, or a fatal wreck, or anything that required on-the-spot reporting, I was their man. The responsibility could be fearsome, and yet there was a thrill in knowing you were at the edge, your job was to hold things together.

You learn crime reporting by trial and error. The errors can be comical or gut-wrenching or anything between those extremes. For example, watch where you step; otherwise you might leave bloody tracks across some woman's kitchen floor, as my fellow crime reporter Harold Williams did one unforgettable evening. The blood was from her brother, who had shot himself on that spot an hour before. Also, keep a grip on your emotions; otherwise you will lose it when the story strikes too close to home—like the time I found myself frozen next to an embalming table where they had placed the decapitated bodies of two little children, roughly the same age as my kids, Mark and Lea. The children had been victims of an auto accident which did minimal damage to their bodies from the neck down but cleanly separated their heads from the major part of their bodies. I learned to remove myself from reality: report it, write, and move on. When my shift was over and the last edition tucked in bed, I found that two beers were good, three were better.

Stay alert. Anything can happen and probably will. I'll never forget one Christmas Eve—it was a slow night and I had gone to the emergency room at Fort Worth's St. Joseph Hospital to cover some minor story. I was about to wrap it up and head home for Christmas dinner when a police squad car and two stretcher bearers brought in a man who had been shot through the heart. "Robbery," one of the uniformed officers told me. I had been hoping for action all night and now, at the last possible minute—exactly when I needed it least—I was neck-deep in mystery. So there I was, standing a few feet away from the ER table where medics were trying to save the man that I knew was dead, when I became aware that someone else had entered the ER. It was a woman. An icy wave shot down my spine as I realized she was probably the dead man's wife. Mistaking me for a detective—sure, I was trying to look like a detective, but not *now*!—she began beating on my chest and crying out: "Where's Ralph? Where's my husband!" As I grappled for something unstupid to say, Detective Grady Haire stepped forward and took the woman very gently by the arm. Directing her attention to one of the attending nuns, he said in a soft voice, "I'd like you to meet Sister Mary Vincent, one of the nicest people you'll ever know." Sister Mary Vincent took the woman aside and whispered something to her. The scream that followed was a sound I can still hear half a century later. Unwrapping Christmas gifts later that night, I hugged Mark and Lea and tried to act happy and hopeful. But it was just an act. Hope is a popular illusion—which is not to belittle it as a link in our salvation. The inevitability of human fate stuck in my breast like a clump of undigested dough and I knew it was there for good.

Vice ran wide and deep in the streets of both Fort Worth and Dallas. When I was in high school, nearly every small walk-up hotel in downtown Fort Worth was a whorehouse. Football gambling cards were sold over the counter by nearly every drugstore, barbershop, or newsstand. You could place a bet at any bar or coffee shop. Just west of the Arlington city limits sat a fancy gambling joint and supper club called Top O' Hill Terrace, which catered to big-shot gamblers like H. L. Hunt and Sid Richardson. Daddy wasn't much of a gambler, but I remember the excitement around our house the night he surprised my mom with an anniversary dinner at Top O' Hill. A day or so later, I asked Daddy if he lost any money and he showed me a silver dollar and told me, "This is all I came away with." It was the last of his collection of twenty silver dollars. But I could tell that it didn't matter. He was still beaming with the memory of that glorious evening. Losing his silver dollar collection had to have hurt, but I could sense the experience had been worth it.

There was a series of gangland murders in Fort Worth and Dallas during the mid-fifties, usually blamed on the Dixie Mafia, a term used by Fort Worth detectives for the hoods who were robbing and shooting up the city. Hardly a week passed without somebody discovering a shallow grave near Lake Worth, containing the bullet-riddled remains of a Tincy Eggleston or a DeLois Green, two of the many outlaws who killed for a living and were eventually gunned down during that bloody period of gang warfare. Every time another grave was discovered, you'd hear a homicide detective speculate, "I'll bet Benny Binion is behind this." Benny Binion was a gambler and a racketeer, the boss of the streets of Dallas — "a cross between John Wayne and Jesse James," or so he was described by Meyer Lansky, the Napoleon of organized crime in America. It was Lansky, not Binion, who bossed the bosses: I learned later that Lansky was the one who sent Jack Ruby to Dallas to front the mob's murder-for-hire operation. People still wonder about Ruby; he was Lansky's guy in Dallas, a certified mobster with a few loose screws. I got to know Ruby fairly well when Bud Shrake and I shared a bachelor apartment in north Dallas, about the time of the Kennedy assassination. I'll tell you about that later.

Benny Binion wasn't the arch-villain people made him out to be, though he killed his share of badasses. It's true that he controlled the rackets in Dallas–Fort Worth for a time after World War II. Eventually, the cost of paying off all the politicians, lawmen, and lawyers got so staggering—more than $1 million a year, by one estimate—that Benny decided it made more sense to put his money in the purchase of a casino in the budding gambling haven of Las Vegas. Even so, he continued to cast a shadow over Texas for many years.

As it turned out, the primary assassin of all those Texas hoods was a professional hit man named Gene Paul Norris, a handsome and, in his own way, charming rogue. The cops had been trying to nail him for years, but nobody could make a good case. My accidental encounter with Gene Paul Norris was one of the high—and low—points of my crime reporting career. By chance, I'd been in the holding area of the city jail when the cops brought Norris in for questioning. Hauling in police characters "for questioning" was a way for cops to get bad guys off the street for a few days without giving them a chance to lawyer up. I didn't understand much about civil liberties back then, or that such heavy-handed police tactics were illegal and should have been reported—not that any newspaper in Texas would touch such honest reporting. All I saw was a chance for an exclusive interview with a famous criminal. I introduced myself to Norris and inquired if he would mind a few questions. "Sure," he said, smiling. "But first I need you to call my lawyer and get permission." He gave me a phone number and I hurried back to my desk in the police press room to do his bidding. Only later, as I watched Norris leave arm in arm with his lawyer, did I realize I'd been had. Like an idiot, I had helped the bad guy get out of jail. Worse still, I never got the interview.

A few months later I listened to the police radio with considerable fascination as a posse of local and state police cornered Norris and closed in for the kill. This was a top-secret operation, available to the media only because the officers involved needed the police radio to communicate. As I pieced it together later, this is what happened: The Texas Rangers had discovered Norris's plan to rob the Carswell Air Force Base payroll and had been planning for several days to use the robbery as an avenue to finally terminate him. This particular operation was supposed to be a dress rehearsal for the real robbery and ambush a day or two later, but when lawmen learned that Norris planned to kidnap a woman bank employee and her young son, everything changed: the dress rehearsal was put on the fast track and became the event itself. Dozens of cops surrounded Norris on a side street near a shopping center, shooting him to pieces. I lost count of how many cops claimed credit for the kill.

One of the amazing things we learned on the police beat was how to handle what were called "nigger deals." We didn't write them, or, if we did, they never got printed. I'll give you an example of how this worked. One night I stumbled into what I thought was a great story. There was this eighty-six-year-old black preacher who every night for fifty years had walked from his home on the south side to City-County Hospital to pray for the sick. Over the decades two things happened that sealed his fate: he went blind, and they built the South Freeway across the path from his home to the hospital. So of course he got hit and killed by a car. Matter of time, right?

I encountered that unfortunate old man for the first time laid out on a slab, another victim of progress. I spent a couple of hours writing and polishing the tale, but when I turned it in to the night city editor, an old hack named Ed Capers, he spiked the story. "Gary," he whined, "this is a nice yarn, but this old man was colored." Well, yes, Ed, I wrote that in the second paragraph. But it didn't matter to Ed. He was buying news, not good yarns, and coloreds weren't news, even those who died violent deaths. "Give us a couple of grafs to protect us," he told me. "Say something in the lead about how many traffic deaths we've had this year in the city."

Police reporters learn to live with idiot editors, just as they learn to tell sanitized versions of stories that inevitably lose their flavor in the sanitizing. A vice squad detective I knew gave me a really colorful account about this old junkie who had "popped his last balloon." He was, in the detective's memorable phrase, "on the down end of the joy train." As the detective told the tale, I started to suspect that he was really telling me about himself, that he had become one of the junkies he was hired to track down, that the story of the old junkie was essentially his own story—his way of speaking the unspeakable. Of course I couldn't write it that way, so I wrote about an anonymous junkie and won that year's Sigma Delta Chi Award for feature writing. Some months later, the detective was busted on drug charges. Well, what do you know? Hell, I knew it would happen sooner or later, but you write what you can prove, not what you know to be true. Truth is nearly always just out of reach or so obtuse that it gets lost in translation. How can you describe Lieutenant Chick Matlock turning to a Houston detective with an opulent lifestyle and inquiring, "How long did you say you'd been in the vice squad?" Or detective Grady Haire, flicking cigar ashes on his necktie and telling you, "That fellow's so crooked he couldn't carry shit to a dead bear." Insights like these are too raw for the reading public, but they make good small talk in the press room.

Television news was just starting to function—a reporter with a handheld TV camera, shooting film that managed to get maybe fifteen seconds of airtime during a fifteen-minute newscast. Radio mobile cruisers, on the other hand, were popular and apparently profitable. Most of them depended on gimmicks to sell authenticity. Once during a storm I heard that a mobile unit reporter was beating on the side of his van with a two-by-four to fake the sound of wind-driven debris. But some really good reporters started on radio news, guys like Bob Schieffer and an old pro named Wayne Brown, who worked for the *Star-Telegram*'s radio outlet, WFAA. They were solid journalists who could think on their feet and write short, action-packed sentences.

There was a lot of dead time on the police beat, so Shrake and I trained a copyboy named Steve Perringer to cover for us while we drank beer at the Office Lounge, a dark little dive across the street from the police station. Steve was a natural. We instructed him to check regularly with the desk sergeant, get chummy with the dispatcher, butter up the nursing supervisors, cross-check emergency room reports against police records, use the crisscross to check out fire alarms before rushing to the scene of a false alarm, and be alert for "nigger deals." He never failed us. If Steve interrupted our beer drinking, it was because a real news story was developing. Our little copyboy was eager, willing, smart, and dedicated. He loved the action, the rush, the thrill of being up close. A few years later he got a job as a TV cameraman and was burned alive when he got too close to a flaming oil storage tank. My little copyboy—I loved him.

NOT LONG AFTER I STARTED AT THE STAR-TELEGRAM, I happened to visit the advertising department of Leonard Brothers department store in Fort Worth, where I had worked for a short stretch before entering the army. That's how I met Barbara Austin, who worked there as an artist, drawing female forms in bargain-priced dresses, usually without heads or feet. She was smart, shapely, and pretty, and from a well-to-do family—her father was a free-spending salesman named Homer Austin, who represented an aircraft supply firm based in Los Angeles. Homer was a big man, hearty, outgoing, and friendly. He had a lot of money, which he loved spending—a boat, a lake cabin, membership in several private clubs. He entertained Barbara and me and my parents several times a week at the Key Club, which was tucked in one corner of the swanky Western Hills Hotel, on the western edge of Fort Worth. I thought the Western Hills was probably the finest hotel in the world, and loved to impress my friends at the newspaper by lighting their cigarettes with Western Hills matches. I was living a dream, or so it seemed at the time. Before I knew it, I had forgotten Kay and asked Barbara to marry me.

Homer and his wife, Evelyn, threw us a grand wedding, and paid for a grand honeymoon in New Orleans. Then they helped us find a nice apartment in an upper-middle-class area of Fort Worth. Barbara's family was Catholic, so most Sundays I joined them at the Catholic church downtown. I enjoyed the Catholic church, or at least the pageantry. It was a real show—fine robes and vestments, bells and music, silly replicas of saints that adorned the walls and ceilings. I never joined the church or paid much attention to its laws and restrictions, but I did agree to take "instructions" and to raise all of our children as Catholics. I mean, what the hell. Catholic, Methodist, Baptist, it was all the same to me. Mumbling oaths, singing about angels, swearing to do stuff or not do stuff—swearing oaths struck me as essentially meaningless. It was easy enough for me to believe in God or to accept Christian dogma. I grew up on that stuff. Go along, get along, don't make waves. It's a philosophy that has worked well all my life. I pray every night before falling asleep, and sometimes in the day. I believe in the words and do my best to follow the teachings of Christianity, but recognize how far short I fall. So sue me.

Less than a year later, our son Mark was born. I was still working the night police beat, getting off just in time to give my little boy his bottle at 2:30 a.m., which became my favorite part of the day. When Mark was asleep in his crib again, I would catch a few hours' sleep and wake in time to make my daily 8 a.m. classes at TCU. Working a full-time job and carrying a full load of classes at TCU didn't seem like an especially difficult path to follow, considering the rewards being offered. I loved Barbara and we spent almost all of our free time together, seeing every first-run movie and having cocktails with friends from TCU. Barbara was very close to her family, and we traveled and socialized with them and their friends. I had my own group of friends, mostly from TCU, and Barbara was never jealous or possessive. She talked a lot about growing up in Los Angeles, making it sound exotic and otherworldly. We took a trip with my parents, through Las Vegas and then to Los Angeles. Life was good.

Homer kept trying to convince me that there was no future for a young man in Fort Worth. Maybe he was right: I was going nowhere fast. Eventually, he promised to help me find a good job in Los Angeles, and I reluctantly agreed. So I resigned my reporting job at the *Star-Telegram* and moved to L.A., living with Evelyn's sister in the San Fernando Valley. The job turned out to be with a small advertising firm: I was hired to write copy extolling the benefits of a vibrating exercise machine and a line of diet supplements that promised to help fat women lose unsightly pounds. I hated the job. It made me feel like an idiot. After a couple of weeks, I left for lunch one day and never went back. I called Barbara and told her I wanted to come home, which she agreed was a good move. Then I telephoned my dad in Fort Worth and asked him to send me some money for the return trip. Barbara still had connections with the advertising department at Leonard Brothers and I returned to my old job, writing copy for grocery ads and men's underwear. By this time we were living in a spare room at my parents' home in Fort Worth and Barbara was pregnant again. Our daughter, Lea, was born in January.

THE VERY BEST RESULT OF MY NEWSPAPER LIFE was that it introduced me to a new crowd of hip-to-the-times wise guys, in particular Bud Shrake and Dan Jenkins, both of whom became lifelong friends and colleagues. Both worked for the *Fort Worth Press*, the *Star-Telegram*'s rival. Shrake was my police-beat counterpart, a brilliant young intellectual with a drive to write great fiction. Jenkins was a born sportswriter and one of the funniest and most original guys I'd ever met: his first novel, *Semi-Tough*, was a runaway best seller and embedded the term "semi" deep in the vocabulary. When the legendary sports columnist Blackie Sherrod left the *Press* and moved to the *Dallas Times Herald*, Dan was promoted to sports editor.

When Dan heard I was back from L.A. and writing ad copy for Leonard Brothers, he hired me at the *Press*. It was 1958, the start of my eight years as a sportswriter—and, in a way I never anticipated, the start of my career as a writer. Bud and Dan became my mates, and Blackie Sherrod was our mentor. It was a time of discovery, fellowship, and opportunity. Bud, Dan, and I drank together, plotted together, and talked nonstop about the books we intended to write, and Blackie led us to bigger and better jobs, first at the *Dallas Times Herald* and later at the *Dallas Morning News*. Sky's the limit, I thought.

If the *Star-Telegram* was the old gray mare of journalism, the *Press* was a frisky, reckless colt. Working there was great fun. It was freedom to explore, to see what you could and couldn't do. Some of Jenkins's best columns addressed themselves to how hard it was to open a package of crackers or buy gasoline. I invented a sportswriter named Crew Slammer and nearly got him voted best sports-writer in Texas. Jenkins recalled that the day when Jerre Todd came to apply for a job, he raced through the swinging gate that divided sports from the city room and did a hook slide at Blackie Sherrod's feet. Blackie loved the presentation and hired Todd on the spot. Though most of us were barely able to pay our rent, we all gambled on football and basketball—and wrote songs about our misfortune. For example: "Duke Over Miami (Why Did I Pick Duke?)." On Saturday night a brace of visiting gamblers with names like Big Circus Face, Puny the Stroller, and Jawbreaker King would drop by to check scores on the UPI sports wire and collect our lost wages.

One of the side benefits of working for the *Press* was hanging out in the composing room and watching through the wide-open windows of the New Jim Hotel across the alley while black hookers worked their little hearts out. When we got off work in the wee hours, a couple of the hookers were usually waiting to proposition us. Shrake told me one offered to trade a blow job for his peanut patty. "I took one look at her and decided to keep my peanut patty," he recalled.

Since the 1950s when it adopted its racy tabloid look, the *Press* was far more fun to read than the *Star-Telegram*. A Scripps Howard paper that the chain seemed to regard as a good tax write-off, the *Press* balanced hard-news coverage against (and between) events like golden wedding anniversaries and spelling bees. Sometimes the crimes were invented from whole cloth or at least twisted beyond recognition. To its credit, the newspaper did take on the Ku Klux Klan and champion Alcoholics Anonymous and soil conservation—which no one seemed to understand or be able to explain—but the only crusade I can remember was its running battle against the evils of pinball machines, which it dubbed "nickel-gulping monsters." The trick of tabloid journalism is the use of headlines so that bland events masquerade as sensational news. The headline might read: GOLF BALL–SIZE HAIL PUMMELS CITY, but the reader has to work through several paragraphs to realize the city is not Fort Worth, as one would presume, but Buffalo, New York. Shrake uncovered an otherwise flavorless account of how some neighborhood kids rescued and made a pet of a wounded deer, only to watch as police confiscated the poor animal. The real story was what happened next and the twist that Shrake—and the headline writer—gave it. The cops barbecued the deer and served it at a police picnic, giving birth to one of my all-time favorite headlines: POLICE EAT KIDS' PET.

One Saturday night a woman called the city desk and said she was about to kill herself. Mack Williams, who was the assistant city editor, yanked Shrake off the police beat and sent him out to interview the overwrought woman. The address was a shanty near the garbage dump and when Shake knocked on the door a dog leaped out and tore his pants leg. Shrake kicked the dog, sending him bounding through a screen door and into the kitchen. At the door Shrake was greeted by a man clutching a shotgun. "Where's the lady who wants to kill herself?" Shrake asked. The man pointed to a heaving lump in a torn slip on the sofa, surrounded by empty gin bottles. "I woke her up and asked if she really meant to kill herself," Shrake told me. "She said damn right, nobody cared if she lived or died. I told her to hurry because I was on deadline. The man with the shotgun said she threatened to kill herself every Saturday night and he wished she would hurry. So I called Mack at the city desk and told him what happened, which was basically nothing," Shrake recalled. "Then I went back to the police station, where all hell was breaking loose. I worked my ass off for two hours on two stories that barely got in the paper, then I picked up the final edition of the *Press* and saw my picture on the front page and a headline that said: I SAVED THE BEAUTIFUL BUT TROUBLED LADY FROM SUICIDE!"

The *Press* wore the label "scandal sheet," which gives you an idea of what passed for scandal in Fort Worth back then. An old editor once explained it this way: "The poor folks take us because we're the least expensive newspaper in town. The rich folks take us to find out what we're telling the poor folks." I respected that explanation. The *Press* was like an old stray dog that nobody claimed but everyone tolerated. It wore the dirt and the grime from years of benevolent neglect as though every stain was a medal of honor.

You loved it and feared for it, feared that every time the presses rolled it would be the last time. "The minute I walked into that old Press Building on Fifth and Jones," Bud told me once, "the minute I heard the teletype machine clicking, I knew that this is where I belonged." Under the influence of the great sports editor Blackie Sherrod, Bud's literary talents began to flower, a phenomenon that had also affected Dan Jenkins a few years earlier, and would eventually affect me, too. Young writers like Jenkins, Shrake, and me arrived, flourished for a time, then moved on, and old-timers like the city editor, Delbert Willis, became part of the scenery. The holy mission of Delbert's life was to find the man who blew off his leg during World War II. To my everlasting surprise, the mission was fulfilled in 1966 when he traveled to Japan for a reunion with twelve survivors of a battalion that his unit had blown to pieces in the Battle of Morotai in 1945. Four of the Japanese soldiers who attended the reunion had held out on the island until 1956. I never really appreciated Delbert Willis until I read his moving account of the reunion and the Battle of Morotai, "a little piece of real estate which no one really wanted."

MY MARRIAGE TO BARBARA LASTED SEVEN YEARS, which seemed like the going rate at the time. All my friends had been divorced at least once. Divorce was part of the deal, what happened next, or so my shallow reserve of experiences led me to believe.

Bud and Joyce got married when they were students at TCU, divorced a few years later, married a second time, and were flirting with yet another divorce about the time I met them. Joyce was the love of Bud's life—and also his lifelong torment.

Nobody understood Joyce, nobody, ever, but a lot of men went mad trying.

Dr. Joyce Rogers, as she preferred being known among her tight circle of scholarly associates, was beautiful, brilliant, unpredictable, and relentlessly romantic. She had short flings with almost all of Bud's friends, including me. She was intrigued by mysticism and by Catholicism, which to her way of worshipping amounted to the same thing. As she sank deeper into the mystic transfigurations of her Catholicism, she couldn't help proselytizing her faith. To this day I get goose bumps recalling Joyce's sweet, sincere, ethereal voice explaining to us of little faith the meaning behind Our Lady of Fatima. At such moments, she could be downright spooky. She wanted desperately to get remarried in the Catholic Church and Bud finally agreed. Though he would certainly have denied it, he had a deep religious streak that could only be articulated in the metaphor of literature. So he signed the papers, promising to raise their sons, Creagan and Ben, in the Catholic faith. Because of their divorce a few years earlier, they were married in the rectory rather than the church. Standing in a corner of the rectory, trying to be unnoticed, I began to realize the marriage was already doomed as I watched Bud mistakenly put out his cigarette in the holy water.

By the time we had moved to Dallas, Bud and Joyce were having serious marriage problems. Part of it was the hard drinking and erratic existence that sportswriters in those days believed was necessary to their success. Bud's day job was covering the Dallas Cowboys, which required him to hang out with club owner Clint Murchison, Jr., and other Dallas high rollers. The rich and famous were always drawn into Bud's irresistible orbit. Among Murchison's coterie were Miami multimillionaire Dick Fincher and his wife, the actress Gloria DeHaven, and two raucous priests, Fathers Higgins and Mulligan, who traveled to all the Cowboys games with Fincher. The priests took a keen interest in Bud, and vice versa. "I was fascinated by their contrasts of life," Bud said. "They got up every morning at four to pray and work in their gardens and live the monastic life. Then on weekends they'd get drunk as pigs and argue religion with guys like me." Higgins constantly advised Bud to "stop kicking against the bricks"—a term that appeared a few years later in Bud's novel *Blessed McGill*.

Bud had his own notions about God and faith. Though raised in Fort Worth's Travis Avenue Baptist Church, he had intellectually rejected the churchgoing experience years before. Whatever the truth about salvation, Bud believed that artistic genius was the great absolution of wretched behavior. Poverty and deadlines are said to be a writer's two motivators, but I'll submit that the agony of love ought to be a contender.

Joyce was a Shakespeare scholar and a true intellectual. "Half the time I didn't know what Joyce was talking about," Bud said. "But I knew that Joyce knew." Jenkins recalled that Joyce "shoved us toward 'great literature' and bolstered us with her humor and good taste." She was beautiful, sexy, and brilliant, but also temperamental and dangerously vulnerable. She could be great fun, but she was high maintenance, too. You were never sure where you stood with Joyce. Later, under her professional name, Dr. Joyce Rogers, she wrote a book exploring the anomaly of Shakespeare's will, in which he left his second-best bed to his widow. The book was titled *The Second Best Bed: Shakespeare's Will in a New Light*, and though it was undoubtedly a work of superlative scholarship, for most of us it was unreadable. It was a metaphor for the constantly expanding universe that was separating Joyce from the recognizable world. Her Catholic faith at times seemed obsessive, as though she were on a vector to sainthood. A second divorce seemed inevitable, though I never imagined that the publication of Bud's first book would hasten it along.

Bud had tried writing a novel while working at the *Press*, a tale about the bitter struggle to integrate Mansfield High School, episodes of which he had covered as a reporter. But the manuscript attracted no interest from publishers. It came as something of a surprise, therefore, that not one but two publishers submitted offers for his second book, *Blood Reckoning*, which he wrote when he was twenty-seven, in the secrecy of his kitchen, in the dead of night, between the hours of three and five. In those days all self-respecting newspaper writers were expected to have an unfinished novel (and a pint of whiskey) in their desk drawer, but nobody was expected to write in the middle of the night. Bud struggled out of bed at that ungodly hour, I learned later, not because he believed that writing was his destiny (though he suspected it was) but to support Joyce and their two sons. Three to five in the morning was his only spare time. We had to be at our desks at the newspaper by six, and our afternoons and evenings were absorbed with the sportswriters' sacred obligation to drink beer and chase around.

Bud chose the larger of the two offers, a $3,000 advance from Bantam, which was about double what the hardback publisher Harper & Row was willing to pay. He used the money to buy a spectacularly gaudy status symbol, a used four-door white Cadillac Eldorado. Joyce hated the Cadillac and refused to ride in it. "It embarrassed her," Bud told me later. "She was afraid that her friends at SMU would see it." I never knew until years later what Joyce thought of *Blood Reckoning*, a book rich in savagery and redemption; she pretended it didn't exist. I doubt she talked about it with her friends in the academic world.

I think it was the combination of the book and the Cadillac that pushed Joyce over the edge. Bud came home one day to find his bags packed and deposited on the back steps. For the next several weeks, he lived in the Cadillac, sometimes sleeping in the backseat while the car was parked at the rear of the newspaper's lot.

Dan Jenkins and his wife June were a steady pair at Paschal High School, but eventually went their separate ways and married other people. Dan married Joan Holloway, daughter of a wealthy Austin real estate developer, and June married Dick Lowe, a TCU football player. Some years later, Dan and Joan divorced, at roughly the same time that June separated from Dick Lowe, and the spark they felt back at Paschal flamed and began to burn brightly. Their romance was supposed to be a secret, but it became known among their wide circle of TCU friends and tongues started to wag. Ironically, it was first exposed at the 1960 edition of the Midwinter, an annual gathering of sportswriters from Dallas and Fort Worth. Staged at a remote farmhouse near Cleburne, Texas, the Midwinter was an invitation-only evening of gambling, drinking, and merrymaking. In one of the event's sideshows, participants teamed up and wrote skits or satirical songs poking fun at one another. The skit that Blackie, Bud, and I wrote exposed the secret love affair of Dan and June and was titled "So Long to the Queen of Mean." Here's a sample verse:

> June is busting out all over,
> She's giggling like a schoolgirl at the fair.
> Jenke has her tipsy, she's chuckling like a gypsy,
> At the way he knots his tie and combs her hair.
> Oh, Jenke's gone and lost his marbles,
> He's thirty but he's acting seventeen.
> He seldom coughs or throws up,
> But when his marriage blows up,
> He's forgotten all about the Queen of Mean.
> And now it's June, June, June . . .

The romance inspired several more song parodies as well. As Dan later recalled, "Journalism didn't always keep us occupied."

Dan and June's marriage has endured with great love and passion for more than half a century. At first I worried that our song might somehow embarrass June, but she loved it and demanded a command performance, even baking a chocolate cake for the occasion. Over the years I've repeated verses dozens of times for her pleasure.

Barbara and I became close friends with Dan and June in the early sixties when I joined the *Dallas Times Herald*. We lived in the same apartment complex as Bud and Joyce, just north of downtown Dallas, near the SMU campus, where Joyce was a member of the English Department faculty. Bud and I quickly became the bad boys of the block, two guys who were forever upsetting the status quo, singing in the courtyard late at night, flirting with all the women, trying to convince them to take off their clothes. We were pretty good at it, too. We invented a game called Naked Bridge, the object of which was to get everyone stark naked as soon as possible. We relied chiefly on a drunken spiel about how God intended the naked body to be a temple to His everlasting glory, and how covering it with earthly garments could be abhorrent in His eyes.

We didn't get within a country mile of persuading Joyce to remove so much as a stocking, of course, but Barbara, always a good sport, went along, and so did a surprising number of neighbor women in the complex. Sex and nudity were dominant themes in our little society. There was a joke going around about this drunk who asks a classically trained singer to do "Melancholy Baby," and when she responds very snobbishly that she doesn't even know "Melancholy Baby," he says, "Okay, then show us your tits." The joke illustrated our guiding principle—nothing ventured, nothing gained. Nothing was too outrageous to try, at least once. Bud and I worked out a truly lamebrain scheme in which very late at night, after everyone had gone to sleep, we would switch beds and climb in with the other's wife. "If we do it right," I assured him, "they'll never even know." Well, needless to report, they did know—at once!

One neighbor started a whisper campaign that Shrake and Cartwright were masterminding orgies. Technically, that was a vicious lie, but it found legs thanks to a very strange report by the wife of a history professor. It seems that one morning she discovered that several pairs of panties she had left drying on the clothesline had been mutilated. We heard her cry out, "Oh, dear Lord, some pervert has eaten the crotch out of my panties!" On closer inspection, it was discovered that the undergarments had been damaged not by human teeth but by some kind of acid. Through a bit of detective work, we learned that the culprit was a teenager in the next block who had some kind of love-hate hang-up with his mother. But Shrake and I remained reliable suspects, crime to be revealed later.

ONE OF THE GREAT REGRETS OF MY LIFE IS HOW my marriage with Barbara ended. We had tried a trial separation, but agreed to go back together. A short time after our reunion, when I had reason to believe she was out of town with her parents, she appeared in our bedroom unexpectedly—and caught me in bed with a woman whose name I have long forgotten. Worse yet, the kids, Mark and Lea, were with her: she tried to shove them into the bedroom, for a close-up of their old dad in action. In the ensuing scuffle, me trying to get her and the kids out of the room, she screaming insults and sobbing her heart out, I took a swing at her. It was just a glancing blow, or so I thought, but somehow I managed to break her jaw.

For almost all of our seven years of marriage, I must tell you, Barbara accepted my careless lifestyle and self-centered habits without complaint. We were mostly happy and content, but a restless wind stirred somewhere in the dark corners of my soul. I wanted something else, something more, something I couldn't name. Barbara was a really good woman, one of the best, and she deserved far better than me, but, sad to say, that's who I was—who I am—careless, self-centered, impulsive, and egotistical beyond all telling. Even now, as I celebrate my eightieth birthday in August 2014, I still have a hair-trigger temper that, when released, can cause suffering and pain to others. Some years after the incident with Barbara, during a similar argument with my second wife, Jo, I hit her and broke her jaw, inspiring one of my son Mark's memorable lines: "Well, Jap, I'm glad to see you haven't lost your punch." I had to laugh at Mark's perceptive humor—remember, Barbara wasn't just my first wife, she was Mark's mother—but of course the situation wasn't funny. I will surely burn in hell for such wanton carelessness and disregard for others.

DALLAS WAS A GREAT PLACE TO LIVE IN THE early sixties. This was a time before Fort Worth and Dallas were lumped together in a unit called the Metroplex: they remained separate places, each with a unique identity and character. Fort Worth was Cowtown, a rough-and-tumble spot where men wore cowboy boots, drank their whiskey straight, and stubbed out their cigarettes on the hardwood floor. It was a good sports town, mostly because of TCU, which nearly always had one of the country's best football teams, and the annual golf tournament at Colonial Country Club, one of the premier stops on the pro golf circuit. But Cowtown had an unmistakable bush-league aura, which it didn't try to hide. (Some people argued that the aura was just feedback from the famous Stockyards, which occupied a large section of land just north of downtown Fort Worth, across the Trinity River.) By contrast, Dallas smelled like Neiman Marcus, cool and fragrant and oh-so-righteous. It took pride in fostering a snobbish cocktail-glass image, coats and ties and big-league ambitions, and fancied itself the New York of the Southwest. But Dallas promised excitement and, to its credit, was beginning to deliver.

Baseball legend Branch Rickey came to town and talked up the possibility of Dallas–Fort Worth getting a major-league baseball team, and though he was a little premature it was obvious that Dallas was ready for its close-up. The NFL had flirted with Dallas in the early fifties, with a really bad cast of second-rate players assembled as the Dallas Texans, not to be confused with the American Football League team that Lamar Hunt started a few years later. The Texans were so underfunded that they couldn't make it through a full season; the franchise was eventually taken over by the league, reorganized under new management, and moved to Baltimore, where it became the Colts. (The organization moved again, to Indianapolis, in 1984.)

A decade later, however, Dallas was ready. The city was on the move and everyone felt it. Blackie Sherrod's decision to leave the *Fort Worth Press* in 1958 and take a position as sports editor and assistant managing editor of the much larger *Dallas Times Herald* was a signal of how far we had all come. Blackie had become a legend at the *Press*, a paper with a circulation of 60,000 that was known and admired all over the country. He was given a mandate to upgrade the staff of the *Dallas Times Herald*, not just in sports but across the newsroom, too. It was a personnel move that jarred the whole state, maybe the whole country. In a short time he had assembled what I believe was the best staff of sportswriters anywhere, ever—Blackie, Bud, Dan, and me. He gave us freedom to write in whatever style suited us, and we took full advantage of it. We made it fun. Any self-respecting writer knows that there is a thin line between fact and fiction and senses the duty to stay as near the edge as possible. Dan invented a character called Billy Clyde Puckett, who started by writing funny, semi-literate letters that Dan published in his column. Billy Clyde later became the central character in his first book, *Semi-Tough*. My invented sportswriter, Crew Slammer, from time to time got his byline inserted on wire stories that almost nobody read, about cricket matches in Leeds, for example, or soccer games between the Tottenham Hotspur and Bayern Munich. Some guy in North Carolina decided to start a national Best Sports Writer contest and sent letters to every writer he could locate. I took this as an opportunity to register the names of several dozen fictitious sportswriters, got ballots in their names, and stuffed the ballot box with votes for Crew Slammer. He won, of course, by a comfortable margin and would have been crowned the best sportswriter in Texas, except for the meddling of Bill Rives, the humorless sports editor of the *Dallas Morning News* at the time, who blew the whistle on my scam.

We were writing to and for each other, not merely sports pieces but satires, parodies, and epic poems that were assembled in a fat volume called "The Pinch Papers" (allegedly the work of a made-up sportswriter named Jim Tom Pinch, who later appeared as a character in a Jenkins novel).

To us, sports were too dumb to take seriously. By common agreement, we only reluctantly permitted the actual score of any game to soil our sterling examples of prose. Bud once began a story about a junior high track meet with this unforgettable sentence: "This is no golden legend, this is the plain unvarnished tale of youth." I once led a report of a game between the Dallas Texans and the Buffalo Bills by writing the "Ode of Momentum." It read something like this:

BUFFALO, NY—You can think of Momentum as a slice of moon buried in the belly of a Frog. That will help you understand how the Dallas Texans lost a game they should have won, and appreciate why all the excuses that coaches use to explain their team's shortcomings stop and start with a rhythm covered with warts, green slime and yesterday's breakfast.

It was a new take on the tradition of sportswriting and in a few years it swept the country and became standard. Everyone everywhere knew about those crazy guys in Texas and wanted to be just like us.

Assuming ourselves superior in every way to the mundane world that we were hired to chronicle, not to mention our superiority to the sports staffs of every other newspaper in the world, we were competitive in the extreme. Between editions, Blackie led us through push-up and chin-up contests and standing broad jumps. Sometimes we raced to the reference room and back again, an activity that failed to amuse the city-side staff.

We were a tight little group at the *Times Herald*. Dating back to our days in Fort Worth, we imagined ourselves as characters out of a Damon Runyon story and assumed colorful nicknames. Jenkins was Jenke or sometimes Pea Mouth. Bud was Thor. Blackie was J. J., named for the ruthless, all-powerful columnist J. J. Hunsucker in *Sweet Smell of Success*, played artfully by Burt Lancaster. I was Jap, or sometimes The Jap. That name came from a casual remark by a retired postman named Puss Ervin—yeah, Puss, how's that for irony? Puss was a colorful old-timer who wrote a bowling column for the *Press* and was kept around for sentimental reasons. It seemed that there had been a real Japanese intern at the paper the year before I arrived, and when my mug shot first appeared in the sports pages—my tanned, round face; my dark, narrow, seemingly Oriental eyes; my burr haircut—Puss groused, "Is that goddamn Jap back again?" Mine was the only name that stuck for more than a couple of years. It is still with me, I regret to say. To Americans of my generation—I was an impressionable seven-year-old when the Japanese bombed Pearl Harbor—the word "Jap" never fails to incite racial hatred, even today. I've learned to live with it, escape having proved impossible, but that atavistic feeling of bad blood does not go away.

THERE WAS AN UNSPOKEN AGREEMENT AMONG THE staff that our mission was to, wherever possible, disrupt the status quo. We did it in the stories we wrote, and we lived it outside the newsroom as well. One evening during the Colonial Country Club's fabled golf tournament, I crashed the exclusive poolside luau and fashion show, dressed in a white waiter's jacket and carrying a basket of rolls. Though there had never been a white waiter in the Colonial's long history, nobody seemed to notice me, until I climbed to the top of the three-meter board. Against a backdrop of floating gardenias and orchids—Miss Universe was singing about the greatness of America—I executed a very imperfect jackknife, scattering lily pads, orchids, dinner rolls, and a great deal of chlorinated water on Miss Universe's gown, as well as on guests who happened to be too close to poolside. Security guards gave chase, but with Shrake's help I climbed a ten-foot wall, leaped down on the soft sands of the bunker that hugged the eighteenth green, and vanished into the trees. Shrake always claimed that I yelled, "Who was that masked man?" but I don't remember that part.

It didn't help that the *Times Herald* was an afternoon paper, which meant that we came to work before daylight. I was chronically late in arriving. Blackie would glare and I would race to my desk and make some kind of dramatic show of attrition—one day I slammed my alarm clock into the trash can—and then settle behind my typewriter and try to look scholarly. Inside, I was terrified; nothing holds the promise of disaster so completely as a blank sheet of paper. For the next hour or so, I would struggle to pull words from the cobwebs of my brain and stitch them into coherent sentences, knowing that each approaching deadline, however dreadful, would be followed by another one just as bad.

Shrake and I sat at adjoining desks, back to back, trying to compose something that wouldn't embarrass us. Every morning we addressed our typewriters like two legionnaires ready to defend our posts against the thundering hordes. Morning after morning, knocking back eight or ten cups of coffee, enveloped in the purple haze of unfiltered Chesterfields, glancing nervously at the clock and at each other, we wondered if this would be the day forecast by the gods of journalism—*the day we'd blow it.* One cold, rainy December morning just minutes before deadline, I leaned over and pulled the sheet of paper from Shrake's typewriter. He had written just one forlorn phrase. It was "Ah, youth!" And that was one line more than I had.

Ah, youth! Half a century later I still remember that line with a smile. The youthful presumption of invincibility afflicted almost all of my newspaper pals in the sixties. We were a generation in which sex, drugs, and rock 'n' roll had replaced sock hops, Juicy Fruit, and Patti Page. That was the decade when I left Arlington behind, once and for all time. Nearly every one of my friends had been divorced at least once. Everyone screwed around. Everyone drank to excess. Everyone smoked. I don't think cholesterol was even a word. Sexually transmitted diseases seemed like something left over from World War I. Amphetamines were those cute pink pills doctors gave people who needed to lose weight or complained of fatigue. Everyone gobbled them like candy. Just outside of the Dallas Cowboys training room, at the entrance to the practice field, hung three five-gallon tins, available to all who happened by. One contained salt tablets, the second had lemon-flavored vitamin C, and the third offered five-milligram Dexedrine pills. I never passed the can without taking a handful. Speed made me smart and funny, or so it seemed at the time. I felt like one of those perpetual-motion gadgets you see in novelty shops, moving effortlessly as long as the batteries last. What seemed like a grand journey into the all-knowing was actually double time to nowhere.

We were finished with the issue shortly after noon, which afforded us long afternoons of leisure, free to drink and carouse. We usually ate lunch at a joint called Nick's, across from the Dallas County Courthouse. A mug of beer and a bowl of beans with onions and cornbread cost about fifty cents. After sucking down beer for a couple of hours, we drifted off to various afternoon amusements, bowling being a favorite at the time. Our colleague from the *Fort Worth Press* days, Jerre Todd, had become a PR man for the Dallas-Fort Worth Bowling Association, and he gave us passes enabling us to bowl free at any lane in town. Our favorite was the Cotton Bowling Palace, owned by Curtis Sanford, the granddaddy of the Cotton Bowl football classic. The bowling alley was a gathering place for guys with time on their hands, including Mickey Mantle and several baseball players who lived in Dallas in the off-season. We usually teamed up with whoever was around and put money in a pot for the team with the best average.

One day I found myself teamed with Mantle: he was the best bowler in our crowd, I was the worst. Now I'm a naturally poor athlete, but I am especially inept at the sport of bowling. I was born with a fused joint on my right thumb, so the only way I can grip a bowling ball is by bowling left-handed. Normally, using my left hand isn't a great handicap because I've lived all my life with the problem, but that particular day I couldn't keep the ball out of the gutter. Mantle was the model of patience, taking me aside for a private lesson. Placing a paternal arm on my shoulder, he demonstrated how to hold the ball, how to move up the lane, when and where to release the ball. But the harder I tried, the worse I got. Not only was I throwing gutter balls, I sometimes launched them into the wrong lane. I was pretty drunk by now, laughing and enjoying the moment, which only increased Mantle's frustration. I recognized, of course, that my partner was a world-class athlete, a genuinely good guy, but a perfectionist who did everything to the best of his ability. Much of Mantle's greatness was attributable to his miraculous ability to prevail over adversity, but my ineptitude was likewise world-class and it stumped him. Finally, he gave up and walked away. So when people ask if I knew Mickey Mantle, I merely nod. I don't want to call him a quitter, but I'll admit that I found him something of a disappointment.

THE SIXTIES WERE A TIME OF HUGE CHANGES, FOR me and my pals but also for the world at large. Just a couple of years earlier, the country was shocked to learn that the Soviet Union had launched the Sputnik satellite, accelerating Cold War fears that thermonuclear war was just a button-push away. The Cuban Missile Crisis reminded us that the world was getting smaller, and more dangerous. Rachel Carson's *Silent Spring* demonstrated the peril of abusing nature and the urgency of supporting an environmental movement. Right-wing nutcases had captured Dallas, which was ripe for the taking. Today, Dallas is one of my favorite cities, but back then it had the heart of a weasel. A gang of wing-nuts had surrounded the front entrance of the *Times Herald* building, where a man in a monkey suit did a jig and railed against integrating the races. Others, led by Congressman Bruce Alger, clogged downtown sidewalks and blocked the front entrance of the Baker Hotel, where Senator Lyndon Johnson was speaking. As Johnson was leaving, one of them spit at him and another hit him in the eye with a sign. General Edwin Walker, who had been cashiered from the military for spreading right-wing propaganda to his troops, was carrying on his campaign of hate from his mansion on Turtle Creek Boulevard. Always hungry for headlines, Walker flew his American flag upside down, his way of signaling that the nation was in distress.

The *Dallas Morning News*, which championed a far-right ideology, hired Bud away from the *Times Herald* and made him the lead sports columnist, with the freedom to cover any major sporting event that caught his eye. Bud wisely avoided subjects with political implications. I was less discreet. I was still covering the AFL Texans for the *Times Herald*, until the team moved to Kansas City, at which time I switched to the NFL Cowboys. The Cowboys were emerging as one of the best teams in football, and covering them was a choice assignment where I thrived for the next four years. I also wrote what we called our "second column" three times a week, musing on a variety of subjects, not all of them related to sports. Jenkins had been stringing for *Sports Illustrated* for some months, so it was no surprise when the magazine hired him to join its staff in New York, opening a new chapter in his magnificent career as America's best sportswriter. (Shrake would join him a year or so later.) I had started writing long feature articles for *Sport* magazine and other national publications and had ambitions far removed from Dallas or Texas.

Bud and I were both going through divorces at the time and

were sharing an apartment on Cole Avenue. Our apartment was a roomy three-bedroom, centrally located in an area of apartments and bars that catered to young singles (not to mention horny divorcés); it quickly became an after-hours fallback for the night crowd, which included a lot of singers, entertainers, and club owners. Somewhere in this time period, Bud and I discovered the pleasure of marijuana. Neither of us knew much about pot and had never smoked it. I had discovered diet pills in high school—amphetamines—when I worked in a drugstore. On a shelf at the back of the pharmacy stood a huge jar of pink Dexedrine tablets, and all of us soda jerks learned that swallowing one or two made us really smart and full of energy. Marijuana, however, was an exotic drug associated mostly with the black population. Then one night a jazz musician friend brought us a lid of weed, the "lid" being an empty Prince Albert tin that was used as a container. As we crowded close to watch, he demonstrated how to roll and light a joint. It was one of the memorable lessons of my life, discovering the joyous and liberating effects of pot and how to make it part of my life. What I remember most about that night is laughing like fools, devoting long intervals to studying a bug that had appeared at a corner of the carpet, and eating several fruit pies and half a gallon of ice cream. I'd never felt so smart, so funny, so ready for life. Colors had never been so bright or interesting. Old episodes of *I Love Lucy* were suddenly profound and tinged with secret meaning. I asked our musician friend if this stuff was habit-forming and he laughed and told me: "That's an old wives' tale. I been smoking this shit every day for six years and haven't got hooked yet." From that night forward, Bud and I always had a lid handy. Now, years later, I can report that, yes, it does appear to be habit-forming.

Our apartment evolved into a crash pad for several writer friends, including the memorable Billy Lee Brammer, whose first novel, *The Gay Place*, was getting rave reviews in New York. Billy Lee always had a pocket full of pills, speed, and God knows what else. Bud was having an affair with an exotic stripper called Jada, who was the featured act at one of Jack Ruby's clubs downtown, and for a time she was a fixture in our lives and a frequent guest at our apartment. Ruby dropped by, too, usually looking for Jada, always pausing to warn Bud that she was "a very dangerous woman." Ruby was a creepy little guy. He always wore a snap-brim hat and carried a gun, but he was anxious to please and seemed harmless enough at the time. Jada warned us that Ruby was "dangerous," essentially the same thing he said about her.

By today's standards, Jada's onstage act was fairly tame—as I recall, it consisted mostly of her dropping to her knees and humping a tiger-skin rug, making orgiastic sounds to the beat of recorded jazz in the background. Though the act was the reason customers paid for watered-down, overpriced drinks, it nevertheless drove Ruby crazy. He thought it far too obscene for such a swanky joint as his. He was all the time pulling her aside and ordering her to tone it down. Jada, of course, told him to get fucked. She was a remarkable woman, with hair the color of Florida oranges— unrestrained, it could reach the floor—purple fingernails that could have shredded an armadillo, lips like red man-eating blossoms. She usually carried a pearl-handled .32 in her handbag and loved to drive around town in her Cadillac convertible, completely naked under a mink coat. From time to time Jada would vanish for a few days, then reappear with hundreds of pounds of the finest manicured pot anyone had ever seen. She told us that her method for smuggling goods across borders involved striking up a conversation with the inspector while allowing her coat to slowly open, fully revealing all of her natural treasures. Yet she could be painfully shy, too, especially around strangers, and at times almost demure. In the morning when she was ready to leave our apartment, she didn't like facing a bunch of drunks who were still milling about the front room. Instead, she preferred to exit through a small window in Bud's bedroom. The window was low and narrow and Jada had to pull her dress up to the waist as she worked her way into position to clear the hedge below. One Sunday morning, just as she was ready to jump, the paperboy happened to pedal by. The sight of Jada coming out the window, crotch first, so unnerved the lad that he crashed his bike into a tree. Yes, a dangerous woman. No question about it.

On the bright side, 1960 was the year I discovered the joy of politics. John F. Kennedy was running for president and I cast my very first vote for him in November 1960. I was twenty-six at the time and just beginning to appreciate the mechanism of government and how democracy made the United States so much better than much of the rest of the world. Events like the Cuban Missile Crisis were scary, but more than that they were perplexing. I couldn't grasp what was happening, but I loved Kennedy and trusted that he would lead us to greater glory and lasting happiness. Shrake and I had several long political discussions, something we had never done before.

I was dating a procession of airline stewardesses, most of whom flew for American Airlines, which had a training school in Dallas, and I was simultaneously enjoying the abundant life of bachelorhood. My favorite hangouts were the End Zone, a shack on Lemmon Avenue that was a popular watering hole for people who worked downtown, and a hip walk-up bar called the Slave Quarters, located in the parking lot behind the Plantation Apartments. The music was jazz and show tunes, and nothing pumped me full of good feelings like listening to the velvet voice of Jeannie Oliver, singing about "girls in white dresses with blue satin sashes." Two or three times a week I'd go there, usually with Dan and June, and stay until closing time, at which time we'd join Bud and who knows who else at the apartment. Life was good and seemed endless.

Even my first novel was a sort of miraculous conception. Someone told me, "Just write a sentence until it seems right, then write another one." I set it against a backdrop of pro football in Dallas because that's what I knew most about at the time—since I was covering pro football for a newspaper in Dallas. I made up not only a team of my own but a league, patterned very much on the new American Football League, which had given birth just before I started the book.

Originally I used Tom Landry as a model for the Dallas coach, only to discover that Landry was too complicated, too cerebral. It was too difficult to get inside his head, too hard to explain what he thought or why he did things. So instead of starting over, I adopted a technique commonly used by football owners—I *fired* him and hired someone else, a coach more like Vince Lombardi. Lombardi was the perfect foil for a happy-go-lucky quarterback modeled on Don Meredith. I wanted a villain so foul and unforgiving you could smell him. I found him in Lombardi.

The book was eventually published in 1968, as *The Hundred Yard War*. It hit the market at exactly the right moment, just as the marriage of television and football was captivating the nation. *The Hundred Yard War* got several nice reviews, including one from the *New York Times*, though another, more astute reviewer called it "a sprawling train wreck." But I had at least published a novel, something I'd never dreamed would happen.

The editors at Pocket Books read *The Hundred Yard War* and decided I would be the ideal guy to write about ice hockey. They didn't know, and probably didn't much care, that I knew next to nothing about this sport. I did know *sports*, however, and it wasn't that difficult to learn pro hockey from books and from a brief field trip to visit the new team starting in Houston. As luck would have it, the team had hired one of hockey's all-time great players, Gordie Howe, who gave me some insight into the sport. I had watched some minor-league hockey as a kid growing up near Fort Worth, and discovered familiar patterns in the rules and composition of the teams.

I decided that the protagonist should be a goalie, a player who maintains a static position on the field of play. I could frame the action mainly from his perspective. I thought that I could fake my lack of understanding of the game more easily if my main character was going blind. What he couldn't see wouldn't hurt me. The plot depended on the reader suspending disbelief and accepting a goalie who was going blind. Gordie Howe had an interesting Canadian accent that worked nicely with the character I was creating. Howe also gave me a sense of what it was like growing up in the frozen north, to be "a river runner," so to speak. After that, everything fell into place.

Bud had started work on a second novel, more serious than his first. He completed *But Not for Love* the following year, typing the pages on his old Smith-Corona Skyriter portable while riding around Europe on a train, getting off in places like Paris, Rome, and Frankfurt. He stayed several months in Frankfurt at the apartment of Dick Growald, another Fort Worth boy who had grown up and gone to Paschal High with Jenkins and Shrake, and who had become chief of all European bureaus for the United Press. While Bud was in Rome, he read about the beatification of Mother Cabrini and was surprised to learn that she was the first North American saint. This provided the germ of the idea that later became his third novel, *Blessed McGill*, which purports to be about the life of the first North American saint. It's the story of a very un-Christlike man who in the end gives his life in a Christlike act to save a mission and the pueblo of Taos, New Mexico.

There was a lot of McGill in Bud Shrake, and vice versa. Many people just didn't get it. I remember talking to an editor who confessed, "I really liked the book, except for all that religious shit."

COVERING SPORTS HAD ALWAYS BEEN FUN, BUT THE job elevated by many degrees when two of Dallas's richest and most powerful families, the Hunts and the Murchisons, decided to invest in pro football teams and fight each other for survival. Lamar Hunt was the youngest son of H. L. Hunt, said to be the world's richest man, and Clint Murchison, Jr., was the son of another pioneer in Texas oil fortunes. A story circulated that when a reporter told H. L. Hunt that Lamar was losing a million dollars a year with his American Football League experiment, the old man growled, "At that rate, he'll be broke in a hundred years."

I got to know Lamar fairly well, and, eventually, Clint too. Lamar had once warmed the bench on the SMU football team and was an unabashed sports nut. He lived in a modest two-bedroom house in University Park, with a basketball backboard fixed to the front of the garage. He invited me to dinner one night and we shot baskets for twenty minutes while his wife finished cooking. The beverage that evening was Coca-Cola. Lamar had an impish grin and a little boy's laugh, and I never got over the feeling that his mother still dressed him every morning. But he was honest, straightforward, and extremely likable. Lamar invited me to join him on a trip to scout a possible location for the team's first training camp, in Roswell, New Mexico. We flew in his private plane, an ancient de Havilland Dove—it was the company plane used by all three Hunt brothers—and we shared a double bed at a Roswell motel. Sometime later I flew in that same plane with Lamar's older brother, Bunker, to watch the Indianapolis 500. Bunker was a likable slob, an overweight hulk with gravy stains on his necktie and part of his shirttail spilling over his belt. I enjoyed Bunker's company and always looked forward to trips with him. One of my fondest memories of Bunker was sitting next to him on the team bus outside the Polo Grounds in New York, on a blustery, bitter-cold day, watching a cluster of freezing fans burn trash to keep from freezing to death. After a while, Bunker nudged me and said: "Now that's what I call the great unwashed."

For the most part, Bunker stayed out of the football business, but his presence was felt. At that first training camp in Roswell, I wrote a critical column about what a second-rate operation the Texans were running. The next day, to my amazement, the team's general manager called me to his office, apologized for any inconvenience, and handed me three $100 bills. Though he didn't tell me, I knew that the money came from Bunker. It was Bunker's artless attempt at bribery, and the message was clear: Stop writing bad things about us. I refused the money, of course, and continued to write what I saw. None of us ever mentioned it again.

The Texans had a good and exciting team that first year and won the AFL championship in an exhausting double-overtime game in Houston. The Cowboys, meanwhile, didn't win a single game that season and became the joke of the NFL. Behind the scenes, both teams were waging a battle for image, busting their butts to court good relations with the media. Lamar invited the writers who covered the Texans to fly (in the Dove, of course) to Las Vegas for an evening of fun, and the Cowboys retaliated by inviting their writers for five days on Clint Murchison's private island in the Bahamas. The contrast in styles of the two owners and the two teams was exemplified by the two trips, the trashy versus the sublime, and that was all Dallas sportswriters talked about for months.

The Bahamas trip became an annual event. When I started covering the Cowboys full-time after Lamar moved his team to Kansas City, I was treated to one of those glorious trips. It was a once-in-a-lifetime adventure where guests stayed in individual beachside cottages surrounded by palm trees and water the color of Windex, and where waiters waded in the surf with trays of icy coconut-and-rum drinks. I'd come a long way from the police beat.

Unlike Lamar and some other rich Texans I met through my association with the Hunt family, Clint Murchison knew how to fully enjoy his money. Droll, reticent, basically shy, he enjoyed life immensely while staying just above the fray. He traveled with a small group of wealthy young friends, nearly all of whom worked for one of his companies, and their mission seemed to be finding ways to keep Clint amused. I couldn't imagine Clint shooting baskets or riding a bus—the Polo Lounge, okay, but the Polo Grounds, not a chance. He owned so many businesses he couldn't keep track of them all. When he asked a business associate to use influence to book a room in Palm Springs, he was reminded that he owned the Racquet Club of Palm Springs.

In the early years the Cowboys lost more than they won, but everyone knew that would change. Murchison had hired one of the sharpest minds in football, Tex Schramm, as his president and general manager. Tex had been a sportswriter before he became the publicity director of the Los Angeles Rams and later their general manager. The Rams were considered the premier franchise in the league, the first to hire a full-time team of scouts and appreciate the wisdom of the draft system. Tex had left football to become supervisor of sports for CBS Television, but football was in his blood—and Clint made him an offer he couldn't refuse. Tex understood that television was about to become a major player in pro football, and he loved and understood the game's complexities. He knew the NFL better than anyone in the business, with the possible exception of Pete Rozelle, the league commissioner. Rozelle and Schramm had been friends since their days working for the Los Angeles Rams, a relationship much resented by others in the league, who believed that Rozelle went out of his way to make rulings favoring the Cowboys. Which of course he did.

Clint Murchison was rich because his father left him a lot of money, but he got richer and more successful as a team owner, because he hired the best and left them alone to do their jobs. Almost everyone knew that Tom Landry was the smartest coach in football, but he was still a lowly assistant with the Giants when Schramm—with Murchison's approval—hired him to coach the Cowboys.

The only times Clint seemed really, truly happy was when he was in the company of his group of merry young pranksters. A few, such as Bedford Wynne, came from old money and were minority owners of the Cowboys. But one of the best was Bob Thompson, Clint's Marine Corps buddy and later his right-hand man and unofficial social chairman. Thompson was tall and lean and had an infectious smile that assured you the fun was just getting started. Thompson loved to belittle the establishment and stayed up late dreaming of ways to torment them and show his contempt. Once at an elite hunting club somewhere in Pennsylvania, he got his entire party kicked out after he attacked a pheasant with a pool cue. When Jim Ling, the billionaire industrialist, was showing off his new mansion in North Dallas, Thompson showed up with his pet turkey, Eric, who promptly relieved himself on the new white carpet. Thompson and the pranksters particularly loved to torment George Preston Marshall, the curmudgeon who owned the Washington Redskins. The Redskins and the Cowboys have been blood enemies since 1960, when Marshall tried to stop the NFL from awarding Murchison the new franchise in Dallas. Clint retaliated by buying the rights to the Redskins fight song from Marshall's ex-wife and holding it for ransom. Marshall's biggest pleasure was staging elaborate halftime shows, with lots of bands, clowns, and live animals. One night before a Cowboys-Redskins game in Washington, Thompson and his cohorts seeded the playing field with chicken feed, with plans to release thousands of live chickens just as a dog team was pulling Santa down the field. It might have been a halftime show for the ages, except the cops got there first.

Thompson, with Murchison in tow, was liable to show up anywhere. I ran into them one night in a black whorehouse in Pittsburgh. Tex Schramm learned to live with their eccentricities. One day at training camp, an aging barroom brawler chewing on a turkey leg and carrying a goat turned up at Schramm's office. He introduced himself as Rufus "Roughhouse" Page and he showed Schramm a Cowboys contract signed by Clint Murchison.

When Thompson and Murchison were out on the town in Dallas, which was fairly often in those heady days, they sometimes dropped by the apartment Bud and I shared. "Just slumming," Bob would grin. Thompson was a man of complexities and contradictions. I never understood the attraction, but one of his dearest friends was J. Edgar Hoover, who made numerous secret trips to Dallas and nearly always stayed in Thompson's guest bedroom. In my opinion, Hoover was one of the most dangerous public officials in American history, but Thompson enjoyed his company. Thompson redeemed himself, however, by hitching a jackass to the staircase that led to Hoover's room.

The last time I saw Clint Murchison, Jr., was the summer of 1996, when he was dying of Lou Gehrig's disease. A mutual friend had called and said Clint wanted to see me. He wanted me to write his memoirs. As tempting as it was, I knew such an arrangement wouldn't work. He would insist on editorial control, which I couldn't permit. It could have been a great story, but only if I told it my way. Nevertheless, I agreed to meet for lunch. I flew to Love Field and Clint and his caretaker-driver met me at the airport. I was astonished to see him so wasted, so thin and crippled. He was confined to a wheelchair and could barely talk. But he insisted that we take him to his favorite barbecue joint. That afternoon, as we were saying good-bye back at the airport, Clint pulled me close and whispered something in my ear. I couldn't understand, so he repeated it. In a thin, hoarse voice, he said: "Roughhouse Page." I laughed and he beamed for me his billion-dollar smile, one final time before the curtain fell.

BUD AND I WERE STILL ROOMMATES WHEN I MET Mary Jo Gross, who would soon be my wife and remain so for the next eleven years. Jo had been a student at Peabody College in Nashville until she got hepatitis and had to drop out. She had always wanted to travel, so after recovering from her illness she got a stewardess job with American Airlines and moved to Dallas. She was twenty-one, eight years younger than me, and had never been married. The only affair she ever mentioned was with a girl she knew when they were students at Peabody. For some reason, I found that really exciting, an emotion that I would reflect on with considerable irony in coming years.

Jo (or M.J., as I sometimes called her) was extremely likable—cute, curvaceous, funny, irreverent, all the things I was looking for in a woman. We hit it off from the start. She lived in an apartment not far from Love Field, next to a guy who introduced himself as Richard Noble. I suspected that wasn't his true name, that he was some type of con man, maybe even a fugitive, but I couldn't help liking him. A lot of suspicious characters were washing up in Dallas at the time. Noble was charming and mysterious, and though he didn't appear to have a job, he always had lots of money, which he spent freely entertaining neighboring airline stewardesses. He had some kind of international telephone hookup and invited Jo and her friends to call anyone they wanted, anywhere in the world. Who could resist such an offer or such a generous guy? He liked Jo and saw himself as a sort of surrogate uncle. He looked me over very carefully before determining that I was acceptable and suggesting that we ought to get married. We laughed off the idea at first. But one night as we were drinking his homemade margaritas, Noble brought up the subject again. He seemed obsessed with finding Jo a good husband and had decided on me. "I know what," he said brightly. "I'll drive you to Durant, Oklahoma, where there is no waiting period." It was a crazy, off-the-wall idea, but as the evening wore on and as Noble continued mixing drinks and telling us what a handsome couple we were, it got more appealing. Finally, we agreed and climbed in his new Cadillac with a bucket of ice, a half gallon of vodka, and some kind of mixer. From Dallas to Durant was about three hours of steady drinking, and by the time we arrived we were past the point of pain, not to mention rational thought. I didn't have a ring, so Noble loaned me his. It was a 1952 class ring from Stanford. As I pieced the evidence together later, I realized there was no such person as Richard Noble and that the ring had probably been purchased in a pawnshop. Noble's life story was a full-blown lie, but that didn't alter the fact that I was now legally married to Mary Jo Gross, a woman I had known for maybe two weeks. When I took her home to my apartment the next day, Bud was shaving. He was rightly stunned when I told him we got married. "If I didn't think you were joking I'd knock your teeth out," he said.

But it was no joke. We rented an apartment and settled in, excited about the challenge of finding a life together. As a wedding gift, Jada gave us a mahogany box full of highly manicured marijuana. As for Richard Noble, when the FBI came looking for him a couple of weeks later, he had vanished. I never heard what happened after that.

A few days after we were married, Jo went to Columbus, Ohio, to visit her mother and sister. I had to cover the Cowboys, who were playing that Sunday in Cleveland. Our plan was for Jo to meet me in Cleveland. She had bought a Buick convertible and we would drive back to Dallas together after the game that Sunday. It was the third week of November, 1963. President Kennedy was scheduled to visit the city that Friday, November 22, as part of the Democrats' strategy to improve his poor ratings in Texas.

The sky was bright and clear, one of those perfect autumn days when you see leaves dancing in the wind, hear the sound of people kicking footballs, and know for sure that, at long last, you have survived another miserable Texas summer. Shrake and I watched the motorcade from an intersection a few blocks from our apartment.

It was a good location because the caravan of cars would slow before making a right turn onto Cedar Springs, which fed into downtown Dallas. A small cluster of people had the same idea, and we found a spot a few feet away, where our view was uninterrupted. As the motorcade approached, Kennedy waved from the rear seat of his convertible and smiled directly at me, or that's how I remember it. Over the years I have sometimes told people that JFK winked at me and mouthed the words "I know what you two bad boys are up to." That's just my imagination at work. Anyhow, we stood there until the motorcade was out of sight and then drove to the drugstore across from the SMU campus, where we usually had morning coffee. The car radio was tuned to a Top 50 station where two moronic DJs played music and made lame jokes about current events. Pulling into a parking place in front of the drugstore, we were vaguely aware that the DJs' dialogue had been interrupted by a grave and frightened voice saying something about gunshots, about the president, about the president being hit, about the motorcade rushing to Parkland Hospital. It took a few seconds for it to register as a genuine news report. "This can't be happening," I said. Shrake shook his head in disbelief. We talked about what to do. As journalists, our instincts were to rush to the scene of the action, but it was hard to know just where the action was: it seemed to be everywhere. Since we were reporters for the *Dallas Morning News*, it made sense to head straight for our office, to report for duty, as it were.

Memories of that day are pretty sketchy. I remember watching Walter Cronkite on a television set in the managing editor's office, remember him saying that it is official now, the president is dead. From the office window, I could see the spot where the president had been shot, the Triple Underpass, the Texas School Book Depository window from which the shots were fired, the freeway leading to Parkland Hospital, where the body now rested. A large crowd had gathered in the street below the window and time seemed to be suspended. Like people on the street, most of the newspaper staff, or at least those not specifically assigned to cover the breaking story, milled about, sad and bewildered, waiting for directions, waiting for something else to happen, waiting for an explanation or an order. There was so much to explain. There had been a full-page ad in that day's *Dallas Morning News*, slandering JFK and inviting universal hatred aimed in his direction. Few people knew it at the time, but the ad was written and paid for by Bunker Hunt and some of his right-wing friends. (I learned about his connection to the offensive ad while joyriding with Bunker and his friends.) Jack Ruby had also visited the newspaper that fateful day, placing an ad touting Jada and the girls who would appear at the Carousel Club the following day. Who could imagine tomorrow? Who knew if there would be a tomorrow?

I tried to call Jo in Ohio, but couldn't get a long-distance line. I assumed she was safe and well, but in the whirlwind of unreality I couldn't be certain. I assumed that the NFL would cancel its Sunday schedule, but I was wrong. I got a call shortly, informing me that the Cowboys charter would leave the next morning at the usual time and that my seat was reserved. The AFL, which was still a separate league then, wisely chose to suspend its games.

There has never been a stranger road trip than that one to Cleveland. Dallas police had arrested a suspect named Oswald at a movie house in Oak Cliff, and rumors were flying of conspiracies and all kinds of weird stuff. The players boarded the team plane and took their usual seats, but nobody seemed remotely enthusiastic about the trip or the game. Guys who normally would have been joking or reading or playing cards sat in stunned silence, looking straight ahead. When we landed in Cleveland a couple of hours later, a small crowd had gathered on a street near the runway. People pointed and whispered but mostly waited in silence, behind police barricades. Players walked with their heads down, as though filing into a room where an execution was scheduled. At the hotel, nobody came to greet the team bus or help us find our rooms. When the team was introduced the next day at Memorial Stadium, some people booed and yelled insults, but most of them sat in silence, wondering what sort of people these were who could murder a president and then have the audacity to come play a football game.

Jo met me at the hotel and drove me to the stadium. We tried to talk, but there wasn't much to say. I had a feeling of deep foreboding, as though I had forgotten something important, as though time was running out. While I was retrieving my typewriter and briefcase from the trunk, I saw Shrake running across the parking lot in my direction. He was out of breath and very excited about something.

"Have you been watching TV?" he asked.

"No, we just finished breakfast. What happened?"

"That guy Oswald, the one they arrested?"

"What about him?"

"Someone just shot him in the basement of the Dallas police station. And you'll never guess who it was."

"Jack Ruby," I said. The name just slipped out of my mouth. Shrake was stunned, and I realized suddenly that Ruby was the correct answer to his impossible-to-answer question. Hundreds and maybe thousands of times I have reviewed that reply. What was I thinking? Why did Ruby's name slip out of my lips? I didn't really think that Jack Ruby had killed anyone. Or did I? No, that name just slipped out.

I've got no memory of who won the game on Sunday. The two teams merely went through the motions of playing football. I didn't bother going to the dressing room after the game, but quickly wrote a bland account and gave it to the Western Union operator. Jo met me at the car and we started a leisurely drive home, taking a route that went through Nashville, where she wanted to stop and say hello to a friend. The Smoky Mountains were aflame with reds and golds and we took a lot of side roads, the better to enjoy the scenery. We were in no hurry to get anywhere.

BUD HAD JOINED DAN AT *SPORTS ILLUSTRATED* and the two of them had captivated the staff with their freewheeling lifestyle. They had pretty much taken New York City prisoner, or so it seemed to me. By the mid-sixties, I was a regular visitor to New York, fascinated to be in their company and witness Dan's patented "whipout" act, the name he gave to the process of peeling off a twenty and slipping it to the guy up front so we'd usually get a table next to Ed Sullivan. Every headwaiter in town knew Dan by name. Our mutual agent at the Sterling Lord Agency, Cindy Degner, referred to Dan as "the Fabulous Mr. Jenkins." His first novel, *Semi-Tough*, wasn't merely the talk of the town; it was changing the language. "Semi" became the country's trendiest adjective. You'd be at a bar and hear some guy say, "My old lady, she's about semi-mean."

Sometimes I stayed with Dan and June, who had a really fine apartment at 86th and Madison Avenue. It was always full of interesting people, including Robert Redford, who lived in an apartment on the floor just below. Sometimes I stayed at Bud's apartment on 16th and Fifth Avenue. One memorable weekend when I was there covering a Cowboys-Giants game, I witnessed Don Meredith challenging Shrake and George Plimpton to a pissing contest off the third-floor balcony. I forget who won, but the losers were whoever happened along 16th Street at that particular time that evening.

You never knew who might show up at Shrake's place. The fabled Billy Lee Brammer, still riding the glory from *The Gay Place*, arrived one day with a portable typewriter and a beat-up suitcase, along with a bundle of manuscript pages that represented his futile attempt to write a sequel that he called *Fustian Days*. He stayed for several months, becoming a sort of writer-in-residence, but he would never finish the book. The idea had been a publisher's knee-jerk reaction to the Kennedy assassination. The plan was that the book would tell the story of JFK's successor, Lyndon B. Johnson, a man Brammer knew well. Billy Lee had worked for LBJ in Washington, and modeled his fictional Governor Arthur Fenstemaker on LBJ. I was with Brammer the day he got the call from the publisher. "I think I hit the jackpot," he told me. The large advance hastened his marriage to the young and very lovely Dorothy Browne, a student at UT. The newlyweds then moved to Washington. Problem was, neither LBJ nor anyone close to him would talk to Billy Lee.

One evening as I was standing on Bud's balcony enjoying a joint, I noticed that I had been joined by a distinguished gentleman in a three-piece suit and horn-rim glasses. He introduced himself as Ken McCormick, a name that at the time meant nothing to me. He said, "Bud tells me that you are writing a novel. I'd very much like to read it." Later, I discovered that Ken McCormick was the internationally famous editor in chief of Doubleday. That casual meeting on Bud's balcony led to my first book contract, an advance of $3,500, and the publication of *The Hundred Yard War*. Who could have guessed it was so easy to break into the writing world? But that's how it was in the sixties in New York, for me at least.

Every night was a night on the town with Bud and Dan. We would usually start at a bar everyone called the Chinaman's (it was a Chinese restaurant, just down the street from the Time & Life Building), where *Sports Illustrated*'s illustrious editor Andre Laguerre held court every evening from five until seven thirty, at which time his faithful driver had orders to whisk him away and deposit him in his own bed, at his own apartment. After an hour or so at the Chinaman's, we would gradually work our way to Toots Shor's for a few "Young Scotches" (to use Jenkins's phrase), and then uptown to P. J. Clarke's, and finally up to Elaine's, which became a sort of late-night base for our crowd. Plimpton, Larry L. King, and David Halberstam were nearly always there, and so were a lot of other writers and celebrities like Woody Allen.

Elaine was like the Godmother of New York (and Texas) writers: when *The Hundred Yard War* came out, she added its dust jacket to the collection of book covers (mostly by much better and certainly more famous writers) that hung from the bar's walls and ceiling. This cluster of Manhattan hangouts spawned numerous off-the-wall deals and assignments. One night at Shor's, Laguerre started talking to Shrake about golf courses in the Far East. What were they like and how many were there? "I know," he said cheerfully, smiling at the whiskey-fueled inspiration that had captured his senses. "We'll send you over to check it out." Andre was as good as his word; a few weeks later, Bud was off on a three-month trip to visit golf courses in exotic locales like Kuala Lumpur, Bangkok, and Sri Lanka, every leg of the trip on *SI*'s dime. Another time he sent Bud to some place in Argentina, where, for reasons I can't recall, he ended up in a jail cell for a couple of nights — until he finally smuggled a message to the local Time-Life bureau. *Blessed McGill*, by the way, is dedicated to Andre Laguerre.

AFTER ABOUT A YEAR OF MARRIAGE, JO AND I started sniping at each other and finding nits to pick, which led to some hellacious arguments. I stormed out of the house a couple of times, always to return after a few hours, reminded how empty my life was without her. Nevertheless, her strong independent streak, which I much admired, now came across as quarrelsome and petty. My ill temper was made worse by the pressure of trying to write articles with more shelf life than the daily newspaper columns that had been my career up to that time. Freelance assignments were few and far between. I was developing a good relationship with the editors at *Sport*, but getting quality assignments from top magazines outside of sports was tricky. Anyway, I was so busy carving out a career that I didn't notice how strained things had become with Jo, until I woke one Sunday morning to find her gone, bag and baggage. She didn't even leave a note. When she finally called a day or two later, she was in Columbus, Ohio, staying with her sister, and told me she couldn't live with me anymore. I was crushed, desperate to get her home again. I took a bus to Columbus and tried to reason with her, but finally accepted that the marriage was history. So be it, I told myself.

Fortunately, I had no time to brood. It was almost July, which meant that pro football camps were about to open. This was my favorite time of year. From the first week in July to the last week of the following January, my job was to hang close to the Dallas Cowboys, go where they went, and write about what they were doing. I would be too busy to lose sleep over a failed marriage.

I turned thirty that summer and enjoyed training camp even more than usual. I didn't hear from Jo, nor did I expect to. I had a brief fling with a nightclub waitress and was secretly relieved when she moved to Las Vegas to become a croupier. I had a lot of time to read, not work-related books but good stuff by writers like Gabriel García Márquez, Dashiell Hammett, James Jones, and John le Carré. A lot of teams in the NFL preferred training camps in small college towns, away from temptations, but Schramm loved the area around Los Angeles. He knew that the weather would be ideal, not too cold, not too hot. Thousand Oaks was less than an hour's drive north of the Los Angeles airport, a built-to-order little town, just across a mountain range from Malibu and the Pacific Ocean. The air was always cool and crisp, and smelled of the sea. You needed a light jacket for afternoon practice, even in August. The Cowboys were a class operation and knew how to pacify the media without insulting their intelligence or interfering with any-one's freedom to pursue a story.

Camp was a paid vacation. I stayed up until two or three every morning and slept until I decided to wake up, usually about lunch-time. I showered, put on a fresh Dallas Cowboys T-shirt that had been delivered to my door, ate a leisurely lunch of salad with cold cuts and melon in the team dining room, then watched the team practice and talked with players and coaches. With the two-hour time difference, I needed to write my story and get it to Western Union by 6 p.m. Then I would join Tex Schramm and a couple of his people, along with a small, select crowd of writers, at this really great bar-restaurant. I can't remember its name, but it was one of those Southern California spots that seemed to have invented hos-pitality and good taste.

As I say, one of the delights of camp was sleeping late, and that's what I was busy doing when the phone rang one morning. To my great surprise it was Jo. "I miss our life together," she said, "and I want to come home." There was a long silence as I weighed many alternatives and tried to compose my emotions. Once I managed to find my voice, all I could think to say was "Okay." Could it be that at age thirty my life was starting anew?

Jo joined me in late August, after the Cowboys returned to Dallas. Our love affair seemed new, fresh and alive with possibili-ties. We hadn't really talked much about having a family, but when we learned she was pregnant we were overjoyed. Shea Duncan Cartwright was born the following August. (The name Duncan, by the way, came from my beloved college professor, Duncan Robinson, who taught journalism at Arlington State and convinced me I had a future as a writer.)

Now, I love children—it's child*birth* that makes me uneasy. I've always tried to stay away from maternity wards. As it happened, Barbara was working in the maternity ward at Fort Worth's St. Joseph Hospital when Mark was born in 1957 and Lea a year later, so there was no way I could avoid being there—though I did manage to convince the nurses I was better off in the waiting area than the delivery room, which was their first suggestion. Almost a decade later, when Shea arrived, I managed to be on a Cowboys charter, flying between Los Angeles and Sacramento. Jo, of course, was a great mom and Shea became a totally irresistible baby, traveling with us everywhere, including a couple of extended trips to Mexico.

SPORTSWRITING MAY NOT PAY AS WELL AS BANK robbing, but it's a lot more fun and promises a brighter future. I met and became friends with some remarkably interesting people during my decade of writing about sports. The most fascinating was Don Meredith, who I think would have become a Hall of Fame quarterback if he had ignored smart-ass sportswriters (like me) and played another six or seven seasons. Dandy Don made playing the game look easy. He made it fun. He made it possible to keep on keeping on. When the outcome turned out wrong—when our team lost—he was a convenient target for our anger and frustration. He had a sense of humor and a style so fresh and original that it took people like me a while to recognize his quality of character. I think that I began to truly appreciate him after writing about a Meredith interception that cost the Cowboys a big game against the Packers in the 1960s.

My lead was a parody of Grantland Rice's famous Four Horsemen story after a Notre Dame game in the 1920s. This is how I started my game story: "Outlined against a gray November sky,

The Four Horsemen rode again Sunday in the Cotton Bowl. You remember their names: Death, Famine, Pestilence and Meredith." A lot of players would have taken this sentence as a cheap shot, but Meredith saw it as an attempt at dark humor. It was a plaintive cry from an admirer keenly disappointed by that fateful interception and the outcome of the game. I was proud of my lead: it became popular and was much quoted by Cowboys fans, but the words didn't really rest easy until I heard that Meredith had laughed out loud when he read it. Dandy Don, what a guy! He was easily the classiest athlete I ever knew or wrote about, and we remained friends until his death a few years ago.

By contrast, I also had a brief, unhappy acquaintanceship with Norm Van Brocklin when he coached the Vikings after retiring as a championship-level quarterback for the Eagles. Van Brocklin was a hothead with no detectable sense of humor. I can't remember how it started, but we got in an argument and finally a fight in the lobby of a hotel in Minneapolis the evening before a preseason game between the Cowboys and the Vikings. I recall standing near a bank of elevators and kicking him in the shin. He swung at me and missed by about three feet. He swung again, and this time accidentally punched Steve Perkins, another Dallas sportswriter. By now we were both on the floor, kicking, cursing, biting, and trying with hardly any success to visit bodily harm on each other. All I remember about that night was going to bed with a headache and a fat lip. When I boarded the team plane for the trip back to Dallas the following evening, Clint Murchison presented me with a gift-wrapped package. It was a pair of boxing gloves.

Somewhere in the back of my closet, I have another gift from the Cowboys from that same period: a plaque that consists of a mounted kicker's shoe and the engraved message "Just for Kicks!" The message celebrates not my scuffle with Van Brocklin, as some people believe, but another incident. This one took place at Tom Landry's weekly meeting with the Dallas–Fort Worth media. Included among the crowd of media representatives was this idiot from a local radio station who kept interrupting legitimate questions to Landry with "I'll answer that for you, Tom!" All of us wanted to kill this asshole, and I got my chance after he opened his radio show by making fun of my new cowboy boots. The following week, I got to the meeting early and waited for him at the top of the stairs, wearing my newly polished boots. When he appeared, I stepped forward, said, "You want to see my boots up close?" and proceeded to kick him down the stairs. When I returned to the media interview area, the other reporters gave me a standing ovation. And when I left the *Morning News* and took a job at the *Philadelphia Inquirer* a few years later, the Cowboys threw me a going-away party and gave me that plaque, which I still treasure. "Just for Kicks!" refers to that specific kick, which I dedicated to the team.

BY 1965, THIS IDYLLIC LIFE WAS SHOWING WEAR and tear, especially at the newspaper. I had several clashes with top editors at the *Dallas Morning News*, who were sadly lacking in humor and increasingly intolerant of some of the political comments I inserted in my column. Sometimes they penciled out lines or paragraphs and sometimes they killed the entire column. One particularly blatant example of censorship occurred when the managing editor killed a column in which I revealed that the Dallas Country Club was planning to cancel its annual tennis tournament rather than invite black star Arthur Ashe. Now this was obviously a major news story—a racist country club that had long hosted an international tournament was junking the whole thing rather than be forced to open its courts to a black man—and I was absolutely correct in reporting it: both Dallas newspapers had always given the tournament more than its share of free publicity. To let it simply vanish without any explanation was not merely bad journalism but cowardly social conduct. To its discredit, the *Times Herald* also chose to disregard the story. To make matters worse, *Sports Illustrated* got wind of the controversy and wrote a story that embarrassed not only the country club but the two newspapers.

Something else happened that summer that put a permanent chill on my relationship with the *Morning News*. I was at Cowboys training camp when I got a call from Billy Lee Brammer. He was in Los Angeles researching a story on a promising heavyweight boxer named Amos "Big Train" Lincoln and invited me to dine at a café that Lincoln recommended. "He's promised to introduce us to what they call soul food," Billy Lee told me, using a term that wasn't familiar to either of us back then. "We're going to a neighborhood called Watts."

Soul food turned out to be exactly what I'd eaten almost every day of my childhood—fried okra, black-eyed peas, fried steak, cornbread, tumblers of iced tea, slabs of apple pie. What's not to like? The streets of the neighborhood called Watts were dark, muggy, and strangely quiet—too quiet, I remember thinking. They weren't exactly deserted: clumps of sullen young men in stocking caps milled around under streetlights. The food, as advertised, was very good, but I was happy when we headed back to Thousand Oaks and the safety of a pro football camp.

Brammer called the next morning and told me to turn on the television: a riot had broken out in Watts. For the next hour or so, I sat in the day room watching in fascination as buildings burned and people died. After a time, Blackie Sherrod and Steve Perkins, my competitors from the *Times Herald*, joined me. As newspaper guys do in times of crisis or upheaval, we concentrated on piecing together what was happening and calculated what we should do about it. The trouble had started when an African American driving in his own neighborhood was pulled over by a white California Highway Patrol motorcycle officer on suspicion of DWI. In a short time the young man's mother, brother, and neighbors joined the confab. The day got hotter and so did tempers. Names were called. There was some pushing and shoving, somebody fired a shot, then another shot, until finally it turned into a full-blown riot, complete with looters and an out-of-control mob of bystanders. A number of deaths and hundreds of injuries had been reported, and nobody knew how much property damage. This wasn't just a riot—it was a race riot, something that hadn't happened in my lifetime.

The Cowboys had provided a rental car that was shared by members of the media, and we decided to use it and head for Watts, as fast as we could. Sherrod called his editor at the *Times Herald*, but

I couldn't get through to anyone on the desk at the *Morning News*. I left a voice message, telling the editor that I was leaving my post at the Cowboys camp to cover the Watts riot, as I was certain he would have me do—if he had been on the job.

By the time we got to Watts, the area was swarming with armed men and burning buildings: more than 1,600 Los Angeles city and county officers were at the scene and police chief William Parker had called in 4,000 National Guard troops.

Sherrod, Perkins, and I had all started out as police reporters and knew how to report on the run. We parked our rental car in a grocery store lot and caught rides in jeeps with National Guard troops. After a couple of minutes, I got separated from my pals and didn't see them again for hours.

I jogged along what had been quiet residential streets, now transformed into a war zone of burning cars, homes, and buildings. People were running in all directions, yelling and sometimes crying or screaming. I was frightened and confused, but also very excited to be on the front line of a major breaking news story. Since I had no map and no sense of direction, I stopped anyone I could find and asked them to tell me what was happening.

"We tired of this shit!" one old man with a stubby gray beard told me. A younger man in a white short-sleeved shirt and a necktie explained that Watts was a hellhole, that people felt trapped in a cauldron of bad schools, chronic unemployment, overpriced rent homes, and racial bondage. "This has been coming on for years," he told me. "Cops treat black people like fucking animals." Chief Parker didn't help the situation by comparing rioters to "monkeys in the zoo."

I had brought only a small spiral notebook. After a few hours the pages were full of my scribbled notes and I was using paper towels gathered from a service station rest room to record my observations. After a time, I found a pay phone in the back of a liquor store whose roof was on fire and called in a running report to the news desk in Dallas. The reporter who took my dictation seemed bored by the whole affair and puzzled about why I was so excited. He kept interrupting and asking, "How much more you got?" Good question, my friend, and one that I will retain for that glorious moment somewhere in a near future when I feel the bones of your worthless throat cracking between my fingers.

I wasn't concerned with details—numbers of deaths, injuries, arrests, property damage; the wire services had that covered—so I concentrated on a first-person account of what it was like to be here, to watch a neighborhood implode, to see people so despairing that torching their own homes and cars made some kind of perverted sense. Over several hours, I revised and updated the story in my head, rehearsing and refining each sentence as though composing for the archives, trying not to think of what I would say when I accepted the awards and accolades that were certain to follow my noble effort. I fell asleep that night dreaming of headlines, bylines, and hero welcomes back home. And I woke to the reality of the brand of zombie journalism practiced at the time in Dallas. While the *Times Herald* spread the story that Sherrod and Perkins had written across the top of the front page, the editors at the *News* cut my beautiful prose to six or eight paragraphs and buried it under a one-column headline, in a section with classified ads and club news. Angry, humiliated, scratched, cut, and sore from a day of running through war-zone streets and dodging police cars and jeeps, I was in a state of shock for several hours, wanting badly to confront the editors and demand an explanation of why my story had been treated with such contempt. But I needed to cool down first.

Several days passed before I came face-to-face with Jack Krueger, the editor in chief at the *News*. I expected him to be embarrassed, for himself, for the newspaper, for the whole world of journalistic honor, but instead he told me in a cool, collected voice: "This was an important story, but we couldn't have it written by *one of our own people*." Say what? Was he really telling me that the *Dallas Morning News*, a paper that had once stood up to the Ku Klux Klan and had won Pulitzer Prizes, had become so cowardly and craven that it couldn't print a staff-written report of a race riot? Yes, that was exactly what he was telling me, in his mealy-mouthed way.

BY NOW I KNEW THAT MY DAYS OF WRITING SPORTS on a daily basis were at an end, that a job that had once been fascinating had become not just drudgery but an embarrassment. One season was running into another: the cycle seemed in danger of repeating itself into infinity. I felt burned out and kept wondering if there wasn't something else I ought to be doing. In my ten-year newspaper career, I had worked for four different papers, two in Fort Worth, two in Dallas. I hoped *Sports Illustrated* would make me an offer, but that didn't happen. While I was trying to decide what to do, Lamar Hunt invited me and four other Dallas journalists to take a trip at his expense to Dundee, Scotland. The purpose of the trip was to educate us about soccer—what the Brits call football. Lamar's newest brainstorm was to start a soccer league, with its headquarters in Texas, naturally. He had already contracted the Dundee United team to represent Dallas until he could put together a team of his own.

I had never been to Europe, or even off the North American continent, so I jumped at the opportunity. The trip was an eye-opener, especially the conversations I had with Scottish sportswriters, who were mostly old, broken down, and very poorly paid. All of them wanted to work in the United States, wanted a job just like the one I was ready to give up. I returned home confused and downhearted. To make matters more bewildering, a few days later I got a totally unexpected call from the sports editor of the *Philadelphia Inquirer*, offering me a job, writing three columns a week and covering an occasional college football game. The pay was more than double what I was making at the *Dallas Morning News*. Flattered by the offer, I talked it over with Jo. She agreed that a new life in Philadelphia sounded like the kind of adventure we needed. That decision turned out to be delusional, though in retrospect it transformed my career in a way I couldn't have otherwise managed.

At first we were fascinated by Philly. It was a big eastern city, a short train ride to New York or Washington. The museums were great and so were scenic strolls along the Schuylkill River and through the historical neighborhoods. Like Boston, Philadelphia is one of those places where the American dream was formulated and fought for, and reading about it isn't nearly as satisfying as walking through its narrow streets and breathing its musty fragrance. Most of our neighbors were friendly and as curious about us as we were about them. We took day trips in our Volkswagen van to places like Valley Forge and Atlantic City, and made friends with our neighborhood butcher and with an Italian janitor who worked at our apartment building. Our apartment occupied the entire third floor of what had been an old warehouse, half a block off Broad Street, just south of City Hall and on the fringe of a black neighborhood that was seething with anger. In big cities all across the East, blacks were protesting centuries of injustice, rioting and burning buildings. From our balcony we got a bird's-eye view of the fireworks. It was a replay of the urban warfare I had seen in Watts, and to realize that it was spreading across the country was frightening but also exciting, like riding a poorly constructed roller coaster. Even so, I began to feel uneasy about the whole Philadelphia scene and wonder if I'd made a big mistake.

I lasted at the *Inquirer* just eighty-nine days, that being one day short of the ninety required to be a member of the guild, at which point my job would have been safe from the arbitrary judgment of a small group of corporate executives who hated what I was writing. In their defense, I hated it, too. I wasn't writing about sports, at least not when I could avoid it. I wrote a column about my Italian janitor, who had started watching bullfights on TV and decided that that's what he wanted to do with his life—fight bulls. On the Fourth of July, I interviewed a group of graying veterans who gathered at Independence Hall and wrote about the pathos of their lives and the futility of the war in Vietnam. When football camps started, I traveled to the Philadelphia Eagles' facility in Hershey, Pennsylvania, and wrote that their coach, Joe Kuharich, ought to give up football and run for dogcatcher. I was beginning to hate Philadelphia, in particular the *Philadelphia Inquirer*. The only friend I made on staff was Joe McGinnis, whose daily column was funny and smart and refreshing. We became friends and drinking buddies and I discovered that he was as unhappy at this newspaper as I was. Joe confided that he was being pressured and censored to follow some unspoken party line, to write "positive things" about the city and its interests. A few days later, Joe's contract was revoked and he was out the door. And a day or two after that, I got fired. I had never been fired before and it came as a shock. But it was also an enormous relief. I remember skipping down Broad Street toward our apartment, feeling a little like Gene Kelly in *Singing in the Rain*, clicking my heels together and singing out, "Free, free at last!"

When I told Jo what had happened, she hugged me hard and said, "Let's get the hell out of this town." I bullied the apartment manager until he reluctantly surrendered a key to the freight elevator, and that night we loaded all our belongings in the VW van and headed for Texas, happy as bluebirds fleeing south for the winter.

Instead of returning to Dallas, however, we decided to move to Austin, where my friend Bud Shrake had recently settled. Shrake had just married a bright, beautiful young woman named Doatsy Sedlmayr, who was an editor at *Sports Illustrated*. Simultaneously, he had somehow convinced his boss at *Sports Illustrated* that he could work out of Austin just as well as he was working out of New York, and had purchased a new home on Bee Creek above Lake Austin, among the cedar breaks of West Lake Hills. Austin had been my favorite Texas locale since the 1950s when I spent two years at the University of Texas, and this was the perfect opportunity to make it my new home and also to be close to my oldest and best friend.

2

WE RENTED A COTTAGE IN WEST LAKE HILLS, on the western bank of Lake Austin, one of the Highland Lakes built in the 1930s when an ambitious young congressman named Lyndon Johnson convinced the federal government to construct a series of dams along the Colorado River in Texas. This particular cottage had been built for the daughter of a former governor, probably as a weekend getaway. It was only partly finished—rough wooden planks, a covered walkway leading from the street to the front door, propped on stilts over what had once been a river or creek. Little Shea started calling it the Brown House, so that became its name. Despite the spare exterior, the interior was charming—two bedrooms with views of cedar and oak trees, excellent hardwood floors, massive windows that stretched from the floor to an eighteen-foot ceiling, a balcony with a spectacular view of downtown, the University of Texas Tower, and the dome of the state capitol. Though we were only a ten-minute drive from downtown, the locale felt secluded, as though we lived in the deep woods. Foot trails where skunks and armadillos frolicked ran off in several directions, and a winding road led to the lake and to one of my favorite bars and hangouts, the Lake Austin Inn.

I tucked my desk in a corner of the living room, where the view was uninterrupted. I had plenty of work to do. Before leaving the East, I made a trip to New York to visit with a number of editors and publishers and got all the assignments I could handle. *Sports Illustrated* asked me to cover the first-ever World's Championship Chili Cookoff in Terlingua, Texas, on the Texas-Mexico border, in the company of my longtime photographer friend Shel Hershorn, a great traveling companion. Willie Morris, an old friend from UT journalism days and now the editor of *Harper's*, asked me to write about my days as a sportswriter, which eventually produced one of the best magazine articles I ever wrote, "Confessions of a Washed-up Sportswriter." The editor of *Sport* magazine assured me that I was always at the top of their list of freelancers.

In the *Harper's* piece I wrote something that remains my firm conviction: "Sportswriting should be a young man's profession. No one improves after eight or ten years, but the assignments get juicier and the way out less attractive. After eight or ten years there is nothing else to say."

Just as "Confessions" was hitting the newsstand and attracting wide attention, I got a completely unexpected job offer to work on the political campaign of a wealthy and prominent Austin attorney named Fagan Dickson. Dickson was a longtime friend and sup-porter of Lyndon Johnson but had turned on the president over his war in Vietnam. As an expression of his stand against the war, Dickson decided to run against LBJ's handpicked candidate in the 10th Congressional District, J. J. "Jake" Pickle. This had once been Johnson's home district, and the symbolism was intentionally framed on an ironic notion: that the way to end the war was to con-vince Johnson that the pointy-headed intellectuals in Washington didn't appreciate him and he ought to come home and be with his own kind. The slogan "Bring Lyndon Home" was meant to produce a smile, not a rush of hostility. That's the part that attracted me— plus the money, which was really good.

I decided to put on my best game face. First, I got a haircut, shaved off my scraggly beard, and bought a suit—I hadn't worn a suit in at least ten years—and began attending Rotary Club lun-cheons, glad-handing other guys in suits, and writing press re-leases. In no time, however, I realized I was a fish out of water. As a PR specialist, I was all thumbs. And the candidate I was backing didn't have a clue what the campaign was supposed to be about. Stopping the war, he confided to me, was secondary to the issue that really got his juices flowing—"returning the country to the gold standard." The gold standard! Who gave a flying fuck about the gold standard? That should have been an unmistakable clue that this wouldn't turn out well.

And indeed, it did not. A couple of weeks later, on March 26, 1968, as Jo and I were preparing dinner, there was a knock on the door. It was two hippies—or at least two young men pretending to be hippies—asking for directions. Mellow guy that I was, I invited them in for a glass of wine and—as misfortune would have it—a puff of really good Mexican boo. One of them asked me to sell them some weed. "I don't sell dope," I said, with a good-hearted laugh. "But I'll roll you a joint for the road." Which I did. Too late, I realized I'd made a bad mistake.

Early the next morning two uniformed officers from the Travis County Sheriff's Office (our house was outside the city limits of Austin), accompanied by the two hippies, now dressed in their DEA best, arrested Jo and me for possession of marijuana, a felony that at the time could have gotten us life sentences. They tore up the place, ripping out the floor furnaces, leaving the icebox door open, throwing garbage all over the kitchen. They also went out of their way to demean us as rotten parents, so uncaring that we used drugs in front of our three-year-old son, too dense and stupid to see through their plot. They ignored our plea to at least allow us to call Shea's babysitter to come take care of him. Instead, they put the little fellow in the backseat of their police cruiser, next to his handcuffed parents. At the police station, I was allowed my one telephone call. I used it to call an attorney friend, Sam Houston Clinton, who showed up a short time later to rescue Shea and, eventually, make our bail.

Our arrest drew headlines all over Texas and caused numerous unexpected consequences. Humiliated, Fagan Dickson withdrew his name from the congressional race that same day—but didn't offer to help me in any way. Larry L. King, a writer friend, relayed the news to his friend Warren Burnett, a prominent lawyer from

Odessa, who agreed to take on my defense. Burnett instructed me to grab the next flight and meet him at his office in Odessa. When I told him I couldn't afford the price of a bus ticket, much less an airplane, he wired the money.

Burnett met me at the airport, a six-pack of beer tucked under one arm. He was a few years older than me and wore a rumpled gray suit and an ironic smile. He didn't seem particularly interested in talking about my case, so we spent the entire day exploring all the beer joints in the Odessa area and talking about politics. He was smart, informed, and a gifted conversationalist. I knew at once that we would be great friends.

In the days that followed, I learned a great deal about Warren Burnett. With the possible exception of Percy Foreman of Houston, he was at the time the most famous and respected lawyer in Texas. Among his many well-publicized victories was the "Kiss and Kill Murder Case," in which a model young man, a scholar and athlete, kissed his fifteen-year-old girlfriend good-bye and blew her head off with a shotgun. Burnett won an acquittal by convincing the jury that his client was "temporarily dethroned of reason" and finally gave way to the young woman's pleas that she wanted to go "live with the angels."

Burnett had a reputation as a gambler, a dice-roller who went by hunch or instinct, but he clearly knew the law, chapter and verse, and understood how to convey its subtleties to a jury. His understanding of human nature was remarkable. "I pick a jury like Karl Marx would," he once told me. "Along economic lines, with a definite notion of class structure. This may not be true across America, but in Texas a lawyer can feel he's done pretty well toward his client if he cuts a jury along economic lines."

One of his first tasks was to deflate my billowing ego. Instead of feeling contrite, I was incensed at my treatment by the criminal justice system. I didn't want a mere apology—I wanted the bastards to give me back my dope. At one of our early meetings, as I was prattling on about the Constitution and the Bill of Rights and such, Burnett interrupted and said, "Eh, Cartwright. If they do send you to the Big Rodeo, don't tell them you're a writer. They hate writers down there." The Big Rodeo! That was Warren's term for the Texas prison system. It was such an engaging expression that I decided to incorporate it into a screenplay I was working on and used it later in books and articles.

FOR SOME TIME I HAD BEEN RUNNING THE OUTLINE for a novel through my drug-enhanced brain. The story was set in the near future, and the main character was a newspaper reporter on a fictional paper in Dallas—which I called New Dynamo City. The broad theme was a critical look at how newspapers had surrendered their historical roles as watchdogs and become part of the establishment. In this perverted environment, honest journalists were driven underground and the whole mechanism of a free press was under attack. The country was sinking into social revolution that threatened civil war. In the story, a bunch of hippies/revolutionaries who lived in a cave outside of New Dynamo City were conspiring to blow it up. I had learned from my research that in reduced temperatures bats go into a state of hibernation. So the hippies planned to cool the bats until they were asleep, attach tiny incendiary bombs to their undersides, then slowly warm and release them on New Dynamo City. I know now how sappy that plot sounds, but, remember, I was smoking lots of dope at the time.

In my current state of mind, I concluded that the perfect place to write such a book was Mexico, land of revolution. I had in mind the village of Zihuatanejo, where Timothy Leary had had his LSD colony a few years earlier. I knew from friends who had lived there that the living was cheap and exotic. I wrote an outline of the book and mailed it to my editor at Doubleday. A few weeks later, I learned that they had accepted my proposal and were sending an advance of $5,000, a fortune in those days. Crazy as it sounds today, that's how things worked in the publishing business in 1969.

First, of course, I had to stabilize my legal situation. By now Burnett had assembled a first-class team of attorneys to oversee my defense—including Sam Houston Clinton and David Richards of Austin, and A. R. "Babe" Schwartz, who was practicing at that time in South Texas. Schwartz was a member of the state legislature and used his office to get me a legislative contingency, a tactic that delayed the trial for several months and thus freed me for the trip to Mexico. Things were working out better than I'd hoped. Our VW van had been repossessed by the loan company after the publicity surrounding our arrest, so Jo and I bought a canary yellow VW Beetle, loaded up my electric typewriter (bad choice, as it turned out) and other gear, secured little Shea in the backseat, and headed south toward Laredo, where we connected with the old Pan-American Highway, down through Monterrey and Mexico City. We spent a couple of days celebrating in Mexico City, which hadn't yet been polluted and was one of the most exciting and totally delightful cities in the world, then headed to Acapulco, and finally Zihuatanejo.

At the time, Zihuatanejo (pronounced see-wha-tah-NAY-ho) was a small fishing village tucked away on a nearly perfect bay, about a three-hour drive up the coast from Acapulco. Zihuatanejo was a sanctuary for Indian nobility: the name translates as "place of women," and it was a matriarchal society when the Spanish arrived in the early 1500s. Spain used it to launch a trade route to the Orient but eventually lost interest in colonizing the area. By the mid-twentieth century, it was populated by just a few hundred fishermen and farmers and a handful of American drug smugglers, expats, and adventurers like me.

One of several interesting people I met was a smuggler and developer named Arty, who in real life was a New York City slumlord. Arty had decided to expand his slum operation to Zihuatanejo, even though Mexican law prohibited non-citizens from owning property. His scheme worked like this: each year he would arrive with a pregnant girlfriend, and when the child was born (automatically becoming a citizen of Mexico) he would purchase property in its name. He had built a fairly elaborate thatched-roof *palapa* on a rocky point on the hillside, with a view of a beautiful beach called Playa la Ropa. If things went according to plan, Arty would someday own most of the land on Zihuatanejo Bay. This was a decade or more before a neighboring village called Ixtapa became a world-class resort, but there were rumors that this would indeed be the fate of Zihuatanejo and other villages in the area. I lost track of Arty years ago. There was no trace of him when I visited Z in 2001, but most of the mountainside where he had had his hut was covered by expensive homes and businesses. Knowing Arty, I feel sure he got his share of the profits.

Jo and I rented a furnished two-bedroom house on the opposite side of the bay. Owned by one of the village priests, it was roomy and open, with wide windows, a sundeck on the roof, and a thatched-roof patio in front, where I hung my hammock. Most of the houses and buildings were brick, covered with stucco. Adobe, the preferred building material of the Mexican interior, didn't work in this damp climate; it turned to goo and melted away during the rainy season.

From the time we arrived in early April until the first week of June, not a drop of rain fell. The earth was as hard as concrete and not a sprig of grass or anything resembling the color green was in evidence. Everything looked dead; even the people seemed to wither and diminish in the heat. But once the rains came, just like magic, the land began to breathe and blossom, becoming green and fragrant virtually overnight. The rains immediately tempered the heat, as if God had decided to adjust the thermostat, and in an amazingly short time the dry season was a forgotten memory.

Our nearest neighbor was the family of John and Madora Brothers, who owned a small café called Los Arcos. The café was also their home, which worked out well, because hardly anyone ever came there to eat. John and Madora were originally from Berkeley and had attended the University of California, before moving to Mexico twenty-some years earlier. They had lived for a time in Mexico City, where John had some type of government position that, among its perks, gave him permission to murder a victim of his choice. The perk was good for life. Of course, he never exercised the option, but he was proud to own it and spoke of it frequently. They had three teenage sons, all born in Mexico but with dual citizenship, and educated by their parents, which is to say they were highly literate and informed about the world. In the company of the boys, I explored the jungles and captured wild parrots, which I kept in a bamboo cage that the boys constructed for me. For a short time I also owned a small burro, which I bought from a passing farmer for $10. I don't know why I bought the damn thing—except that $10 seemed so reasonable at the time. The burro, which I called Morono, soon became a pain in the ass. I tried to run him off, but he seemed to enjoy the field of weeds below my house and stayed around until I persuaded John Brothers to find a man willing to take him off my hands. At first the man wanted to be paid to take the animal away, but John convinced him that a free donkey was a good bargain and the guy finally led Morono away, to a better life, I trust.

John and I spent many hours talking about our shared views of the world and drinking rum at a seaside café near the zocalo, where he was widely known as El Professor. He owned thousands of books, many of which I borrowed and read in my hammock. This being the wild tropics, the electricity was reliably unreliable—once the rainy season arrived, power went off three or four times a day. Before long I put away the electric typewriter and wrote in longhand on yellow legal pads. After a few weeks, I gave up writing altogether and spent my time reading.

Jo and I explored miles of unoccupied beach, which ran off in both directions. Every afternoon, we ate a hearty lunch of fresh seafood, made love in our sweaty bedroom, and took a long nap. Our stretch of beach ended abruptly in places too steep and overgrown by jungle to permit passage, so we searched out mountain trails that bypassed the problem areas. Sometimes Jo and Madora shopped together at the market, leaving John and me to amuse ourselves with booze, books, and exploration. One day John said that he wanted to introduce me to a friend who occupied a section of Playa la Ropa. You couldn't reach it on foot, so we rented a skiff with a small motor. When we landed, he introduced me to La Ropa's single resident, a Frenchman called, of course, Frenchy. He lived in an open-sided *palapa*, with dozens of women's bras dangling from the ceiling. Frenchy had discovered a recipe for absinthe, which he made by fermenting wormwood. I never learned where he got the wormwood, or how he processed it, but the resulting brew was an aromatic green liquid that turned cloudy once water was added. It tasted like licorice. The effect was mildly narcotic and I understood at once why it was so popular in Europe back in the twenties. I had read about absinthe in Hemingway (and other places) and understood that the narcotic effect caused brain damage. Though I've never believed the tales about brain damage—believe me when I tell you I've researched this with great diligence—that was the reason absinthe was universally banned years ago. When I asked for a refill, Frenchy reluctantly mixed a second drink, but refused my requests for more. John declined the drink, for reasons I can't explain. All I know is absinthe was one fine drink. Though I only tried it that one time, I've never forgotten the warm, secure sensation. Can it be that after all these years, I'm still hooked?

John tried to teach us Spanish, at $10 a lesson. We mastered a few phrases but never got comfortable with the language. Our attempts, however, led to some awkward, often very funny situations. Trying to buy a type of popular redfish from a local fisherman, Jo confused the fish's Spanish name and asked for some *chinga sus madre*, which means "fuck your mother." We hired a very proud but prissy retired teacher to take care of Shea. His name, as I recall, was Epollito, which was too foreign for little Shea's uneducated tongue. Shea kept calling the old gentleman "Pollo," which means "chicken." We could see Epollito cringe every time Shea crooned his name.

After we'd been in Zihuatanejo about three months, Bud and Doatsy came for a visit. They were formulating a plan to rent a villa in Acapulco for a month, with Dan and June Jenkins, their three kids, and five or six longtime friends from Texas. We had had enough of Zihuatanejo by then and decided to join them.

We spent a fabulous month in Acapulco, in a beautiful villa once owned by the Mexican movie star Dolores Del Rio. It had six or seven large bedrooms, arranged around a central *sala* or family area, and a large swimming pool that sat on a high cliff, over a stretch of water favored by tour boats. We spent much of our time poolside. One day we got the bright idea to hang a banner over the side of the cliff, greeting tourists passing below. In bright red capital letters it read:

DOLORES DEL RIO SAYS HI TO ALL OUR BOYS IN KHAKI.

It was fun to wave at the passengers who aimed cameras in our direction and no doubt speculated among themselves as to the mental state of the strange group of people at the top of the cliff. Life drifted by unhurried and without apparent care.

The meals at the villa were always good and interesting. The old woman who ran our kitchen was supposed to be one of the best cooks in Acapulco, but Dan Jenkins, who was famous among our crowd for refusing to eat anything that wasn't brown or white, didn't trust her even a little bit. Every morning he'd send Marty, Sally, and Danny to the kitchen to check the groceries and report what the cook was preparing for lunch. "We don't know what it is, Daddy," they would tell him, "but it has lots of arms and legs." Dan loaded them in his rental car and drove the family to lunch at Denny's. This became a daily ritual. Half an hour before lunch or dinner at the villa, as the rest of us began to assemble for the meal, Dan and June and their three kids would head for Denny's. Dan was also discomforted by the little geckos that played on the walls and sometimes hid in your shoes or crawled down the neck of your shirt. All of us thought of the geckos as pets, except Dan. One day as he was ranting about all the Mexican things he was learning to hate, he paused and added, "And another thing I don't like is those damn little lizards."

One guest who shared the villa with us was a vice president of a large bank in downtown Dallas. I'll call him Skidmore and tell you just a little about him. He had a brilliant mind and was an insatiable reader of all sorts of books, and he loved to smoke dope and play games that challenged his mind. One was a board game called Pro Football. During the previous football season, a group of us had gathered at his apartment for a rousing game of Pro Football every Tuesday evening; the contests became at times so spirited that we almost came to blows. Skidmore and several of us had been friends for a couple of years, and in a way none of us ever understood, business associates. Skidmore would have us sign blank loan applications from his bank, after which money would mysteriously appear in our accounts. We could use the money as we pleased, no strings attached. After a length of time we'd get a thank-you note from the bank, informing us that the note on our pickup truck had been paid in full. This arrangement ended some months later, when Skidmore suddenly vanished from our lives. I like to think that he is living comfortably in some South American country, where he is on a first-name basis with the dictator.

Life in the villa was mostly sanguine, due in part to a kilo of Acapulco Gold that Bud and I brought from Zihuatanejo. The problem was, nobody had thought to bring cigarette papers. It is far easier to buy drugs or even a submachine gun in Acapulco than a pack of Zig-Zags. Jo and Doatsy wandered the back alleys of Acapulco for most of a day before they were able to purchase a single package of papers—for $5!

Everything was expensive. Our VW broke down and it cost us $500 (and took two weeks) to get it repaired. Even so, it was great fun being there with our friends. Doatsy's sister Andy and her mother visited us in July. They stayed at an expensive hotel, Las Brisas, and invited us to dinner. As it happened, it was the night that Neil Armstrong made his historic walk on the moon: July 21, 1969. We had planned to listen to the broadcast of the landing on my shortwave radio, but instead we watched it on a giant television while dining at the hotel's lavish open-air restaurant. What a magic night: tropical breezes, big steaks, endless margaritas— and a moon so gigantic and brilliant that it took my breath away. As we looked at it, an American astronaut was up there claiming it for all mankind. Best of all, I was there with the people I loved most: Bud, Doatsy, Jo, and, now, Andy and her mother. Not only were they good company, they picked up the check.

FROM OUR FIRST MEETING IN THE POLICE STATION press room in Fort Worth in 1956 until his death in 2011, Bud Shrake was my guiding star, the force that gave me light, hope, and direction. He was a big brother, a loyal and steady friend, a co-conspirator, and, thank God, a reliable bad influence. We shared a burning need to seek out trouble, to make sure that things happened, even when they weren't otherwise inclined to happen. We excelled at testing limits and spreading joy. This required an extensive wardrobe of costumes, which we always managed to have available. I have a photo of me wearing a World War I helmet and Bud decked out in a red fez—for what occasion I can't imagine. We were our own occasion. Sometimes he dressed as Batman and I presented myself as Robin. This was years before the Caped Crusaders became public icons. In these outrageous costumes, we cruised around Dallas, looking for people who would appreciate being liberated from the ordinary. I remember a night when Batman and Robin paid a surprise visit to the home of Cowboys president Tex Schramm and his wife, Marty, who, to their everlasting credit, welcomed them and served cocktails. Other times we dressed as Les Flying Punzars, claiming to be a team of Italian acrobats with a shady history, something about having been expelled from the 1956 Olympics after failing a gender test. We found the word *punzar* in an Italian dictionary (it means, as I recall, "prick," as in pricking your finger with a pin—which didn't really translate our true meaning, but was as close as we could come at the time). The original Punzars were me, Bud, and our esteemed boss at the *Dallas Times Herald*, Blackie Sherrod. Our wives stitched together our costumes, using scraps from their sewing boxes and a few swatches of cloth purchased at a fabric shop. The Punzars made their first appearance in 1958, at an annual gathering of North Texas journalists, called the Midwinter Follies and Fashionable Freak Show. Over the years Blackie dropped out, but Bud and I carried on the tradition, recruiting different friends to fill out the trio. Singer-songwriter Jerry Jeff Walker sometimes filled the bill, with his own distinctive flair.

The Punzars spoke broken English and were totally inscrutable. We kept a footlocker full of Punzar paraphernalia—black tights, pink tunics with the letter *P* in reverse on the chest, green capes—in case a third Punzar happened along.

The Punzars might show up anywhere and try anything. I recall being at a nightclub in Dallas with Lamar Hunt and some other swells, all of us wearing red Dallas Texans blazers. Bob Halford, a good friend and the publicity director of the Texans, got to the microphone and announced that the world-famous Flying Punzars were in the audience and might be persuaded to perform their death-defying triple somersault. Without waiting for applause—which almost never followed such announcements—we leaped onstage and proceeded to take numerous bows. As a snare drum began to roll, Bud stationed himself at one corner of the stage, his arms dangling from his chest and his hands cupped to catch my foot. I positioned myself across the stage. At the roll of the drum, I raced toward him, fully believing for at least that particular moment that my foot would meet with his cupped hands, and that he would toss me gracefully into the air. I would then execute the perfect triple and land in an upright stance on his broad shoulders. Of course that's not exactly what happened. My foot missed his cupped hands by seven or eight inches, slamming instead into the middle of his chest, at which point we both tumbled off the stage and into a set of drums and cymbals. What a memorable clatter! We bounced back onstage in triumph, taking numerous bows while the audience sat in stunned silence.

Though he seldom talked about it, Bud always had a novel in the works, subjects ranging from events in his life to the incomprehensibly mysterious. *Strange Peaches* is based on what was happening to us and people we knew during the time of JFK's assassination. The character of Ben Carpenter is Bud, as he saw himself at the time. He used me as the model for his friend Buster. Dorothy was based on a girl named Diane Dodd, a stunningly beautiful University of Texas student that Bud met in Austin and invited to come live in our apartment in Dallas. The character called Franklin was a version of our friend Bob Thompson, who was a close friend of Clint Murchison, Jr., and who allowed us to share his high-living lifestyle.

I think Bud really loved Diane Dodd, but wouldn't admit it, even to himself. He took her to Acapulco for a few weeks in 1965 or 1966, where she caught some kind of disease that eventually killed her. Before she got sick, however, she wandered away to Houston, where, we learned later, she climbed aboard Ken Kesey's Merry Pranksters bus in Houston and left for San Francisco. Diane was very much a child of the sixties, free, fun-loving, and doomed.

This book was followed by *Peter Arbiter*, a satire in the manner of *Satyricon* in which three social misfits amble through the world of Dallas moneyed society. Neither book made much money.

Bud moved for a time to the Left Coast, living at the Beverly Hills home of Don and Susan Meredith and looking for a foothold in Hollywood. Then, out of the blue, he and I both received identical telegrams from someone claiming to be actor Cliff Robertson. The telegrams—yes, there was such a thing as telegrams back in the day—asked if we would be interested in rewriting a screenplay written several years earlier, titled "Ride the Wild Lightning." It was about life on the professional rodeo circuit. Since the telegrams arrived on April Fool's Day, 1970, each of us assumed the other was playing a joke. A couple of phone calls, however, revealed the offer to be legitimate.

Having never read a screenplay, I had not a clue about the format or the length. Bud had read a copy of William Goldman's screenplay *Butch Cassidy and the Sundance Kid* and told me, "It looks fairly simple, a whole lot easier than writing books." After reading the screenplay that Robertson sent us, we decided that it wasn't worth rewriting. But we were willing to write an original on the same broad subject—life on the rodeo circuit. I recalled Warren Burnett's cutting reference to the Big Rodeo, meaning the Texas state prison, and we began plotting a new story about a character we named J. W. Coop, who learns to rodeo while in prison. When the time comes for his release, he joins the rodeo circuit, working at the only profession he knows. He is successful at first and wins some prize money and meets a girl he might learn to love, but the world has changed greatly while he was away. He can't adjust to modern life. He can't fit in. In the end he robs a grocery store, knowing that this is a sure way to return to prison, where he'll feel safe and secure. Robertson liked our broad outline and thus began our grand Hollywood adventure.

A week later, we met Robertson at Love Field, which was at that time Dallas's major airport. He was handsome, but shorter than I'd expected, and full of kinetic energy and a practiced charm. I've seen this sort of thing before in certain show biz types, a professional affliction in which a person's eyes become too bright to focus. I liked him well enough, but suspected from the beginning that there was something artificial about his good-ol'-boy act. We took him to a party that night at the home of former Dallas Cowboys wide receiver Pete Gent. Don Meredith and several other players were there. Robertson had cautioned us that he didn't want people to recognize him, so we introduced him as our friend "Biff." By the end of the evening he was royally pissed that nobody had recognized who he really was.

We had already contacted Larry Mahan, whom we knew through mutual friends. Mahan was at that time the most famous rodeo star in the country, five-time World All-Around Rodeo Champion, television celebrity, and brand name for a line of western wear. He agreed to personally guide us on a tour of the rodeo circuit. With Biff and a two-man camera crew in tow, we followed Mahan to four or five events within driving distance of Dallas. Like good reporters, we took extensive notes on the language and customs of cowboys, how they prepared for an event, what they wore, the gear they packed, the highs and the lows of constant travel, the constant risk and often reality of injury. Some of the more interesting cowboys became characters in our screenplay.

We finished the first draft in about five weeks, extremely pleased with our work. Biff responded with a memorandum of questions and suggestions that was longer than the screenplay itself.

We were about half finished with the rewrite when he showed up in Austin. Bud and Doatsy invited him to stay in their guest bedroom, so we were in very close quarters for a few days, during which time we heard a rumor of an impending drug raid. Such rumors were commonplace in Austin at the time, but were almost always false alarms. Nevertheless, Bud gathered his small stash from its hiding place under his bed, and hid it instead inside a pipe, half buried in the dry creek bed behind his house. Biff watched all this with great interest, then gathered his own small stash and asked Bud to hide it in the same pipe. Biff stayed up late reading the screenplay, then woke Bud up about 2 a.m., saying he needed to get back to Hollywood and would Bud please retrieve his stash, which Bud did, in a driving rain, holding a flashlight in his teeth.

Months passed before we heard again from Biff. He didn't expressly reject our work, but he didn't pay us, either. As weeks passed, I nearly forgot about it, but Bud didn't. One day as he was thumbing through a Hollywood trade paper, he spotted an article in which Biff took credit for a new film at Columbia Pictures called *J. W. Coop*, which he claimed was produced in secrecy to protect it from other rodeo movies in production. He claimed to be the producer, director, and sole author of the film.

As Robertson toured the talk shows, magazines, and newspaper offices, he got more and more carried away with the story he had invented. At first he claimed that he sent us the original story in a two-page memo before we wrote a word—he even submitted a fraudulent copy of the nonexistent memo to the Screen Writers Guild, dated, unfortunately, a year later than the time frame when all this actually took place. Later, he told a group of New York film critics that he sent us a *finished* script, which we returned in three days, unchanged. After being courted by Robertson, the critics compared our movie to *Hud*, *Grapes of Wrath*, and *Hamlet*. Elston Brooks, amusements editor of the *Fort Worth Star-Telegram*, called *J. W. Coop* a major statement of our time. On reading Brooks's remarks, I told Shrake, "Anyone who thinks that movie is a major or even a minor statement is the sort who would enjoy reading the Waco telephone book." In a previous column, before he had even seen the movie, Brooks wrote of his visit with Cliff Robertson and referred to Robertson as "my best friend in Hollywood." Though Shrake and I both knew Elston Brooks well—Bud had gone to high school with him, and I had worked with him at the *Star-Telegram*—he didn't bother to call and ask our version of what happened. Bud telephoned and asked Brooks when he got to be such close friends with Robertson. It turned out that Brooks had met the actor once, at a party before the premiere of *Charly*. "What impressed Elston," Bud told me, "was that after all these years, Robertson still called him by his first name."

We were forced to sue, not just for the money (about $10,000) but for the screen credit and some peace of mind. Our attorney friend David Richards took the case and after numerous delays got it on the docket in Austin, where we mistakenly believed a jury would side with its two homeboys against this slick Hollywood type. We couldn't have been more mistaken. When Biff showed up for the trial wearing what looked like a big-game-hunter outfit, members of the jury panel swarmed him for autographs. "If this was a capital trial," Bud whispered, "they'd hang us."

Lucky for us, Biff didn't really have much of a case. He had hired a team of lawyers who knew Hollywood but not Austin. Their star witnesses were the two lackeys from the camera crew Biff had hired to follow us during our research trip. They testified that they had read an outline for the play, written by Biff, long before we appeared on the scene. This was a bald-faced lie. Fortunately, we still had our handwritten notes from the trip, supporting our contention that the screenplay was our original work, augmented by a few suggestions from Biff. Clearly, the jury would support our position. Biff agreed to settle out of court.

Still, Biff managed to have the last word. When we saw the finished film later, we had to smile at the way he'd designed the credits. Against a clear blue Texas sky, in dark letters you could read a mile away, it said: "Written by Cliff Robertson"; then, below, in yellow letters, camouflaged against a field of yellow flowers, so you had to strain to read the words, ". . . and Gary Cartwright and Edwin Shrake." Ol' Biff! Hiding our names in yellow-on-yellow type was far and away his most creative contribution to the whole project.

NOT LONG AFTER THE TRIAL, FLYING HOME FROM a trip to San Francisco, Bud and I conceived an entity that over time became Mad Dog, Inc. Mad Dog wasn't an expression of our experiences with Cliff Robertson, though it could be seen that way. Instead, it began (as all things Mad Dog seemed to) with several martinis and some drunken babble. The conversation started with us lamenting our government's war in Vietnam, and its equally stupid battle against peaceful dope smokers. Big government and big business were like a pair of malignant octopuses, we concluded, squeezing the life out of people, taking the law prisoner, employing highly paid lobbyists who wrote self-serving laws and bullied them through a subservient Congress. "What we need is a Citizens Lobby," Bud declared, the rigor of a founding father underpinning his voice. "We need a system that directs power to the people."

In the week that followed, we shared the idea of a Citizens Lobby with a government class at the University of Texas, taught by our friend Paula Sornoff. The students loved the idea. That night we talked it up at Scholz Garten, where our crowd of beer drinkers included David and Ann Richards, Mike and Sue Sharlot, Pete and Jody Gent, and a few other young couples who were politically active and looking to stir things up. The idea was radical, meaning that it had almost no chance of success, making it therefore irresistible. We needed a founding organization with a marketable name and decided on—Mad Dog. If you can follow that train of logic.

Dave Richards filed articles of incorporation with the state in 1970, making Mad Dog a legal entity. We printed up cards and letterhead. Our slogan was "Doing Indefinable Services to Mankind." Our credo was "Anything That's Not Mystery Is Guesswork." An artist friend, Jim Franklin, whose work also made the armadillo a symbol of Austin's hip culture, designed our logo, a crazed caricature of Abraham Lincoln taken from a $5 bill he happened to have in his pocket. The caricature of Abe was superimposed above the words "Doing Indefinable Services to Mankind." Since we were the founders, Bud and I reserved the right to select members when and if the notion occurred. The initiation ceremony required us to give each new member a slug of tequila, two pesos, and a kiss on the cheek.

Mad Dog was like a running shaggy dog story, its own reason to be. By pretending to be a powerful force for good, we mocked the idea of good. Mad Dog would be a rallying point for writers, artists, radicals, politicians, anyone who felt stifled by the times. The grander and more impossible an idea sounded, the better Mad Dog liked it. We planned to produce and distribute books and movies, open an all-night general store that sold 88 flavors of ice cream, and start a sanctuary for depressed greyhounds. One of the books we wanted to publish was a manuscript written by Taddy McAllister, granddaughter of the former mayor of San Antonio. The book was Taddy's stunningly frank tale of her sexual adventures with a wide assortment of politicians and well-known Texans. She called it "Sweet Pussy." Who could resist the title? We also wanted to publish the prison poetry of Candy Barr, the notorious Dallas stripper who thumbed her nose (and other parts) at Dallas society and was duly framed and locked up on drug charges. I'll tell you later about a memorable night I spent with Candy and how our friendship started.

Mad Dog tapped into Austin's counterculture of live music and rebellion, and it suited the times perfectly. From all evidence, the United States was in the process of going bonkers. We had just invaded Cambodia, wherever that was. The war in Southeast Asia seemed endless. Blacks and Hispanics were, as always, treated as second-class citizens. Young people caught puffing a handmade cigarette could face life in a Texas prison. Protests on a variety of issues were erupting on college campuses all over the country. The demonstrations in Austin, I'll confess, were relatively benign. One was a sit-in at the UT Student Union cafeteria protesting a policy that banned non-students—a category that included most of us activists. A second was a rally that attempted to save a small grove of trees that UT's autocratic board chairman, Frank Erwin, wanted to cut down. Though both protests started without Mad Dog's assistance, we believed that Mad Dog gave them institutional gravity.

Our grandiose plans included buying our own town, which

would be governed by laws that we drafted and approved. Dope smoking, of course, would be legal, maybe even mandatory. As Bud explained in an interview with *Playboy*, Mad Dog, TX, would have the potential for "heavy tourist traffic in expatriates, the smuggling of Chinamen and extensive trade in the Far East in jade, fine silks, and frankincense."

The search committee for the right town included Les Flying Punzars, of course, and also David and Ann Richards. Ann sometimes dressed like Dolly Parton, wearing a giant blond wig and a tight red dress, her bra stuffed to overflowing with rolls of cotton. David and Ann's home in West Lake Hills was a sanctuary for Mad Dog and the scene of some of our greatest gatherings. One famous party honored Abe Rosenthal, editor of the *New York Times*. Ann greeted Rosenthal at the door dressed as a giant tampon. Bud stood just behind her, wearing a large Afro-style wig that we'd found in a box of costumes. We began to pretend that he was Dr. J—pro basketball star Julius Erving. Rosenthal got into the spirit of our game and started asking Dr. J some questions.

"How can someone achieve your type of stardom?" the *Times* editor asked.

"Learn to dribble, white boy," Bud replied.

Rosenthal wrote in his column later: "One of the best parties I ever went to was in Austin, Texas. . . . I realized later why I had such a good time. None of it was catered, a form of surrogacy that dominates evenings in most big cities. . . . The crayfish were cooked in Ann's kitchen and she spread them out on the table herself. There was music—not a hired band, but some guests picking on guitars . . . and a standup comic [Shrake] right there in the living room, not on television."

Our first choice as a locale for Mad Dog, TX, was the old silver mining town of Shafter, an hour's drive from the Mexican border, in the Chinati Mountains. Problem was, it was an eight-hour drive from Austin. Then we thought about Theon, a small settlement just northeast of Austin. Our scouting trip to Theon was made memorable by a pit stop at the Squirrel Inn, a honky-tonk of no particular distinction except that customers were invited to serve themselves. Thinking he was taking a pitcher of ice water from the fridge, Bud mixed it with a heavy slug of the J&B that he always carried along. Turns out it wasn't ice water at all, it was kerosene. He might have died except that the quick-thinking woman who owned the place forced him to swallow some goat's milk. On the way home, reeking of whiskey, kerosene, and goat's milk, Bud did his best to keep his aging Ford van on the highway, but still we got pulled over by the highway patrol. Somehow the cops thought we were security risks and we ended up spending the night in the Williamson County jail in Georgetown. Viewed from the outside, the building looked like a medieval castle. Judging from the smell inside, the dump probably hadn't been swept or mopped since Robin Hood was a juvenile offender. Friends bailed us out in time for breakfast.

The most promising locale was Sisterdale, west of Austin, in Kendall County. After a phone conversation with someone in the mayor's office, David Richards believed that we could buy the whole town for $6,000, a sum that was within our margin of error. Among those who crammed into Bud's old van for the visit to Sisterdale was Donald Ward, one of Elaine Kaufman's partners at the famous New York watering hole Elaine's. Donald had long red hair and wore a pair of floppy seven-league boots like one of the Three Musketeers. The good burghers of Sisterdale took one look at our party of nonconformists and jacked up the price by a factor of ten—to $60,000. That was far out of our range. In the end, we never did buy a town.

Mad Dog really blossomed, however, when we traveled to Durango, Mexico, for the filming of a screenplay Bud wrote, called *Dime Box*. He had been working on the play for a while, but was momentarily blocked when I happened to mention that I'd read in Frank Tolbert's column in the *Dallas Morning News* a claim that the airplane was invented by a Baptist preacher from Dime Box, Texas. That sparked a new direction for Bud's story.

In the movie, set in the early 1900s, an outlaw (Dennis Hopper) trying to go straight moves to the town of Dime Box, where he accepts work in a factory that makes ashtrays shaped like sombreros.

He soon realizes that he hates the job, not to mention the snobby, self-righteous people who make the rules, and he starts hanging out with some dope-smoking Comanches. Meanwhile, another citizen named Preacher Bob (Peter Boyle) is building a flying machine. When Hopper loses his job, he decides to rob the factory payroll and escape in the flying machine. In a nutshell, that's the story.

OUR MAD DOG CONTINGENT DROVE TO DURANGO IN two spacious vehicles, Bud's old Ford van and a Winnebago that Pete Gent had borrowed from a dealer in Dallas. Both vehicles sported banners across the sides, proclaiming us to be employees of Mad Dog Productions, Inc. We crossed into Mexico at Eagle Pass, where I convinced an overly diligent Mexican customs agent who was about to refuse Pete entrance because of his long hair that we were filming a movie about Jesus. Pete had been obliged to grow the facial hair, I explained to the confused customs agent, in order to convincingly portray the role of Our Savior.

Located in central Mexico, Durango sits like a baked buzzard, near the tectonic seam that centuries ago erupted into the Sierra Madre Occidental. It is centered in a vast chaotic valley of dust, cactus, and volcanic boulders, of arroyos, of changing shadow, delirious sunsets, and hair-raising mountain roads that connect nowhere to nowhere. Until John Wayne discovered it on behalf of the motion picture industry in the 1950s, Durango's two principal industries were mining and the manufacture of ashtrays and key rings constructed by pressing the bodies of scorpions between layers of Plexiglas.

The film company arranged accommodations for us in a large four-bedroom house in the central part of town. Bud and Doatsy shared the largest of the bedrooms on the ground floor, and Jo and I and Pete and Jody took smaller upstairs bedrooms. The two children, Shea, who was only five, and Holly Gent, who was ten, shared a small room just off the kitchen.

The actual movie set was twelve miles northeast of Durango,

in the mountain village of Chupaderos, an Indian word for the witches who used to suck the blood and brains from deformed and disabled children. It had been used as the set for a number of period westerns, including several by John Wayne. Our producer, the incomparable Marvin Schwartz, had used it once before, for his film *War Wagon*.

On our way out to the set, we passed a five-story building that looked like a potbellied stove, belching white smoke across the valley. Our driver, Ricardo, informed us that this was the local telephone-pole plant. The owner of the plant had moved into the Hotel Durango for the duration of the filming and rented his home to Hopper and his girlfriend, Daria Halprin, a beautiful actress who had been in *Zabriskie Point*. Since such things as water and electricity were still years away in this village, I asked Ricardo what they planned to do with all those telephone poles. "They are going to line the road with them," Ricardo told me. "Then if they ever get telephones out here, you can see that they will have no difficulty stringing wire." Smoke from the waste of the plant filled the northern sky and seemed to grow denser by the day, though it hadn't yet reached the village. When it does, I wondered, what will happen to Chupaderos? "Then you gringos will go somewhere else and film your movies," Ricardo told me.

"Well, at least when they finish the movie," I observed, "the people of Chupaderos will have a nice new town."

"When they finish the movie," he said, "the people of Chupaderos will tear it down and use the lumber for something else. Lumber is very precious. Anyway, another movie company will start soon and then there will be another new town. Only it's a pity. This was a very nice town for Chupaderos."

Visiting the set was like falling into a time warp. Behind all the false fronts was a real village, coexisting in adobe squalor with pigs, chickens, goats, cows, and burros. Hollywood paid the rent—to whom, it wasn't clear—and the single sign of American charity was a tile-roofed laundry trough, donated by John Wayne, and a Sears jungle gym, a gift from Dean Martin.

Dozens of extras overdressed in 1902 costumes milled about;

technicians swarmed among spools of cable, giant lights, and portable generators; wranglers positioned horses and wagons such that no matter where the camera swung, it recorded an atmosphere of mobility and change. In Bud's screenplay, Dime Box was a busy, ambitious place that greeted change while also stubbornly defying it. An old Indian warmed himself beside a fire of dried dung and cactus. Bite-sized pigs nursed a sleeping dog. A goat chewed a rusted Pepsi Cola sign. Old women and young girls scrubbed clothes in an inky green stream and spread them over thistles to dry. A funeral procession bearing a wooden casket moved from the door of the white-steepled movie-set church, which covered the village's real place of worship.

Curious to see the real church, I stepped inside. Despite its adobe walls and dirt floor, the church had the requisite seven stations of the cross and an altar of shimmering candles. Above the church's mantel stood a replica of Our Lady of Guadalupe. In my notebook, I wrote: "If man can conceive of that which is holy, what's the difference between this place and St. Peter's?" It was a question that had no answer.

Once again, some ingenious Hollywood set designer had transformed the Street, as they say in show biz, into a 1902 Texas town, or something close to it. The Street was actually cross streets—a cantina, a tent city, a land office, and a chicken-plucking establishment along a secondary street that intersected with a primary and much nicer main street that included the fake church. There were also false fronts that represented a bank, a dry goods store, a hotel, a livery stable, a blacksmith shop, and a grocery store. At one end of Main Street sat a full-size replica of a boardinghouse, where all respectable citizens ate. Across a meadow from the town was the central metaphor of Bud's story—a full-size, working ceramics factory, where Dennis Hopper and co-star Warren Oates work making ashtrays until Hopper decides that he's had enough and hatches his plot to rob the payroll.

Producer Marvin Schwartz had decided to cast Shrake as the Town Drunk. Bud was a towering figure anyway, but in the costume of the Town Drunk he loomed bigger than life—black cowboy hat, Indian boots, an incredibly filthy white suit once worn by movie legend Hans Conried, a bottle of brandy sticking out of his rear pocket, which was held together by a safety pin. Though he had no dialogue that I recall, he filled many frames of the movie.

Schwartz, a slender man with graying Buffalo Bill hair, a droopy mustache, and flinty mother-of-pearl eyes, had taken a calculated risk in casting Hopper for the lead. I asked him how this had happened. "I loved Bud's screenplay and my original idea was to do a low-budget movie, under a million dollars," he told me. "But when I showed the script to Fox, they flipped. It was one of those rare scripts that had everything. They doubled the budget and said they wanted a big name."

Several actors were considered for the part—Hopper, who was still riding his success in *Easy Rider*, Dustin Hoffman, Jack Nicholson, and Jon Voight. Schwartz's first choice was Hoffman, but he was such a big name that just getting him to look at a script was a major undertaking. Besides, Bud hated the idea of Hoffman in the role. Hopper was a good second choice, but there were downsides, as we would all discover. Hopper was at the time a notorious head case, a doper, a drinker, a man absorbed by his own image as one-who-rides-alone. As it happened, Schwartz had a friend named Eddy Donno, a veteran stuntman and tough from the toughest part of Philadelphia. Donno knew Hopper well and could handle him, or so it was hoped.

Schwartz, Donno, and Shrake visited Hopper at his seventeen-room mansion near Taos, New Mexico, a villa made famous when it was the home of heiress Mabel Dodge Luhan, who shocked society by entertaining her gentleman friend, D. H. Lawrence, while she was still wed to an Indian named Tony Luhan. Hopper had spent a fortune restoring the house, and it had become a rendez-vous for his dope-fiend friends. The liquor bill was said to exceed $10,000 a month. Among the constantly changing cast of residents were two young women whose only purpose was to sit at a table and roll joints. Hopper glanced at the script and pronounced it "a piece of Hollywood fluff," but agreed to play the role for a fee of $400,000, which was big money back then. Donno was signed as a special assistant director, in charge of keeping Hopper more or less straight.

Marvin Schwartz had virtually reinvented himself in recent years. Divorced from his second wife, he lived in a large home in Benedict Canyon, with a perpetuating string of full-breasted "housekeepers" recruited through ads in the UCLA student newspaper. After the divorce, he got rid of his turtlenecks and outfitted himself in custom-made Levi's and boots. He traded his sports car for a Ford Ranch Wagon, and burnished his image as a cowboy by spreading some strands of hay in the back. He was the key cowboy on this set, no question about it. He controlled every aspect of the filming, somehow retaining his sense of humor against incredible odds. His main assets were brutal honesty, a high tolerance for the absurd, and a low tolerance for bullshit. He usually carried a giant cigar, which he never smoked or even lighted but used as a pointer when gesturing to subordinates. Whereas an actor like Hopper might survey Durango's indomitable sky and decide it represented man's attempt to alter his doomed soul, Marvin would see X hours of daylight. Movies were movies and life was reality to Marvin. If an actor needed a ration of dope to get through the day, Marvin found it. If the police were nosing around the set, he paid them off. When his mostly British camera crew complained of fatigue and heat exhaustion, Marvin laced their cocoa with amphetamines. One afternoon when the crew was slow setting up a scene, Marvin told them: "You guys are British, aren't you? You speak *English*? Then hurry the fuck up!" Warren Finnerty, the New York actor who did such a fine job in the Broadway production of *The Connection*, kept pestering Marvin to read a stage play that he wanted to direct. Marvin stalled as long as he could, then read the play and told Finnerty: "I hate it, man. What else can I say?"

The strain of production was eased by regular Saturday-night parties at Marvin's palatial rent house. The guest list was like something out of a Fellini film. One night a woman named Maria, identified as "Durango's No. 1 bull dyke," showed up with her companion, who looked like a ten-year-old Tricia Nixon in a snow-white ice cream dress. Maria looked like an aging jockey, in a tight red dress and spike heels. She danced with all the men and goosed all the women, generally making herself obnoxious. Finally, she walked over and kicked Marvin hard on his ankle. Before she could blink, Marvin embedded the toe of his boot deep in her shin, sending her sprawling under a table. "I deal with them in kind," he explained.

One early problem was finding extras among the citizens of Mexico who could pass for turn-of-the-century Texans. Schwartz solved it by recruiting a colony of Mennonites, who had settled near Durango in the 1860s. In one memorable scene, actress Janice Rule, who plays the role of a hooker, rides into town in her carriage. When she spots her old flame Hopper, she cries out in delight: "Bick Waner! You son of a bitch!" But as soon as she spoke the line, all the Mennonites walked off, complaining that they were not accustomed to such language. Schwartz huddled with assistant director Tony Ray, then shouted to one of his assistants, "Hey, you. Go get me twelve Mennonites, and make sure none of them speak English."

Schwartz had somehow put together an all-star cast, which included not just Janice Rule, Peter Boyle, Howard Hesseman, and Lee Purcell, but the great Ben Johnson, who played the role of Sheriff Mean John Simpson. Casting Purcell as Molly, a tart who tries to seduce Hopper's character, turned out to be a big mistake. In one memorable scene Purcell had to read a Dear John letter to Hopper from his former girlfriend. The letter played into her plan to seduce Hopper and should have been very good news for her, except every time they tried to film her reading the letter, Purcell burst into tears. Director Jim Frawley tried repeatedly to explain the scene to her. "No, no, dear," he told her. "You're supposed to act happy." Finally after about twenty takes, Schwartz decided to take charge. He took Purcell aside and whispered something in her ear. Whatever he said, it worked. She nailed it on the next take. When I asked Marvin later what he whispered, he said dryly: "I told her to imagine she had Dennis Hopper's cock in her mouth."

Most of the cast stayed at the Campo Mexico, a prong of motel rooms arranged around a palm-lined drive, semi-famous as a home-away-from-home for movie people for many years. Next to the motel was a concrete patio with signatures and handprints of some of the actors who had stayed there. In John Wayne's case, the print wasn't a hand but a fist. Members of the cast could be seen milling around the patio, sharing gossip or just enjoying the evening air. One night, for reasons I didn't understand, actor Bobby Hall, a former football player from Oregon, threatened to beat up Ralph Waite, a former Presbyterian minister turned actor. "This happens on every movie set I've been on," Waite told me later. "I walk into a room and there is one guy who smells me for the coward that I am. Then it happens . . . he goes after me."

Ben Johnson, his wife, and his mother-in-law stayed in a camper they had driven from Ben's Limousin cattle ranch in California. I had been a Ben Johnson fan for years. One day I spotted him sitting alone between takes, an imposing figure of a man in black frock coat and a six-shooter that must have weighed twenty pounds.

"I loved you in *One-Eyed Jacks* and *The Wild Bunch*," I told him. "But I thought your job playing Sam the Lion in *The Last Picture Show* was one of the great moments in the history of film."

"That so?" Ben growled, smiling as he spit a long stream of tobacco in the dirt.

"You were great," I said.

"It was a dirty picture," Ben's wife interrupted. She said it without malice, just a statement of opinion. Mrs. Johnson was a handsome woman with a tough Agnes Moorehead face and an Oklahoma directness. She and her mother had the same organic earthiness I'd seen in Ben. During meals, they waited around until the cast and crew had finished and distributed the remaining food to the children of the village. They also took up a collection to buy 250 sweatshirts for the kids of Chupaderos. One of my lasting memories was watching the children seated in neat rows in their new shirts that advertised Lamar Tech or the San Antonio Toros, like a tableau in a classroom. The scene being filmed was full of action, Ben Johnson and the townspeople, armed with guns, rocks, and pitchforks, charging up the hill where Hopper is attempting his escape in the aerocycle—but the children had their *backs* to the action. What fascinated them was a parked helicopter that would be used later to hoist the aerocycle off its ramp and make it appear to be actually flying.

There are men who look like cowboys, talk like cowboys, and act like cowboys, but Ben Johnson was a sure enough cowboy. (So was his father. Ben Johnson, Sr., had been a world champion steer roper, as well as manager of the legendary Chapman-Barnard Ranch in Osage County, Oklahoma.) Ben Jr. got into the film business when his father sold some livestock used in Howard Hughes's film *The Outlaw* and sent his son along to help manage the stock. Ben Jr. went on to become one of Hollywood's best stuntmen. He eventually got a break as an actor from the great John Ford. After some time, he took a year off from acting to go on the rodeo circuit, hoping to match his father's achievements, which he did, winning the world team-roping championship. Then he returned to Hollywood, "broke and with a wore-out car and a pissed-off wife." On days that he wasn't required to be on the movie set, Ben worked with fifteen horses he had purchased in northern New Mexico. I had read a story out of New York to the effect that Ben at first hesitated to take the role of Sam the Lion but changed his mind after director Peter Bogdanovich called John Ford, who asked Ben to do it as a favor. I asked Ben if that story was accurate. "Yep, that's about the way it was," he admitted. "It wasn't just all those four-letter words. I didn't like a part with so much dialogue."

Ben always referred to John Ford as "Mr. Ford," as though talking about a beloved high school science teacher. This seemed strange to me. Their ages weren't all that different; they had been friends, contemporaries and even dinner companions for years. Why this inexplicable deference? When I pressed Ben for an answer, he told me a story about having dinner at Ford's house years ago. They were sitting around the dinner table, talking about a scene Ford had directed that afternoon. "Well, we sure shot a lot of Indians out there today," Ben had remarked. From a corner of the room, John Wayne downed a shot of whiskey and yelled out, "Yeah, but none of them fell." Ford spun around, outraged that his judgment had been questioned. He thought that Ben Johnson, not John Wayne, had made the remark. "Mr. Ford was a good man," Ben said, looking me straight in the eye. "But he didn't use me in another picture for eleven years."

Hopper was always a problem, or at least the threat of a problem. Between takes, he liked to hide out in one of the Mad Dog vans, and when a bottle of tequila or a joint was passed around he never refused. And yet, when the cameras rolled, he didn't appear drunk or stoned, merely crazy. Crazy was the edge he gave to the character. One day we realized that he nearly always carried a loaded pistol in his overalls pocket, or sometimes tucked in his boot, another way of getting close to his character.

There were an alarming number of firearms on the set, not counting the unloaded guns put there as props. Pete Gent had a small arsenal of firearms and often had fast-draw contests on the set with Warren Finnerty or others. Gent nearly always won these contests, throwing a match occasionally to keep his competitor interested. Nearly all the male actors were obsessed with demonstrations of manhood. Two aging actors, Finnerty and Bobby Hall, staged a footrace up a small mountain and nearly collapsed from exhaustion.

Many of the actors were hounding Shrake to make changes in the script, invariably to somehow alter the characters they played. Warren Oates thought his character had too many homosexual overtones. Janice Rule wanted to be seduced by Hopper, not the other way around. José Torvay, a marvelous old Mexican actor who had been in 520 movies, became convinced that *Dime Box* was the story of an old Indian, played by himself. Ironically, it was Hopper, despite having originally called the script a piece of fluff, who worked hardest to defend Shrake's work. At least half a dozen times I heard him complain to director Jim Frawley, "Man, you're cutting out the best part of the movie."

Schwartz did his best to humor Hopper. One day while the producer was attempting to explain how a scene should play, Hopper pretended to concentrate instead on trying to suck tequila from one of those Mexican bottles that are designed to drip instead of pour. The drink was running down his chin and into the bib of his overalls, which, I'm guessing, was part of how he saw his character. He was the consummate pro, one of the great actors of the film business. We eventually became friends, but during this stage of his career he could be a real jerk.

On the last day of the year, as Mad Dog was busy planning its New Year's Eve Masked Ball, Hopper tried his best to sabotage Warren Oates's big scene. In the plotline, this is the day when he learns that Hopper has been screwing around with his wife, Lee Purcell, and confronts Hopper with a shotgun: the audience isn't sure if Oates plans to kill Hopper or himself. The crew had already filmed Hopper's close-ups, while Oates stood patiently to one side, hour after hour, feeding Hopper lines. When it came time for Oates to show his stuff, he was nearly exhausted. While Oates tried to pull himself together and concentrate on getting the scene just right, Hopper stood to one side, doping and joking and feeding Oates all the wrong lines. Since they were not recording Hopper's voice, the lines didn't really matter to anyone except Oates, who had to react to them. One of Hopper's more asinine ad-libs was, "Hey, Warren, have you read *The Golden Stream* by I. P. Freely?" To this bit of stupidity, Oates had to reply: "You said you were my friend." Somehow he prevailed and played the scene much as Shrake wrote it. But Oates was furious. He told us later: "I don't know what kept me from killing that little shit. I guess I wanted to save the movie, but Christ, I wanted to kill him! I'll never work with that cocksucker again."

There was another dustup that day too, this time over a scene where Hopper gives a raw chicken to the Indians and one of them starts to bite into it. The argument was about the morality of having the Indian actually bite into an uncooked chicken. That's how Schwartz wanted it shot. Frawley wanted to shoot it the way Shrake had intended, with Hopper stepping in to prevent the Indian from looking like a savage. Hopper was appalled at the whole thought and pointed out that he was a personal friend of the real Taos Pueblos and that even suggesting that an Indian would chew a raw chicken was demeaning to an entire race. The argument went on for hours, during which time I consumed a great deal of tequila and then decided to join the discussion. "Look, Dennis," I said, butting into the conversation. "My old granny was half Comanche and I've seen her drink hot blood out of a spurting chicken's neck many, many times. She claimed it was good for her liver, and she lived to be ninety." Now, in truth, Granny was part Comanche and she did live to be ninety—and while I used to marvel at the way she could wring the necks of two chickens at once, separating heads from bodies that continued to flop around the backyard—the part about drinking hot blood was a total fabrication. True or not, it had the effect of lighting Hopper's fuse. He launched into a long tirade about how the world was conspiring against not just Dennis Hopper but against his ancestors as well, including his great-uncle Daniel Boone, who according to this telling invented the closet.

This monumentally silly argument flared up again that night at the New Year's Eve party at Marvin's house. It took place in one of the bathrooms where a bunch of us had gone to snort coke. Only this time it got physical. The details are fuzzy, but I vaguely remember calling Hopper "a goddamn actor!" I was turning to leave the room when Hopper grabbed me by the shoulders. I wheeled around, grabbed him by the neck, and slammed him into a wall. "What did you do to Hopper?" Gent asked me later. "He came out of the bathroom crying and saying that you said things that broke his heart. He said you called him an actor." Only later was I reminded about the loaded .38 that Hopper always had in his boot. Or that many actors, never sure about the level of reality at any given moment, might be crazy enough to shoot me.

Joel Schiller, the Hollywood set designer hired to do the movie, did the decor for the Mad Dog Masked Ball, rearranging Marvin's place with sheets of transparent plastic that hung like Spanish moss. The scene resembled an out-of-focus time warp. A Christmas tree was gaily hung with toy cap pistols. Most guests came in costume and everyone had some kind of mask. Jo Cartwright was dressed in Shrake's filthy Town Drunk suit, which would easily have fit four women her size. Peter Gent wore a rugby sweater and a baseball cap that said BAND. Jody Gent arrived as Harlow. I hadn't brought my Flying Punzar costume, but I created a suitable replacement with a cape, some long johns, and a Day-Glo vest on which I printed a backwards letter *P*. The letter *P* in reverse looked like the number 9 and people started referring to me as Captain 9.

Sometime that day two guests arrived to stay with Bud and Doatsy—football and television star Don Meredith and his girlfriend (and soon-to-be wife), Susan. Various other characters began arriving as well, including a handsome Los Angeles woman named Olivia who wore a convict's burr haircut and had fingernails that resembled sabers. Another recent arrival was one of Hopper's friends, a mad chemist named Arthur, who had flown in from New York with a nose-drop bottle filled with homemade vanilla-flavored LSD. Arthur had a silky red Fu Manchu moustache and beard, and he walked with a crooked staff. He created an instant sensation in Durango, first by trying to score coke from the chief of police, then by stumbling on-camera while Peter Boyle as Preacher Bob was delivering his big sermon.

Arthur's magic drops were only one of a smorgasbord of chemicals in attendance at the Mad Dog Masked Ball. Warren Oates brought a bag of magic mushrooms, which guests were chopping in Marvin's blender to create a paste that they smeared on crackers. (There are twenty-five varieties of narcotic plants that grow wild in the states of Durango and Chihuahua.) Mad Dog had also ordered two tanks of nitrous oxide from Mexico City, which, as luck had it, never arrived. A couple of days earlier, Jo and I had simmered a kilo of finely manicured marijuana in butter, blended it with some cookie dough and baked some cookies that were so powerful that we were stoned for twelve hours and dared not try them a second time. Unfortunately, however, a large platter of the cookies remained on the table, along with cheese dip, chips, and pico de gallo.

Of all the drugs assembled at the party, the cookies were by far the most lethal. I didn't think much about it at first, but deep into the party Jo drew me aside and informed me, "Meredith and his girlfriend have been wolfing down those dope cookies like it's Halloween. They've had at least ten each. I'm getting worried." So was I: the Masked Ball was racing out of control and there was nothing anyone could do about it. Walking across the room to warn Meredith, or at least give him a heads-up on what was about to happen to him, I was stopped by Bobby Hall, who was seated at the bar. He had pulled his gorilla mask to the back of his head and was eating from a giant salad bowl with both hands. I had the strange sensation that Hall's voice was coming from the gorilla mask. I tried to ignore him, but he insisted on telling me about a diary he was keeping, revealing his experiences in Hollywood. He called it: "SOBs I Have Known." "I'm up to page thirteen thousand," he said proudly.

Even across the room I could tell that Don and Susan were zonked out of their minds, helpless to understand what was happening to them. But it was about to get worse. Arthur the Mad Chemist had cornered Meredith. I heard him say, "Open your mouth and say 'Peep.'" Before I could intervene, Meredith opened his mouth like a baby bird awaiting a worm and Arthur squeezed a few drops of vanilla-flavored acid through his lips. The low dementia in Meredith's eyes changed to wild fear. He started coughing and spitting and tearing at his clothes.

"You've killed him!" Susan cried out.

"I've got to get out of here," cried Meredith. "They've tricked us." He put an arm around Susan's shoulder and hurried her to the door. I heard they took the first plane out of town, not even bothering to say good-bye to the Shrakes. Weeks later, Shrake still hadn't heard from Meredith, though they were and would remain close friends.

Back at the bar where I'd seen Bobby Hall, some sort of commotion had started. From out of nowhere actor Cliff James, who had scuffled with Hall on the patio at Campo Mexico, rushed at Hall with a whiskey bottle, screeching, "You had no right to do that to Ralph [Waite]. Now you're going to get yours!" Hall threw up his arms to protect himself, as a writer I hadn't met before (his name, I learned later, was Brian) quickly disarmed James. But nobody had yelled, "Cut," so this scene wasn't yet finished. Hall grabbed two beer bottles, one in each hand, and smashed them against the bar, as he had no doubt seen Errol Flynn do in many old films. But these bottles were made of real glass, not spun sugar, and at first they failed to break. Hall smashed them harder until the necks broke away, then went after Brian, shouting incoherently, "You dirty little fag, you can't do that to my buddy!" Arthur flew across the room and rode Hall piggyback to the floor, where Pete Gent helped remove the jagged bottles from his hands. "Look at this!" Hall said, lifting a giant bloody hand from the glass on the floor, which was covered now in a pool of blood. "I believe I've cut off my thumb." Sure enough, his right thumb hung by a thread of skin. There was blood everywhere—on the floor, the furniture, the stereo, the salad. It was a Hollywood moment, but with real blood. By now people were running screaming in all directions. Olivia was racing in circles, screaming at the top of her lungs, "They're killing Brian!" She turned and ran through the swinging door into the kitchen, shouting over and over, "They're killing Brian!" Lee Purcell was crying hysterically, barely able to walk. I wrapped my Captain 9 cape around her and held her close, saying in what I hoped was a calm, soothing voice, "It's okay. It's okay. You're offstage now. The door is closed. No one can hurt you."

"I wish I could be sure," she sobbed and I could feel her heart pounding against my chest.

"I promise you, it's okay. You're out of the movie. They can't get you here." Then Olivia reappeared from the kitchen, shouting, "They're killing Brian!" At that precise moment, Cliff James turned casually to Pete Gent and said, "So what do you hear from Brad Ecklund?" naming an old footballer both had known years ago.

By now we were starting to calm down and consider the question of the moment: what to do about Bobby Hall? Apparently, he was in danger of bleeding to death. "Maybe we should take him to the hospital," Cliff James suggested. "No way," Shrake decided. "They'd send the whole batch of us to Star Chamber purgatory." The group agreed that we would drive Bobby Hall downtown and drop him off in easy walking distance to the hospital. So that's how Mad Dog dealt with that problem. Miraculously, Hall got to the hospital in time to save his life and even his thumb.

Throughout this psychodrama, Hopper had remained secluded in Schwartz's bedroom. We didn't see him again until we were leaving, shortly before dawn. By this time the house looked as though the Turkish cavalry had been playing all-night polo, using someone's head as a ball. There was blood, broken glass, broken phonograph records, bits and pieces of flesh and salad, all covered with soggy, bloody, transparent plastic. Someone had managed to fall through the Christmas tree, which now looked like a secret cache of toy pistols concealed on the floor of a flattened pine forest. As we were leaving, we broke toy pistols from the branches and ran out pretending we were in a gunfight. You know: Bang, bang, you're dead!

I was crawling into the back of Shrake's van when I spotted Hopper, ready to climb into the backseat of his chauffeured car across the street.

"Bang, bang, you're dead!" I said to Hopper.

"Bang, bang," said Hopper, and I realized I was looking down the barrel of his cocked and loaded .38.

DAY AFTER DAY, AS THE CAST AND CREW WORKED, Gent sat at the kitchen table of our communal apartment, chainsmoking pot and writing a novel about his pro football experiences. Turned out to be the best-selling book and later the hit movie *North Dallas Forty*. Meanwhile, I worked at a desk in the production office, writing a third draft for a screenplay titled *Rip*, on which Shrake and I were collaborating. It eventually became *A Pair of Aces*, which was filmed twenty years later by CBS and eventually spawned a sequel called *Another Pair of Aces*.

During post-production, some wise guy at Fox decided to change the title of the movie from *Dime Box* to *Kid Blue*. The film had only modest success at the box office but became a minor cult favorite. It almost ruined Dennis Hopper's career, and so disillusioned

Marvin Schwartz that he got out of the film business, moved to Nepal, and became a Buddhist monk named Brother Jonathan. Several weeks before we finished up in Durango, I learned that I had won the Dobie-Paisano Fellowship, co-sponsored by the University of Texas and the Texas Institute of Letters.

I FIRST LEARNED ABOUT THE DOBIE-PAISANO Fellowship from my friend Bill Wittliff, one of the writers and literary lions who founded both the Texas Institute of Letters and its fellowship, named after our state's landmark man of letters, J. Frank Dobie, and his ranch west of Austin, which he called Paisano, the Spanish name for the varmints more commonly called roadrunners. I was in Mexico working on a movie when Wittliff telephoned and suggested I apply for the fellowship. The nine previous winners included such established Texas writers as Billy Porterfield and A. C. Greene; that someone as gifted as Wittliff thought I was worthy to join such company remains one of the supreme compliments of my career.

In my application, I wrote: "I have published one novel (copy enclosed), one screenplay and numerous magazine articles, and my shelves sag with other manuscripts—including a finished novel— which haven't been published because they are not good enough. I have known some success and a lot of failure, and I am blithely ignorant of other forms of work. I am at the moment embarrassingly destitute, in great need of the physical and spiritual benefits of this fellowship. I need to lean against Dobie's rock."

At that time I had been collecting scraps of information about villains of the Southwest and thought they would make a good subject for a book. I planned to write a series of character studies done in the New Journalism style. "Maybe I will discover something about the nature of villainy, maybe not," I wrote in my application. "But I ask you to consider my case. Otherwise, I may have to rob a bank, thus becoming the subject rather than the author of this concept."

I'll never know why I didn't follow through on this idea. I got sidetracked on other pursuits, none as rich in potential as the original plan. As I have many times in my career, I let the moment slip away. Why? I think it was because I didn't really believe in myself. Part of learning to be a writer is knowing when and how to make your moves, and having the guts to try. In that respect, I was an extremely slow learner.

Paisano is the ultimate writers' retreat. It sits atop three hundred acres of some of the most scenic land in the Texas Hill Country, and has a special magic, known to just a select few. It is surrounded by a deep, mysterious woodland of oak and cedar. In one isolated pasture sits a tumbledown log cabin, whose history is long forgotten except that it apparently dates back to the late 1800s. The crystal-clear waters of Barton Creek flow through the property, which is several miles upstream from Austin's famous swimming hole, Barton Springs. During heavy rains, the low-water bridge leading from the highway to the ranch house is usually under water, cutting off access to the outside except by a circuitous route that crosses several fence lines. It's a perfect place to work or just sit back and breathe the sparklingly fresh air. Giant boulders line the sides of the creek above the swimming hole, making ideal places to sunbathe or simply enjoy the solitude. There were usually a handful of naked bodies on those rocks.

As it turned out, there wasn't much solitude for the first several weeks because some of the cast and crew members from the *Dime Box* set decided to come for a visit. Marvin Schwartz and his new girlfriend stayed for several days, as did Jim Frawley and his female companion, but Peter Boyle and Howard Hesseman stayed for a couple of weeks, and Pete and Jody Gent were there for more than a month. I didn't mind. Jo and I welcomed the company and gave ourselves over to the pleasures of the moment. I worked at a desk in the bunkhouse to the rear of the main house, but instead of writing the book I had planned I wrote a long essay about our experiences in Durango, some of which appears as passages in the above paragraphs.

Pete armed me with one of his pistols, which made me a menace mainly to myself. I took aim at a few turtles, but never came close to hitting anything. Pete, on the other hand, could quick-draw and shoot the head off a turtle or a rabbit from fifty yards. He was a great natural athlete.

Part of the fascination of living at Paisano was watching the weather come roaring down from the north. We witnessed several spectacular lightning storms; during one of them, Pete and I climbed to the roof and hoisted straightened-out coat hangers, daring God to strike us down. Fortunately, God was busy with other problems and chose to ignore us.

After Pete and Jody moved on, I spent a lot of time alone with Jo, just the two of us enjoying life and each other's company. I was partial to the rocking chair on the front porch, just as Dobie and his friends Bedichek and Webb had been years before, and I found an isolated bench—Dobie called it his "philosopher's bench"—along a narrow trail between the house and a bend in the creek. I would sit on the bench, composing sentences and paragraphs in my head until they sounded right, then go to my small office and write them in longhand on a legal pad. Eventually, I had stacks of legal pads full of scribbling, but, alas, nothing I could call a composition. One morning as I was strolling through the woods, I saw a small cat in some distress, stuck in a high tree. I climbed the tree and brought him down. The cat's ears were pointed, like a wildcat's or a mule's. So I named him Muley. Though he looked more wild than domesticated—and had probably never had a human companion—he was docile in my arms and became my good and constant companion—until one morning he simply disappeared. Back to the wild, I guess. It was a choice I understood.

The ranch house was cozy and well made, with a small fireplace in the living room and a kitchen that looked like the kitchens I remembered as a boy—a small stove, a small refrigerator, a freestanding sink, a wooden drainboard, a table with four chairs. Just outside the kitchen door loomed an oak tree that must have been at least three hundred years old, a sentinel assigned to protect the family.

Life was slow and easy, and after a while it got even slower: by the second or third month I found myself missing the chase—the give-and-take of reporting, the thrill of discovery, the challenge of storytelling, even the risk of failure—or, more specifically, the daring that the risk inspired. Then, out of the blue, I got a call from an editor I knew at *Rolling Stone*. He asked if I was interested in writing about Delbert McClinton. I greatly admired Delbert's music and knew a little about his private life: he was about my age and grew up in Fort Worth about the same time I was growing up in Arlington, listening to the same music, probably fighting the same demons.

I'd been a fan of Delbert McClinton and the Straitjackets since my first year of college, in 1952. They were the house band at Jack's, an infamous beer joint just beyond the Fort Worth city limits, patronized by gangsters, gamblers, and students without IDs. On weekends, the Straitjackets played backup to such featured bands as B.B. King, Lightnin' Hopkins, T-Bone Walker, and Big Joe Turner; on weeknights, they played until closing time, the only white band ever to play at Jack's. Except they didn't sound white, which was what made them so exciting. They were the only white band heard regularly on Fort Worth's black radio station, KNOK. Racial mixing was so rare back then that people like me hardly noticed what was happening, just accepted it the way we accepted changes in the weather or the confusion of first love. Jack's was where I came of age, in a way of speaking. It was where I discovered how much I loved the action, the music, the new freedom embedded in the rock 'n' roll scene. You could always tell the night a raid was planned: the jackass on the neon sign out front stopped kicking. I saw my very first marijuana cigarette in the parking lot at Jack's. I remember it well, because the cops were *inside*, raiding the joint.

I was a little nervous meeting Delbert for the first time, but he soon put me at ease, opening a couple of beers and motioning for me to find a seat on one of the packing crates that jammed the front room. Delbert, his wife, Donna, his son, Clay, and a cat named Wild Kingdom were getting ready to move to L.A.—or rather to a cliffside home in Malibu, which said a lot about this stage of his life and career. He had put great trust in his new album, a bluesy, jazzy collection called *The Jealous Kind*. It could be a ticket to better things. "I still don't have a penny," he told me. "Trying to keep a ten-piece band and a bus and a road crew alive, it's taken everything. I've been too busy making a living to make any money. Maybe this year."

"So after twenty-five years of one-night stands," I asked, "how does it feel to be an overnight success?"

"I decided for once to do an album sober," he laughed. "I want to *remember* doing it. I'm forty now, and at this age I want to be responsible for myself. If there are happy times, I want them to be happy for real. If it's a bummer, I want to handle it like a grown-up. You can only fool yourself for so long."

We talked for a while about how a man needs to find his roots, agreeing that you have to grow some before you can remember what roots are about—before you can translate them into meaning and write something that makes sense. Success is something you measure in scar tissue: fame and fortune are products of luck, but success is an element torn from its socket, organic and dangerously alive. He told me about hitting bottom ten years earlier, fed up with his first marriage, fed up with working beer joints, fed up with Monday-morning trips to the unemployment office. When his unemployment benefits ran out, he hit the road for the West Coast, with a beautiful divorcée who had just come into a pile of money and a new Chrysler. They were crazy in love, or so he believed. Then, without any notice, she split and left him alone and confused. Nothing in his misspent youth prepared him for the shock. That night he picked up his guitar and wrote his first really good song, "Two More Bottles of Wine."

> I thought I'd be a star by today, but I'm sweeping out a
>   warehouse in West LA.
> (But it's all right, 'cause it's midnight, and I've got two
>   more bottles of wine.)

LIFE HAS A WAY OF DOUBLING BACK ON ITSELF, and then—when you're not paying attention—doubling back again. Living at Paisano didn't exactly change my life, but life nevertheless changed while I lived there. I didn't know it at the time, but Jo was looking over my shoulder and planning a future that didn't include me. Not long after we returned from Mexico, she enrolled in nursing school. I learned later that one of the main reasons for this sudden change of direction was that she was having a love affair with a woman who was the supervisor of the nursing school. At long last, the dormant lesbian side of her personality had won out.

The only way I could deal with the situation was to get as far away from her as possible. I went to the bank, withdrew my savings, then caught a flight for New York. I called Dan and June and told them I needed a place to stay for a few days—or a few weeks, I couldn't tell. As always, they welcomed me in. After a couple of weeks I rented a furnished apartment on the lower West Side, on 23rd Street, between Seventh and Eighth Avenues. Strolling along 14th Street one day, I spotted in a shop window a pair of sturdy hiking boots. Just looking at them made me feel better, and I bought a pair and wore them everywhere for the next several months. With the boots and a warm, fleece-lined coat, I felt secure and able to fight off the challenges of winter in the big city.

The Jenkinses had leased a weekend home on Long Island, in the village of Bridgehampton, and for the next few months I divided my time between my apartment in the city and the house on the island. Dan and June only used the Long Island place on occasional weekends, so I had it mostly to myself. It was a good place to write, and to be alone with my thoughts. Willie Morris had dissolved his arrangement with *Harper's*—in a burst of acrimony and injured feelings. He had left the city and moved to Bridgehampton, so we spent almost every evening together at a gin joint called Bobby Van's.

I had known Willie briefly when we were undergraduates in the journalism department at the University of Texas in the mid-fifties, but we weren't close until years later—when as editor in chief of *Harper's* he worked over my original manuscript of "Confessions of a Washed-up Sportswriter" until it was worthy of publication in a first-rate magazine like *Harper's*. That was the first time I appreciated what a fine editor could bring to a story. He cut a lot of deadwood from the story, but he also encouraged me to expand passages or tell him about other adventures that I had mentioned during our drunken conversations.

Willie loved to talk, especially about growing up in Mississippi, and I enjoyed his company and listened with interest. My own growing-up tales paled in comparison. North Texas seemed so drab, so pointless, so lacking in the stuff of life that Willie saw sprouting from every bush in his native state. Thinking back, I believe Willie didn't fully appreciate Mississippi until he moved away, until he found himself living in Austin, working for the *Texas Observer*, and absorbing a Texas point of view.

Editing rather than writing was Willie's real talent. He loved editing and appointed himself as my mentor, encouraging me to stop overthinking what I was trying to say and just let it flow. That may have been good advice, but I never trusted myself enough to just let go. I required a structure, and structures took considerable—well, *structuring*. For me, writing was very hard work, but I learned that if I did it with enough diligence, it paid off.

Willie and I were both working on various projects at the time— I was writing a screenplay for director Harold Becker—and we talked about the work we were doing, and what we wanted to do. Willie was writing a book about a woman he had once loved and probably still did—I think her name was Barbara Howar—and he talked about her almost as if she were dead and gone from his life. There was something sad about Willie, something remorseful and hurting, as though he believed that the best part of life had already passed him by. And yet he was full of life, more than almost anyone I ever knew.

I was terribly lonely and sometimes miserable during my interlude in New York City, but was determined to hold it together. After a time, I was reintroduced to an interesting, attractive woman whom I'd known briefly a couple of years earlier when I was working on a long piece at *Life* magazine. Her name was Dina and she'd been a fact-checker at *Life* but now worked as an independent film editor. She lived alone in a third-floor walk-up, not far from my apartment.

We had dinner together two or three times and very good sex, usually at her place. Soon I was spending most of my nights there. She left early every morning for her job, but I slept in and woke when I pleased, usually in the late morning. Alone in her apartment, I made coffee and inhaled her essence, feeling happy and maybe in love. I wondered who Dina really was and began exploring her apartment, opening drawers and cabinets. It was basically a single room, divided into compartments by bookcases, curtains, and stacks of books. I discovered to my amazement that she was part of the Greenwich Village bondage community, where she was known by her nom-de-orgy, Sasha. She kept a trunk loaded with whips, handcuffs, and costumes, and bondage magazines and books were piled high in every available space.

It was an exciting if completely confusing discovery and I didn't mention it to Dina for a few days. I could tell, however, that she had something on her mind, that she was wondering where our relations were headed. One night over drinks she asked me, "Have you ever been to an orgy?" I laughed and said with exaggerated bravado, "Are you kidding? I'm from Austin. All we ever did was orgy!" "Good," she replied, "because we're invited to one." What a dope I was.

That night she led me deeper into the Village, to what I took to be an abandoned warehouse. She rang the bell on the heavy wooden door and it was opened by a man wearing a thong and a pearl necklace. He looked us over quickly, then smiled at Sasha and kissed her on the mouth. I took that to mean I was also welcome. The interior was one enormous room, with very high ceilings and wall-to-wall people. At first it looked like a bunch of ordinary people, laughing, drinking, having a very good time. Then I noticed that some of them were getting undressed and a few were already naked and locked in hot embraces. I was suddenly aware of a young woman suspended from an overhead beam, her hands bound with leather, naked from the waist down. A cat-o'-nine-tails hung from a nearby hook and a sign encouraged guests to use it to whip her bared ass. Laughing at myself, I gave her a couple of gentle whacks and was startled to hear her cry out, "Harder, you son of a bitch!" I tried to really lay into her but couldn't make myself do it. Somebody passed me a joint and I took a hit and started coughing. I was sweating like a hog, finding it hard to breathe, hard to think. Dina had disappeared in the crowd and I started pushing people aside, looking for her and for the exit. I waded through piles of copulating couples and naked bodies doing things to one another that I hadn't seen or even read about. Finally I spotted her, laughing at something said by a woman with huge tits and a mop of red hair in which was nested a small sparrow. Pushing through the mob, I grabbed Dina's arm and said, "I got to get out of here." She seemed disappointed but allowed me to lead her out.

We took a cab to Elaine's, me trying to compose myself and Dina no doubt wondering where our romance was headed now. We made really wild love that night, but in the days that followed she cooled down and I knew it was over. Gradually, she vanished from my life. I still thought about her, and a couple of times after drinking way too much called her in the wee hours of the morning. But there wasn't anything to say. I missed being with her, but I'm sure she knew that and didn't much care.

I was working eight and ten hours a day on a couple of projects. One was a short story about a cult of rednecks and cedar choppers who lived in the hills west of Austin and enjoyed the sport of dog fighting. I'd gotten to know them the previous summer when I took a minimum-wage job on a construction gang, something I did from time to time to prove to myself I could still work with my hands and muscles. These two guys on our crew, who I'll call Crater and Stout, owned and bred pit bulls and talked about the sport of dog fighting with the same passion heard when devoted fans talk about football. It was almost a religion, not just with Crater and Stout but with their parents and all their close friends as well. For whatever reason, they invited me to join them one Sunday at a makeshift dog arena in the cedar breaks west of Austin. I didn't care for the blood sport of dog fighting, in fact found it repulsive, but I was fascinated with the subculture of fans and participants for whom it was part of life. I knew I had to write about it someday.

The experience eventually evolved into a story called "LeRoy's Revenge." It's still my all-time favorite story, maybe because it was turned down by nearly every magazine in the country. *Rolling Stone, Esquire, Playboy, Sports Illustrated*—they all had a shot at the story and rejected it. It wasn't just a judgment call; they truly hated the piece. "Good Lord, dogs killing dogs," *Sports Illustrated* editor Ray Cave told me. "My wife would never speak to me again if I printed that." The story touched some primordial sense of revulsion in all these editors; people were killing people daily, in Vietnam and everywhere else, but there was something about dogs that was too much for their sensibilities. I had to beg *Texas Monthly* editor Bill Broyles to accept the story, though he loved it once he saw it in print. Everyone did. Not long after publication, I received a call from *Esquire* editor Geoffrey Norman, who had rejected the piece when he was still articles editor at *Playboy*, but apparently didn't remember. Norman wanted to know why I never sent any really good pieces like this to him.

I doubt if "LeRoy's Revenge" could get past today's fact-checking standards. I changed names, combined several dogfights into a single big event, and took large liberties with the plot. The story revolves around some guys like Crater and Stout who run a scam on a wealthy and well-known dog fighter from Phoenix: they disguised one of his own prize dogs as an ordinary animal called LeRoy. The part of the story where the man from Phoenix pays off the bet but then takes his revenge by killing LeRoy with his .44 Magnum is a legend among fanciers, as the dog crowd calls its devotees. I didn't actually witness this famous fight or the execution that followed, only heard about it and used it as needed for my plot. But it's an honest story, something that really happened in that shadowy underworld. To paraphrase Margaret Mead, "I don't judge 'em. I just write down what happened."

The other project that occupied my time while living in my small apartment in New York was a film deal with the director Harold Becker, who had made his reputation as a still photographer and would later direct some fine films like *The Onion Field*, *Taps*, and *Sea of Love*. Becker had read a story I wrote in *Rolling Stone* and wanted to develop it as a movie. The story was also set in the Hill Country, and its characters were cedar choppers who raised and fought dogs. But dog fighting was only a small part of this story, background stuff: it was a tale of a man who discovers his beloved older brother is a serial killer and is forced to deal with it. The screenplay changed names several times, but finally emerged as *The Devil's Backbone*. I wrote it over a six-month span, moving between New York and Los Angeles, depending on Becker's schedule. The project bounced around various studios and attracted some interest but finally died for lack of financing.

By this time my divorce from Jo was final. She offered to give me custody of Shea, who was about to start first grade. I flew to Austin with the notion of renting a temporary apartment until I finished my screenplay; then I planned on bundling up Shea and his belongings and returning to New York. I had decided to make New York my permanent home. But fate had other plans.

I found an apartment on a hillside overlooking Zilker Park. The apartment was just across the alley, as I soon discovered, from Willie Nelson. I had been a Willie fan since my days covering the Dallas Cowboys, when Don Meredith and I used to debate the merits of country-and-western entertainers. I was a George Jones fan, but Meredith kept telling me about this guy I'd never heard of, Willie Nelson. One afternoon in the Cowboys locker room, Meredith called me over and handed me a copy of Willie Nelson's *Live at Panther Hall* album. I played it at least a dozen times that night and was forever hooked. It was a life-altering experience.

Willie's music was perfect background for what was happening in Austin at the time. Austin was going crazy and finding its soul. In the old days the only hangout place was Scholz Garten, but new places were opening every day and young musicians from all over the country were streaming into Austin. An acid-rock group, Shiva's Headband, was knocking down the walls of a jam-packed club called the Vulcan Gas Company, attracting a curious mix of hillbillies and hippies. Shiva's was managed by a beer distributor and hippie entrepreneur named Eddie Wilson, who more than anyone else on the local scene understood the chemistry that was inspiring the great change. When the landlord forced the Vulcan to close, Eddie found an abandoned National Guard armory on the banks of the Colorado River, just south of downtown. With a few upgrades, he transformed it into what became Austin's most famous venue, the Armadillo World Headquarters. The armadillo became mascot and symbol of a free-spirit movement that forever changed the city and shaped its counterculture. Artist Jim Franklin was obsessed by the strange little animal and crafted drawings that featured the armadillo prancing about or sticking his snout aboveground next to a hovering space capsule. Mad Dog was still going strong, and we donated $200 to help Armadillo get started. In return we got the use of one of the spare rooms as our first headquarters.

The acts that Eddie Wilson booked at the Armadillo—Ravi Shankar, Earl Scruggs, Jerry Jeff Walker, Willie Nelson—set the tone for the progressive country/redneck rock craze that was becoming wildly popular in Austin and was about to sweep the country. The Armadillo wasn't just a venue for music, it was a community center for arts and crafts and the beer-drinking culture that became the city's artistic core. I was first introduced to Willie one afternoon as his band was rehearsing at the Armadillo. I didn't really get to know him, however, until I moved back from New York and dived headfirst into the swirling mix of music, dope, and art.

My friendship with Willie Nelson was typical of Austin's special chemistry. We met through a mutual acquaintance, Phyllis Sickles, whom I knew only slightly through yet another mutual acquaintance. She was married to a Dallas musician at the time, but by 1976 she was single, unattached, and mighty appealing. She had a son, Michael, who was about a year older than Shea. One of her close friends was married to Paul English, Willie's longtime drummer and sidekick. In this particular episode of small-world dealing, I began to hang around Phyllis and the Austin music scene, and before the summer ended, we were living together. A few months later we decided to get married.

The wedding was held in a fitting venue—the back room of the Texas Chili Parlor. It was officiated by the Rev. Edwin "Bud" Shrake, who had had the foresight to mail $100 to a post office box in New Jersey, which acknowledged the money by ordaining him as a Doctor of Metaphysics in the Universal Life Church. Though the title carried no official weight, it gave him a degree of respect among those of us in his circle: he had officiated in several previous ceremonies, including the marriage of Hollywood producer Craig Baumgarten. As it happened Phyllis and I had purchased a marriage license that same week, betting on the come, as they say in gambling circles. Bud wrote some vows on the back of a napkin, Doatsy made a quick trip to gather up our sons and pick some Texas wildflowers, and soon we were legally man and wife. We knew it was real a few days later when a woman from the Travis County Clerk's Office telephoned for clarification. Assured that, yes, the Rev. Shrake was indeed certified by the Universal Life Church, she entered us in the official record, a marriage as valid as the Law of Abraham. That night, full of good cheer and all kinds of mood elevators, I climbed onstage with Willie and his band and composed on the spot a song that I called "Main Squeeze Blues." The words were soon forgotten, but Phyllis became the love of my life.

Me as a sophomore at Arlington High, 1948.

Dan Jenkins (left) and Bud Shrake, at the Fort Worth Press, *1955.*

Bud Shrake and me at the Dallas Times Herald.
That's Blackie at the desk behind us.

The original Flying Punzars: Bud, Blackie, and me.

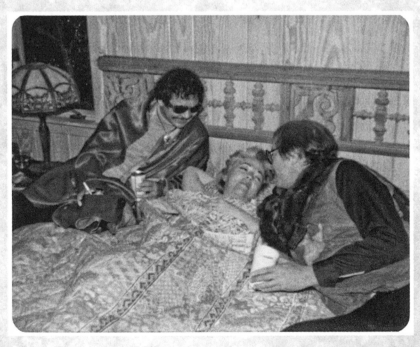

Bud Shrake and me, dressed as Flying Punzars, wake Ann Richards early one Sunday morning. Photo © Doatsy Shrake. Courtesy of Doatsy Shrake.

*Don Meredith and me. Though we became good friends,
I sometimes wrote caustic reviews of his performance as a Cowboys
quarterback. This photo, taken after a skeet shoot, was a gag—mostly.
Image courtesy of* The Dallas Morning News.

Mad Dog Productions. Photo © Doatsy Shrake. Courtesy of Doatsy Shrake.

*Jim "Lopez" Smithum, to my left, at a Dallas bar called Bud Shrake West.
An elegant boulevardier, he was my running mate until
he died of lung cancer in 1996.*

The original staff of Texas Monthly *from 1974. Editor Bill Broyles is wearing a sweater and standing in the front row. I'm on the back row, right, behind Greg Curtis, who would follow Broyles as editor.*

Phyllis and me with her son Mike (left) and my son Shea. The dogs are Abby and Kilo, a pit bull Phyllis rescued off the street.

That's me in the dumb hat, watching Mark (right) and his pal
Sammy Rawlins jam, during the week of Mark's wedding to Helen.

Ann Richards and Phyllis, with a crazed Shrake looking over their shoulders.

Phyllis and me with our Airedale terriers Bucky and Abby.

This is my favorite picture of Bud, my lifelong best friend and guiding light.

3

T HE NEXT MAJOR DEVELOPMENT IN THE twisted trajectory of my fate was the founding of *Texas Monthly*. Writers had talked for some time about the need for a statewide vehicle to match up with the abundance of unused talent in our state. Unless you were willing to move to New York, the writing trade was a juggling act that few could manage. But starting with the magazine's first issue, in February 1973, it was apparent that Mike Levy and the two young editors he had hired, Bill Broyles and Greg Curtis, were shaping *Texas Monthly* into a great magazine.

For the first issue I wrote a story about Duane Thomas, the talented but extremely reclusive running back for the Dallas Cowboys. I had come to know Duane fairly well when I worked for the *Dallas Morning News* and had smoked dope with him and his roommate, a linebacker from Tennessee. By 1973, however, Duane was refusing all interviews. He agreed to talk with me for just a couple of minutes, but by this time I knew him well enough to write a coherent and interesting story.

Since there had never been a magazine or even a statewide newspaper that explored the entirety of Texas, *Texas Monthly* had a virgin field from which to select story ideas. I wrote about Candy Barr, Jack Ruby, Tom Landry, and other famous names in the first couple of years, to considerable acclaim. One of my most memorable stories was the discovery that the flamboyant El Paso private detective Jay J. Armes was running what amounted to a magic lantern show.

Armes had attracted considerable attention in magazines like *People* and *Newsweek* with stories of his daring adventures as a private eye, including the helicopter rescue of Marlon Brando's son from kidnappers who were holding him in a remote seaside cave in Mexico, and the tale of a beautiful model who shot her aging husband and then turned a shotgun on herself because Armes refused to sleep with her. These super-sleuth adventures were made even more spectacular by the fact that both of Armes's hands were blown off in a childhood dynamite accident and had been replaced with two gleaming steel hooks, which he used so skillfully that they had become a character trait rather than a handicap. The hooks were what attracted the attention of a number of national publications, but Armes embellished his story with each telling and reinforced it with some impressive props. *Newsweek*, for example, reported that Armes "keeps a loaded submachine gun in his $37,000 Rolls Royce as protection against the next—and fourteenth—attempt on his life. He lives behind an electrified fence in a million-dollar mansion with a shooting range, a $90,000 gymnasium and a private menagerie, complete with leopards that prowl the grounds unchained at night. He is an expert on bugging, a skilled pilot, a deadly marksman and karate fighter and, perhaps, the best private eye in the country."

As I discovered during my own investigation, there was more to Jay J. Armes than met the eye—and also a lot less. As I say, all of his stories were highly exaggerated and mostly concoctions of smoke and mirrors.

EVEN NOW, MANY YEARS AFTER OUR MEETING, I think fairly often about Candy Barr, the stunningly beautiful stripper who scandalized Dallas in the fifties and did prison time for the effrontery. I spent a memorable afternoon, evening, night, and following morning with Candy back in 1976. I'll tell you what happened presently, but first let me introduce her to an audience not old enough to remember that strange era.

To place Candy properly in time you have to go back to Sugar Ray Robinson, James Dean, Marilyn Monroe, Joe McCarthy, John Foster Dulles, RAF Group Captain Peter Townsend, Mort Sahl, and Sputnik. The Dodgers were still in Brooklyn, Russian tanks rumbled through the streets of Budapest, and Fidel Castro hadn't yet poked his nose out of the jungles of Cuba. Texas was still the largest state in the Union, Elvis Presley's "Don't Be Cruel" topped the Hit Parade, and *Playboy* magazine was an under-the-counter novelty, less than three years old and tame as a pet goose. It was a time of paralytic conservatism and raw censorship. Something called the National Organization of Decent Literature was putting pressure on bookstores and publishers to stop selling such purveyors of filth as Hemingway, Faulkner, Dos Passos, Zola, and Orwell. In this atmosphere, you can imagine what the good housewives of Big D thought of a woman whose act was to take off her clothes and drive their husbands and boyfriends crazy. Someone with a dark sense of humor labeled this "The Age of Innocence."

When I decided to write about her for *Texas Monthly*, Candy was living in Brownwood, alone and very much out of the public eye. It took two weeks to track her down and another week of fast talking before she agreed to be interviewed. I made contact with the assistance of another stripper who was a mutual friend, Chastity Fox, who lived in Dallas and sometimes worked in the legitimate theater. Chastity telephoned Candy and vouched that I was a good guy, and Candy reluctantly agreed to an interview.

I already knew a little about her background. She was born in the tiny Texas town of Edna, as Juanita Dale Slusher, one of thirteen children fathered by Doc Slusher, a whiskey-drinking, harmonica-playing brickmason and all-around rowdy. Her mother died when she was nine and she ran away from home at age thirteen, using her babysitting money to buy a bus ticket to Dallas. She made her reputation stripping at the Colony Club in downtown Dallas, and appeared in what became a famous underground stag movie. The rest, as they say, is history, and that's the history that I wanted to learn.

By the mid-fifties Candy was the talk of the town, especially among wives, girlfriends, and professional bluenoses like Lieutenant Pat Gannaway, head of the vice squad for the Dallas Police Department. Gannaway saw himself as the terrible swift sword of Dallas's moral climate. He made it his mission to bring Candy to justice, even if he had to create a crime. Gannaway hatched a plan involving another stripper who had run afoul of the law and needed help to get out of jail. The stripper was given a small amount of marijuana and instructed to prevail on the big-hearted Candy to hide it for her. Candy agreed and stuffed it in her bra. A short time later, Gannaway and his boys forced their way into her apartment and found the "evidence." The raid made headlines all across Texas, and as far away as New York and Los Angeles.

Like the arrest itself, Candy's four-day trial was a farce—and a foregone conclusion. Judge Joe B. Brown, who would later make headlines as the buffoon who sat on the bench during the Jack Ruby trial, borrowed a camera and snapped pictures of "the shapely defendant." Bill Bracklein, one of her lawyers, told me later: "Candy was a very naive young lady. While we were waiting to come to trial, she was out in Las Vegas, doing her act. One week before we came to trial, I got word that she was going to be a bridesmaid in the wedding of Sammy Davis, Jr. [to a white actress]. Anyone who grew up in Texas knew you couldn't do that right before a trial." The jury found Candy guilty and gave her fifteen years. While her attorneys were appealing her conviction, she made new headlines by moving into the Los Angeles penthouse of mobster Mickey Cohen. Candy was always her own worst enemy. But she did her time like a good girl, sewing men's trousers in the prison workshop and appearing as the star of the Texas Prison Rodeo.

When she got out of jail in April 1963, overweight, overwrought, and badly shaken by the experience, she moved back to Edna and became friends with a woman named Gloria Carver. When Gloria moved to Brownwood a few years later, Candy followed her. "I felt safe here," she told me. She was broke and jobless. Old friends like Mickey Cohen and Sammy Davis, Jr., had problems of their own and didn't offer to help. She considered making a comeback, but under the conditions of her parole, she couldn't even set foot in a place that sold alcoholic beverages. "What was I supposed to do, work in a root beer stand?" she said. "They were pushing me into a corner all over again. It was either get on my back or do something silly." The one old friend who did help was Jack Ruby. Jack gave her $50, an air conditioner, and two breed dogs "so you won't have to go out and sell yourself."

Abe Weinstein was finally able to pull a few strings so that Candy could make a brief comeback at the Colony Club. Abe even spread word that her prison poems were "in the hands of Doubleday this very minute." To Abe's way of thinking, this was mostly true. He had stashed the pages with his friend Bill Gilliland at the Doubleday bookstore in downtown Dallas. Candy ultimately saved and borrowed enough to publish her own book, then began to make brief, unannounced appearances at events like the chili cookoff in Terlingua, where she sold copies. She made many tentative agreements with writers and editors to sell her life story, but for many years none of them resulted in a book or movie deal. As Larry L. King once noted, "She must have sold ten percent of herself about two hundred times."

She disappeared from public view for a while. Then in October 1975, *Oui* offered her $5,000 to pose and be interviewed, an idea that originated with writer Gay Talese, who suggested to a friend at the magazine, "Instead of those teenybopper dipsos, how about some pictures of a mature woman?" Or, to state it more bluntly, how many forty-one-year-old grandmothers are willing to pose for split-beaver shots? More to the point, how many of them is the public willing to look at?

Talese's motive was not altruistic. A year earlier, he had visited Candy in Brownwood, hoping to do research on his own much-anticipated book on sex, society, and the law. The interview was a disaster. Candy refused to talk into a tape recorder, and when Talese asked specific questions about Jack Ruby, Mickey Cohen,

Joe DeCarlo, prison, and Dallas in the fifties, she wouldn't talk at all. Instead, she wanted to talk about "my memoirs," which she assumed Talese wanted to write. Talese tried to explain that he had enough problems with his own book, which he had been working on for several years. After a day and a half of getting nowhere, Candy did one of her dramatic flip-flops. She stripped naked and positioned herself on the floor, as she had so many times when there didn't seem to be another choice. What happened next depends on which story you believe, but shortly thereafter Talese grabbed the next plane out of town. The interview, such as it was, was finally accomplished a few weeks later, by flying Candy and her companion, Gloria Carver, to the Chicago offices of the magazine.

I never got to see her perform when she was a star, though I tried on one occasion. It was February 1956, the day after I got discharged from the army. My friend Jim Frye and I were walking down Commerce Street in the direction of the Colony Club, which was easy to spot because outside the front door was a life-size cardboard cutout of Candy wearing a very brief cowgirl outfit and brandishing a pair of six-shooters, one of which she was firing under her hiked leg. Without warning, a cop car stopped in front of us, blocking our path. Two Dallas cops jumped out, clapped us in handcuffs, and took us to jail. They said we were drunk. We were not drunk, though I'll admit that was our intention. Those were the days of what I call the "How Dare You Squad" in Dallas: intent was sufficient cause for arrest and confinement—a lesson that Candy learned the hard way.

In 1976, a year after the famous photo spread in *Oui* and twenty-something years after my first attempt to see Candy ended with me spending a night in the Dallas jail, I finally made contact with her. She agreed to an interview but wouldn't tell me how to find her house. "Drive to Brownwood," she instructed. "Then telephone me."

I made the three-hour drive from Austin and called her from a phone booth outside a liquor store, only to have her tell me that the house was a mess and I needed to call back later. So I did. I called back four or five times. During one of the calls, she told me, "Why don't you look over the town while I'm getting dressed?" I had already experienced the pleasure of touring Brownwood. It was a pleasant enough town, a place where men wore business suits to visit Main Street and women dressed up to shop at the Safeway. Motorists thought nothing of parking in an intersection to exchange gossip with pedestrians. Everyone went to church, not just on Sunday but two or three times a week. It was a town supported by a few small industries, a pecan research station, a model reform school, and a farm where workers potty-trained little pigs, dressed them in plastic boots, and made sure their feet never touched the ground from conception to skillet. In the summer people played softball all night, and the remainder of the year they drank coffee and talked about the 1940s when a wee halfback named Chili Rice personally defeated archrival Breckenridge for only the second time in thirty-six years. People were friendly and proud. They all knew Candy Barr, of course, but they didn't, you know, *know* her. If you asked nearly any businessman about Candy, he was likely to shriek, "For Godsake, don't use my name. My wife would leave me if she knew I'd even spoken to her."

Candy lived a very private life at her lakeside cottage, with no visible means of support. She aroused only mild curiosity. The menfolk assumed she was supported, at least partially, by a certain local banker, or by a former member of the Texas Board of Pardons and Paroles who at one time "kept her." The women just naturally assumed she was a hundred-dollar-a-night hooker (when I mentioned this to Candy later, she joked, "That's a hundred dollars an *hour*"). But most people respected her privacy. Nobody was shocked when she made an unexpected appearance at a fundamentalist church to give a brief testimonial to Jesus as a "superstar."

When I telephoned again for what I'd already decided would be the final time, Candy invited me to come for supper and spend the night. Five minutes later I was standing at the door of a small white clapboard cottage, shielded from the street by an unpainted plywood fence and a yard of junk. She called her cottage Fort Dulce, *dulce* meaning "sweet." Like candy. The license plate on her Cadillac parked in front was DULCE 1. Dulce Press, Inc., was the name she gave the company that published the book of poetry she had written in prison, *A Gentle Mind . . . Confused.* On the shelves that separated the living room from the kitchen were many jars of sweets—candy kisses, lemon drops, jelly beans, peppermints, candy corn. I was greeted at the door by her seventeen-year-old niece, Susan Slusher, and by her twenty-two-year-old boyfriend of the moment, Scott. Three dogs and four cats crowded up to compete for attention. Susan informed me that Candy was still dressing and asked me to make myself comfortable on the couch. Two hours later, Candy was still dressing.

When she finally made her appearance, shortly before 10 p.m., she hit the room like one of Sgt. Snorkel's Ping-Pong smashes. Her blond hair was in curlers. She had scrubbed her face until it was blank and bleached as driftwood. Her green eyes collapsed like seedless grapes too long on the shelf. She wore a poor-white-trash housedress that ended just below the crotch, and no panties.

"Don't think I dressed up just for you," she told me.

The next twelve hours were like being trapped on the set of a Fellini movie, without Fellini. Candy had changed into jeans and a blue work shirt. On one level she was doing her best to cook supper, and on another I was trying to interview her. The stereo blasted at top volume with rock and the kind of blues you heard in the black hovels of Dallas in the fifties. Dogs and cats prowled underfoot. A pet spider named Brutus spun a web above a portrait of Jesus saving New York City. I was confused because I couldn't hear what she was saying, and she was angry because she thought I wasn't listening. I asked questions about her life as a teenager on the streets of Dallas and she rambled about Jesus, daddy, and Lord Buckley, three of the men she found worth remembering. She accused me of having a secret tape recorder, and when I told her that I hated tape recorders, she scolded me for using the word "hate" in her presence. She smoked Virginia Slims and made bad puns about "coming a long way" and sometimes broke out with a few lines from a song that happened to cross her mind. Susan watched the TV set with the sound turned off, and every ten or fifteen seconds walked to the door to let the dogs and cats in or out. Scott attempted to make himself invisible.

I already knew that Candy could blow without warning: try to imagine a hurricane in a Dixie Cup. The laughing green eyes would begin to boil. The innocence that had made that perfect teardrop face a landmark in the sexual liberation of a generation of milquetoasts would twist into the wrath of Zeus. I'd read that she once sat waiting in a rocking chair for her ex-husband, and when he kicked down the door she blasted him with a pistol that was resting conveniently in her lap. She was aiming for his balls but, unfortunately, hit him in the belly. When she caught gangster Mickey Cohen talking to another woman, she slugged him in the teeth. She carved her mark on a dyke in the prison workshop: this was not a lovers' quarrel as an assistant warden reported, but a disagreement stemming from Candy's hard-line belief that a worker should take pride in her job. Candy had a cosmic way of connecting things.

So it was that presently I got to watch her blow. Without warning, she hoisted a dripping black skillet from the dishwater and shrieked at Susan: "My God! What have you done!" I jumped out of the way, but Candy ignored me and continued to yell at Susan. "Don't ever, *ever* put that skillet in the dishwater," she shouted. "And I told you to sharpen this knife blade. Look at it!" Candy whacked the blade into a tomato, disfiguring the inoffensive fruit. Susan said in a meek voice that she would try to do better.

"Before my mother died," Candy went on, her voice and demeanor again serene as a spring morning as she continued to dip pieces of chicken in flour, "she instilled in me a lot of wonderful things like tolerance and patience. After she died, I talked to Jesus a lot. I wanted to be a missionary."

"Then tell me about that."

"I walk around talking to the Chief a lot," she went on. "I tell him: you're a groovy cat. He was far ahead of his time. I argue with Him. I ask a lot of damn questions and get some answers. Sometimes I don't agree. Sometimes He seems too severe. Hey! Give me some slack! Daddy never gave me pain seven days and seven nights. But nobody is gonna make me change what I feel about Him. Not even Him."

In disjointed bits and pieces, her story unfolded.

Many talent scouts have taken credit for discovering Candy Barr: Barney Weinstein, who paid her $15 a night to act as a shill at his "Amateur Night" at the Theater Lounge, though she was so obviously superior to the other contestants that nobody believed she was an "amateur"; his brother Abe Weinstein, who hired her away to become his headliner at the Colony Club, and who gave her the name Candy Barr because she was always eating candy; Joe DeCarlo, a Los Angeles entrepreneur and pal of Hefner and Sinatra, who got her away from Abe; and Gary Crosby, Bing's son, who once admitted to Mickey Cohen: "Goddamn, she can make you feel like a real man."

To be technically correct, it was the old Liquor Control Board (LCB) that first discovered the girl who would become Candy Barr. They discovered her posing as an eighteen-year-old cocktail waitress—the minimum legal age. Candy wouldn't turn eighteen for another four years, but girls from tough backgrounds develop early, or they don't develop at all. Candy credited her impressive balcony to the fact that as a fourth grader she had to hurry home and wash bedsheets on a rubbing board. "Honey," she advised young girls looking to improve their figure, "get yourself a rub board." She kept changing jobs, she told me, but the LCB kept tracking her down. Once they even sent her home to Edna, but she caught the next bus back to Dallas. The only place a teenage runaway could count on steady work was at the Trolley Courts or the other hot-pillow motels, located out Harry Hines Boulevard, or along the old Fort Worth Highway. Pimps, thugs, and night clerks traded young girls around as they pleased. Candy's arrangement with the motel consisted of making beds by day and turning tricks by night.

An old crook named Shorty Anderson decided she had too much class for the Trolley Courts, so he claimed her as his property and took her to live in his trailer under a bridge where he ran a school for young burglars. Candy's first husband, Billy Debbs, was a graduate of Shorty's academy. Billy was a good lover but a poor student. He went to the pen, got out, and got shot to death. Somewhere in there, a pimp who spotted her jitterbugging in a joint called the Round-Up Club launched Candy's film career.

She must have been about fifteen when *Smart Aleck* was filmed. A million guys must have seen this classic over the years: all of them surely recall that she was a natural brunette. *Smart Aleck* was America's first blue movie, the *Deep Throat* of its era, only infinitely more erotic and less pretentious. It was just straight old motel room sex: the audience supplied its own sound. I remember seeing it at the Wolters Air Force Base NCO Club in Mineral Wells about 1955. There had never been anything to equal this film, not for my generation. We had all seen stag movies, threadbare sweathogs wrestling around with some jerk hung like Groggin's mule. But this was different: this was a strikingly beautiful fifteen-year-old sweetheart type, and you could just tell she was enjoying it.

When I talked to her twenty-something years later, Candy could barely recall even making the film. "I had been forced into screwing so many times I wasn't really aware that this was any different," she told me. "I don't think they even paid me. I've read that that movie made me Candy Barr. That movie made it because I *became* Candy Barr."

One of the fringe benefits of her new film career was that Candy got invited to all the best stag parties. Several prominent business and professional men, on my oath that their names never be revealed, recalled a Junior Chamber of Commerce stag where Candy was the star attraction. Bill Gilliland, the manager of the Doubleday bookstore, told me that when he was a student at SMU in the mid-fifties Candy was the sensation of the Phi Delta Theta stag, held at the Alford refrigerated warehouse.

"What I remember about Candy was her enthusiasm," Gilliland told me. "Here was one woman willing to flaunt it."

I offered Candy a cigarette and asked her to verify a story I'd read about Mickey Cohen and about her years living in a villa at the famous Garden of Allah on Sunset Boulevard. Cohen had personally guaranteed her $15,000 bond while the marijuana appeal ran its course. In a cruel way, these were peak years for Candy. She was earning $2,000 a week, stripping in L.A. and Las Vegas, but simultaneously, a pack of lawmen and profiteers howled in her shadow like hungry dogs. The pressure was so great that the El Rancho Vegas decided to replace her with a less controversial act—Nelson Eddy, of all people.

"I was in and out of the hospital with hepatitis," she recalled. "The first time I ever heard of Mickey Cohen was when he sent an orchid in a champagne glass to my hospital room. There was a note, saying, 'Don't worry, little girl, you've got a friend.'"

"I've read that Cohen finally got rid of you because you were giving him a bad name," I said, trying not to sound prosecutorial.

She nodded, biting her lips. "When I finally went to prison," she told me, "it was with a great sense of relief. Otherwise, I would have been dead or laying on some gangster's couch." I was still standing behind her dressing table, watching her face in the mirror, which was the only way she was comfortable answering questions. "Of course, I didn't know what prison was," she continued. "I guess I thought it was a country club. I ordered all these new clothes from a place in Florida—ten dresses, twenty bras, cosmetics. Hell, I was going to be there for a long time. The only thing I didn't think to take with me was the only thing I really needed—money. Everything else they took away."

As the evening wore on, Candy paced about the bedroom and living room, trying to concentrate but mostly rambling. She would begin a story, get distracted, and jump to another subject. She started several times to tell me about a terrible night when she was babysitting, how she almost killed a baby. "I was dead tired from washing bedsheets all afternoon and trying to study," she said in a soft voice. "The baby wouldn't stop crying, so I walked over and put my hand on his nose. That's all there was to it, a moment of darkness . . . when I knew I was capable of killing. I thought about that many times in prison. Women who had killed or harmed children were ostracized in prison. I could understand why the others struck out at me, but why those poor women—didn't they understand how those women hurt inside?"

She looked straight at me, her green eyes swimming, and said: "This is very hard for me . . . talking to you . . ." I could see that it was. She required the illusion of control, no matter how chaotic the situation. While Clyde McCoy blew his bluesy harmonica on the stereo, Candy began a monologue recalling her daddy, old Doc Slusher—how the deputy back in Edna used to ride up on that big white horse to question Doc about some groceries that had gone missing from the local market, how when they came to repossess his car, Doc sloshed a ring of gasoline around it, struck a kitchen match on the seat of his pants, and invited them to come ahead. "Ride the rhyme, that's what Lord Buckley taught me," she sang out, obviously enjoying the telling of these stories. "I learned to dance when I was two . . . on my daddy's knee. Daddy played the French harp. He was a blues man. Saturday was his blues day. He'd set a bottle of whiskey on the table for anybody who came around and he'd play the blues on that harp." She went on about picking cotton and making soap and bacon for her family, about that great big wash pot in the backyard and hunting with the hounds and the taste of possum, which she couldn't stand, and fried armadillo, which was still a favorite.

After some time, she tired of pacing and sat on the couch, motioning me to join her. She was sifting through a new stack of fan mail; her fan mail had greatly increased since Talese's article. There were some old publicity pictures, too. Maybe it wasn't much of a legacy, she conceded, but it was what it was. "I know my kids have been hurt by what's been written," she said, close to tears again. "I'm not saying it's totally incorrect. It's the *way* they say it." Sure, she had done a little dope and turned some tricks. But she had never stolen, or hurt anyone—except when it was necessary.

Looking again at the famous photograph of the young Candy Barr with the twin toy pistols, she told me: "I almost let them make me feel ugly."

By now she had willed herself to stop sobbing, to stop beating herself up. "Goddamn it!" she snapped at me. "I'm supposed to be in there cooking supper. See what you're doing to me!"

It was after 4 a.m. when we sat down to a meal of fried chicken, potato salad, corn, red beans, sliced tomatoes, canned biscuits, iced tea. Candy's spirits improved with each mouthful. It was nearly dawn when she made a bed for me on the living room couch, covering me with an imitation bearskin rug and tucking it in.

An early cold front had passed through West Texas. I lay there in the changing shafts of light, thinking not so much of the woman whose essence filled the house but of that life-size cardboard cut-out of Candy Barr that Jim Frye and I saw so many years ago. I knew what Frye would say when I told him about this night. He would ask: *Did you get any?* No, Jim, and you ought to be ashamed of yourself for even asking.

After a few hours' sleep, we all felt better. I walked down by the lake and watched Scott dig the cottage intake pipe from the mud and blow it clean so there would be clear water for Candy's morning shower. After her shower, Candy invited me into her bedroom with its pink wallpaper and lacy dressing table. It was the dressing room of a star, though one fallen on hard times. The floor was covered with badly worn carpet and old publicity photos collected dust on the wall. The bed was extra large and so was the bathtub. Carefully crossing her legs, Candy seated herself in front of the mirror, so that the face I saw was her reflection. She arranged the clutter of tubes, jars, and brushes in an order that pleased her. Like one of those time-lapse Disney films where a desert flower appears to blossom before your eyes, she performed the ancient miracle of her sex. The blond hair brushed out soft and glossy. Mascara arches defined her eyes, which now sparkled like polished turquoise. The cave-dweller's pallor that had appeared so unflattering in the harsh light of the kitchen the night before now took on tones of finely dusted nutmeg. In her tight hip-hugger jeans and red halter, she looked like a young girl ready for a hayride.

Momentarily, she reappeared in the kitchen as Candy Barr, a lost vision of great beauty, warmth, and charm.

"Now we can talk," she said. "What do you want to know?"

"I want to know how you feel," I said.

"I feel like . . . like I'm not vulnerable anymore," she told me.

That's how my story ended, with that plaintive line about not feeling vulnerable anymore. The story created great interest at *Texas Monthly*, among editors and readers alike, and became a measure for how I think a good profile should develop. Candy loved it and wrote me a thank-you note. A couple of times she even drove to Austin for a brief visit. Phyllis and I were living on West Avenue at the time, with our two preteen sons, Mike and Shea, when she dropped by one afternoon. The boys were so stunned by the beautiful visitor that they sat still and silent for nearly an hour.

When I read that she had died in June 2006, I felt a great wave of sadness, but I felt deep gratitude, too. I am glad I got to know her.

SPENDING TIME WITH STARS LIKE CANDY BARR was the exception rather than the rule during my writing career. Most of the stories involved the antithesis of glamour—ventures into the seedy, depressing, and sometimes dangerous side of life. One of the most memorable was "The Endless Odyssey of Patrick Henry Polk," an inside look at the life of a family on welfare. The story was a great success—it won the 1977 Stanley Walker Award from the Texas Institute of Letters—but I've never spent a more miserable two months.

I had picked my subject with some care. I didn't want to write about a stereotypical welfare mother, I wanted a welfare *family*. At the time I wrote the story, only a small percentage of the poor families in Texas got any kind of public assistance. The popular misconception was that most people on welfare were black or Hispanic women, but that wasn't true. I picked the Polks because they were fairly typical of those on the public dole—Anglo-Saxon Protestant, nearly illiterate, and totally puzzled by the complexities of life. Polk wasn't the family's true name. I changed the name because that was the only way they would agree to a series of interviews that must have perplexed the flow of their lives and nearly drove me crazy.

I ended up spending eight or ten hours a day with Henry Polk, his wife, Cynthia, and their seven children, because that was the only way I could get to know them and understand what their life was like. Hard-luck stories had become routine for this family, which included not just Henry and his wife and kids, but a long string of cousins, uncles, aunts, and in-laws, every one of them a medical and social basket case. Polk was a brickmason by trade but had a bad heart and hadn't worked for a year or longer.

For weeks now, they had been living in roadside camps, or jammed together in their ancient Buick. The car was a rattletrap that was constantly breaking down, but it was all they had. A few days before I met the family, a welfare worker helped the Polks move into a subsidized house in South Austin. It wasn't much of a house, sterile and unfurnished except for an old sofa and a few kitchen chairs, but at least they had a roof over their heads. They got an old king-size mattress and box spring from Goodwill. Henry, his wife, and three of the kids slept in the bed, the two youngest girls slept on cots at the foot, and two boys slept on pallets spread on the dining room floor. Henry's brother Obie eventually moved in with them: I never figured out where he slept. Cynthia found some patches of cloth and sewed some curtains, and Henry improvised a coffee table from a piece of glass and some scrap lumber he found in the alley. They were living hand to mouth, literally.

Their welfare check was overdue. Now all they could do was huddle together and wait for the mail. But at least they had a street address. Before this they had been constantly on the move, never staying at a single location for more than a few days. Nobody at the welfare office could say exactly when the check would catch up with them. Hopeless days followed hopeless days, an endless chain of misery.

Cynthia was a good-hearted and well-meaning person, but she understood almost nothing about homemaking. The living room floor was often littered with spilled chocolate milk or chicken bones. Still, she was a good improviser. She measured out the food stamps carefully, loading up initially on staples like sugar, flour, potatoes, and lard. While the stamps held out, there was usually a little meat or chicken, always fried. Every meal included potatoes, beans, and cake: Henry's favorite meal was red beans and chocolate cake, mixed together. Nobody in the family liked vegetables or fruit. In the afternoon when the kids came home from school, Cynthia would drive them to a bakery outlet and treat them to day-old fried pies. There was one particular supermarket that the Polks visited regularly, a chain that sponsored the television sweepstakes *Let's Go to the Races*. Cynthia would select four or five items, and then they would head to separate checkout lines, thereby multiplying their allotment of sweepstake cards. On Friday night, they would gather in front of a small black-and-white TV and cheer home their horses. Henry thought this was foolish. He thought it was equally foolish when his older brother, Obie, kept reminding him of stories they had heard as boys, that there was a cave on the west bank of the Colorado River where the Comanches had once buried a cache of silver.

One day all nine of them climbed into the bed and discussed what they would do when the check arrived. Cynthia wanted a washing machine. The kids wanted a drive-in movie and a bucket of fried chicken. Another day brought total panic: the supply of medications that one of the little girls required was about to run out. Without it, she would lapse into a coma, but a refill cost $27, more money than they could manage. They got it together long enough to rush her to the ER—where one of the social workers reminded them that they already *had* a Medicaid card, that it came automatically with the welfare package, and that it would pay for whatever medications they needed. For some reason, none of them had figured out this elementary process. "I had the card right here in my purse and didn't know it was any good," Cynthia said, laughing and crying at the same time.

Obie always had a little money in his pocket, from where I never learned. One day he came home with something that he called "a dowsing instrument," a cheap, finger-sized piece of hollow aluminum, dangling from a cheap chain. Obie had bought it from a man he met down the street, who assured him that it could detect the presence of water, oil, and precious metal. He opened an old, badly soiled magazine called *Treasure Hunting Unlimited* and pointed to a diagram for aligning the dowsing instrument with the shadows and rays of the sun. "Exactly half way between the marks is where the treasure is buried," he told Henry.

"What treasure?" Henry demanded to know.

"Them nine jackloads of Meskin silver buried by the Old Confederates Home. 'Member, that ol nigger lady told us about it? Long time ago?"

At the mention of treasure, all the kids started yammering at once, but Henry ordered them to shut up. "Obie," he said, "you're touched is what you are." Obie began to protest, but Henry turned his back to him, took his Bible from the top of the TV and walked to the bedroom.

I was with them the afternoon the welfare checks finally arrived. Henry had been feeling poorly, complaining that "the Claw's got me again," his way of indicating the pain that sometimes stabbed at his chest. "I'm just a backsliding Christian, banged up, beat up, wore out." Then we heard the girls squealing and saw the postman at the front door. Suddenly, Henry was on his feet, dancing around the room.

Three checks arrived at once, totaling more than $600. An hour later, I followed Obie, Henry, and the family to Payless Shoes, where they bought some cowboy boots for the two little girls. It had been almost two weeks since they had eaten meat, so the next stop was the supermarket, where they got $5 worth of round steak, some cigarettes and candy, and a stack of *Let's Go to the Races* cards. The kids were still bellowing for some Kentucky Fried Chicken, so that was their next stop. One of the older girls confessed a hankering for some peach-scented stationery from the drugstore. Henry gave her a dollar, then peeled off a dollar for each of the kids. Cynthia bought some thread, and the following day a used washing machine. Henry got a new water pump for the Buick, paid the gas, water, and electric bills, and ordered a telephone (and paid an extra $5 for an unlisted number). He also purchased a used twenty-five-inch color TV, paying $55 down and agreeing to pay $59 a month for eighteen months—or a total of $1,117. Then they bought another bucket of chicken, spent $108 for a new supply of food stamps, filled the Buick with gasoline, and went to the drive-in to see *The Town That Dreaded Sundown*. Two days after its arrival, their welfare money was reduced to $60. It would have to last them for another month.

Stories like this one have no ending. It's just one miserable day following another, a break here and there, but nothing a family can hold on to—no place to get a firm footing. That's what welfare is about. It's the best we can do with a bad system, and it won't get any better as long as society keeps producing illiterate and clueless families like the Polks.

IN THE LATE SEVENTIES, TWO TEXAS MURDER CASES occupied much of my time and ultimately turned my career in totally unexpected directions. It all started when I wrote about them in *Texas Monthly*. The first was a sensational murder in Fort Worth, in which a multimillionaire oilman named Cullen Davis was charged with shooting his estranged wife, Priscilla, and murdering her lover, Stan Farr, and her teenage daughter, Andrea. Cullen was the richest man ever tried for murder in Texas, and the case dragged out through three separate trials and consumed me for months. The story eventually evolved into a book, *Blood Will Tell*, and then a four-part television movie. Income from the book and the TV movie supported me for the next few years.

The second was the murder of the flamboyant El Paso attorney Lee Chagra, which was the foundation of a far more complicated case that involved the murder-for-hire of federal judge John Wood. This became another compelling book and later a movie, *Dirty Dealing*.

When I think about the Cullen Davis case, I think first of the many hours I spent talking to Priscilla in the $6 million mansion that Cullen had built to immortalize their marriage. People in Fort Worth simply called it "the mansion." It was an eye-popping sprawl of trapezoids, parallelograms, and blinding-white walls that covered 10,000 square feet and could be seen for miles. It was more on the order of a museum, something cool and impersonal, perched on a windy hill adjacent to the Colonial Country Club's golf course in the heart of Fort Worth, a silhouette that protruded from the landscape like an ocean liner.

The divorce of Cullen and Priscilla had been the talk of the town for weeks. Cullen deeply resented that Priscilla had custody of the mansion pending settlement. Even more, he resented that she was living there with her lover, Stan Farr, a onetime basketball player at TCU. Cullen was from one of the wealthiest families in Fort Worth, a sort of nerd who had never attracted much attention until he married Priscilla. The busybodies of high society spoke of Priscilla as that platinum hussy with silicone implants who wore a diamond necklace that spelled out "Rich Bitch" and took pleasure in dragging her mink across the carpet at Shady Oaks Country Club. Middle society saw her as a knockout blonde with the enormous breasts and hip-hugger jeans and Indian jewelry who was always getting her picture taken at the Colonial golf tournament—in the words of one advertising executive, "a lady who looked like she had spent too much time in bowling alleys." I just saw her as an interesting woman from the other side of the tracks who had tried to better herself and had almost been murdered for her effrontery.

The murder of Stan Farr and Priscilla's daughter by her first marriage, Andrea Wilborn—and the shooting of Priscilla and a friend who happened on the scene of the violence at the wrong time—took on all the elements of high drama when the district attorney announced that he was seeking the death penalty. Nobody of Cullen's stature had ever been tried for capital murder in Texas. Here's what I knew at the start of my own investigation: One hellish August night Priscilla and Stan Farr drove back to the mansion after a night on the town. He headed upstairs to the master bedroom and Priscilla went to turn off the kitchen lights. That's when she noticed a bloody handprint on the basement door—she didn't know it yet, but the killer had already stashed Andrea's body down there. Suddenly Cullen Davis emerged from the laundry room, dressed all in black, wearing a woman's black wig, both his hands in a black plastic bag. Said "Hi," then shot Priscilla through the chest. At the sound of the shot and scream, Stan ran down the stairs, whereupon Cullen shot him four times. Priscilla staggered to her feet and ran down the grassy slope of the 181-acre estate, toward a neighbor's home. "My name is Priscilla Davis. I live in the big house in the middle of the field off Hulen. I am very wounded. Cullen is up there killing my children. He is killing everyone."

Cullen was being held without bail, pending the trial. Because of all the publicity, the trial was moved to Amarillo, in the Texas Panhandle. Everyone in Fort Worth had a firm opinion about the case, which spun off a bevy of related suits and countersuits and brought employment to bushels of lawyers and private investigators. PIs were thick as lightning bugs, investigating every aspect of the case and often one another. Cullen hired famed Houston trial attorney Richard "Racehorse" Haynes, who was making maximum use of media accounts and gossip about Priscilla's private life. Haynes and his associates would portray her as a money-grabbing slut and worse, a Dragon Lady who corrupted youth and trafficked in drugs. There were rumors that hit men were lurking in the shadows, that Priscilla wouldn't live to testify. She was advised to "stay off the street."

I was one of the few people Priscilla trusted. We talked for many hours, sometimes in the mansion, sometimes at a private club on Camp Bowie Boulevard where the owner was a good friend of mine. Whenever we went out, Priscilla wore a silver-plated .32 strapped to a custom-made holster on her right boot. I got to like her and I believed her story. Most people took the position that if a man as rich as Cullen Davis wanted someone dead, he would hire a hit man. But the more I got to know about Cullen, the more I realized this was something Cullen would want to do himself. That's who he was.

At the trial in Amarillo, Cullen was treated like royalty. Though he had been held without bail for many weeks, he was enjoying the attention. In a jail so overcrowded that some prisoners slept on the floor, Cullen had a private double-bunk cell with a color TV. He always appeared in court freshly groomed and immaculately dressed in an expensive business suit. A stream of beauties escorted by his subordinates sat in the front row, behind the defense table, and shared catered luncheons with Cullen and his girlfriend (and later wife), Karen Masters. Housewives and groupies fawned over him like loving aunties—the Menopause Brigade, one bailiff called them—baked him cookies, and scolded a deputy sheriff for not making sure his bed linens were changed regularly.

At first glance, the prosecution's case appeared open and shut: Priscilla and two other eyewitnesses identified Cullen as the man in black who did the shooting. But Racehorse Haynes reminded members of the jury, "The opera ain't over till the fat lady sings," and by the time he finished tarring Priscilla, even some reporters had forgotten what the trial was about. In retrospect, a trial that appeared to be a foregone conclusion in favor of the prosecution turned out to be an easy win for the defense. Even as the jury was returning with its not-guilty verdict, Cullen's Learjet was warming up at the airport to whisk him off on a skiing vacation in Aspen, Colorado.

BLOOD WILL TELL WAS STILL IN THE BOOKSTORES when I began researching a *Texas Monthly* story that appeared under the title "The Black Striker Gets Hit." The Black Striker was a name I gave famed El Paso attorney Lee Chagra, who was murdered in his fancy law office just before Christmas 1978. The killers were a couple of lowlifes who left behind his vial of cocaine but took $450,000 in cash. What was an El Paso lawyer doing with a vial of coke, you might ask? No, the real question was: where did that huge amount of cash come from? Looking for answers led me on a long journey along the Texas-Mexico border, where I found an underworld of crime, murder, and multimillion-dollar drug deals. This search resulted in my next book, *Dirty Dealing*.

The Chagras were a handsome, adventurous family of Lebanese migrants who arrived first in Mexico and later in El Paso, near the turn of the last century. Lee was the first college graduate in his family and the first professional. He worked his way through law school at the University of Texas in Austin, graduating fourth in his class in 1962, gaining a reputation as a champion of social justice and an outspoken critic of segregated dorms and football teams. Setting up law practice with his brother-in-law back in their hometown of El Paso, Lee took on hard-core criminal cases and won almost all of them. He adopted a wardrobe suitable to his self-image: black cowboy hat, matching black jeans and shirt, fancy handmade boots, and an assortment of expensive jewelry, including a gold bracelet that spelled out the word "Freedom." He carried an ebony cane with a gold satyr's-head handle, and he walked with a well-deserved swagger. He loved to gamble for high stakes, and he thumbed his nose at drug enforcement cops who became convinced that he was the kingpin of a big smuggling operation. He wasn't, but his younger brother, Jimmy, was, and the heat would eventually burn the whole Chagra family.

The federal agents reasoned that Lee had to be the mastermind behind the operation for the simple reason that he was so smart. They were so preoccupied with this theory that they failed to see the obvious: Lee was *too* smart to play that role. And yet, right under their noses was another Chagra not at all handicapped by brains or good judgment—Jimmy, who grew up hustling and hanging out with some of Lee's more prosperous clients. Jimmy wanted nothing more than to be recognized as Mr. Big.

The consensus had always been that Jimmy Chagra would never amount to much. He was the black sheep, the all-star goof-up. He nearly bankrupted the family carpet business to support his floating crap game. He was in a hurry to get rich, so he started peddling dope, even as he ran up large gambling debts in Las Vegas.

Instead of flying in small loads of marijuana from Mexico in small airplanes, which was the custom of the times, Jimmy used tramp steamers, bringing to the American market not just hundreds of pounds but thousands with each shipment: one such shipment, which landed at an isolated cove on Massachusetts Bay, exceeded 50,000 pounds. Soon the money was rolling in by the hundreds of thousands—and then millions—of dollars, and the Chagra brothers were in a race to see who could spend it the fastest. Folks in Vegas thought they had seen it all—Hunter Thompson once described how a casino shot a three-hundred-pound bear out of a cannon right in the middle of the floor and nobody bothered to look up—but Vegas had never seen anything that surpassed the show put on by the Chagras. On five minutes' notice Caesars Palace would send out a Learjet to fetch Lee or Jimmy. The brothers didn't even bother to register at the hotel: they simply walked into the lobby and someone handed them a key to a six-room suite. Jimmy preferred the Sinatra penthouse with its white baby grand piano and spiral staircase. Food, drink, girls, anything they desired was delivered in a flash. Jimmy played blackjack for $10,000 a hand and had almost unlimited credit. Lee loved sitting in the middle of the table, flanked by armed guards and at least one beautiful "broad" who acted as his lucky piece. They could barely deal fast enough for Lee, all the spots covered with white chips, $21,000 riding on every deal.

Lee worked like a dog to pay his gambling losses, winning case after case, most of them involving major drug dealers. But he paid a steep price for success. His trial record made him many enemies, in particular a hard-driving prosecutor named James Kerr.

A zealot who abhorred not just drugs but the lifestyles of people like Lee and Jimmy Chagra, Kerr made it his mission to bring them down. To help in his crusade, he enlisted his good friend Judge John Wood as an ally. Wood had an almost irrational hatred of drug dealers and sentenced them with great relish, always to the maximum allowed by law. Soon he was known widely as "Maximum John."

Meanwhile, Lee played into their hands, allowing himself to get sucked into Jimmy's smuggling operations, first by setting up a dummy corporation in Florida where Jimmy could launder his dirty cash. The youngest of the three Chagra brothers, Joe, who had been Lee's law partner, was so concerned about the smuggling that he quit the firm and started his own practice.

One fateful weekend while Jimmy was in Florida awaiting a shipment of weed from Colombia, Lee realized that his personal finances were running dangerously low and decided to remedy the problem with a trip to Vegas. He was absolutely certain of his gambling skills, and his luck. He was overdue for a big score. "This is going to be one they'll write a book about," he told his friend

Clark Hughes, an El Paso district judge who made frequent trips to Vegas with Lee. "I'm going to take the joint apart."

In their adjoining suites in Vegas, Hughes watched in fascination as Lee transformed himself into the Black Striker. "For sheer élan," Hughes told me later, "I don't think I ever saw Lee higher." It was almost midnight when the Black Striker made his grand appearance on the casino floor. Bored by now by the tame pace of blackjack, Lee marched directly to a craps table and told the pit boss to clear away the riffraff, give him plenty of room. The pit boss snapped his fingers, motioning for guards to bring a velvet rope to restrain the crowd that always gathered when Lee went into action. "Gentlemen," the pit boss announced, "this table is now reserved for a private game." As he reached for the dice, Lee recited a spiel that was part of his ritual: "This joint ought to pay me fifteen hundred dollars an hour to entertain the customers. Where do you get off? Who do you think you are?" The pit boss had heard the spiel many times and he smiled as he counted out stacks of $500 chips. In the first minutes of Lee's run, a little old lady burst through the crowd just as Lee released the dice. "Any craps!" she shouted, throwing a $5 chip on the table.

But it wasn't Lee's night. After about an hour, he had lost $90,000, a sum that he laughed off. "That's small change for a stepper," he told Hughes. Lee returned to his suite to refresh himself with some cocaine, then headed back into action. In short order he had lost another $80,000 and was screaming at the floor manager, who was threatening to cut off his credit. To change his luck, Lee decided the next night to play baccarat instead of craps. Twenty-four hours after their arrival in Vegas, Lee was stone broke and had signed markers totaling about $240,000.

On the way home, Hughes asked how his friend was ever going to pay back all that money. "I don't know," Lee admitted. "But like Teddy Roosevelt said, it's better to try. It's better to bust your ass trying and get kicked all over tomorrow than live all your life like those gray bastards out there."

If Lee was at all concerned over the large debt, he didn't show it. Back at his plush El Paso office, life resumed as usual. The secretaries who worked for him knew that on any given day he had large amounts of cash in a safe in the bathroom. Every few days he would pay out or sometimes receive new shipments of cash. Everyone suspected that the money came from Jimmy's operation, but no one knew for certain. The mere idea that he, Lee Chagra, was somehow dependent on Jimmy was unthinkable, at least in Lee's mind. But money was like cocaine, something he was powerless to resist.

As the prosecutor James Kerr was redoubling his efforts to nail Lee, something astonishing happened: On his way to the courthouse one morning in November, Kerr's car was suddenly blocked by a van and two gunmen jumped out of the rear door and opened fire. Somehow, Kerr escaped unharmed except for a few minor cuts from shards of splintering glass. The attempted assassination of a federal prosecutor unleashed the most sweeping drug investigation in the history of the Southwest. The next morning FBI agents called on Lee Chagra, confiscated his gun collection, and asked him to take a lie detector test.

Pushing life to the limits was one of Lee Chagra's great pleasures, and in the end it cost him his life. Lee was murdered a few days before Christmas, 1978, in his luxurious new apartment and office complex on the edge of downtown El Paso. He had just returned from winning a big court case in Tucson and was flush with cash and a feeling that he was, at last, back where he belonged—on top of the world. The new complex was his gift to himself, a combination of plush bedrooms, kitchens, and office suites, equipped with luxuries he had dreamed of when he was an altar boy at St. Patrick's Cathedral across the street. The office complex was a grand fortress with an elaborate and very expensive security system. Only a handful of close friends and associates could have gained entrance. One of them was Lou Esper, a seedy, rat-faced ex-con who supplied cocaine for Lee's growing habit.

Esper was the lowest of El Paso's impressive cast of lowlifes, but he was exactly the sort of misfit with which Lee loved surrounding himself. Esper operated a small-time ring of burglars and robbers, using mostly black soldiers from Fort Bliss to do the dirty work.

He knew that Lee kept large amounts of cash in his office, to pay for drugs and gambling debts, and he arranged for the two soldiers to bypass security and grab the money. It was planned as a simple robbery, no rough stuff, no gunfire. Esper had guessed there might be as much as $100,000 in the office, but Lee was sitting on $450,000, most of which was earmarked to settle a debt to mafia chieftain Joe Bonanno, who had fronted one of Jimmy's smuggling operations. Unfortunately, one of the young soldiers Esper had assigned to the job was trigger-happy: when Lee appeared to be resisting, he shot and killed him. Thus was written an inglorious finish to one of the great high rollers of the day.

Over time, it began to dawn on the feds that the guy they really needed to question was Jimmy. Jimmy's cockiness and arrogance inevitably collided with his natural recklessness. Even as the FBI and other federal agencies had him in their crosshairs, Jimmy spent money with wild abandon. Records at Caesars Palace showed that in the fall of 1978 his winnings totaled $2.5 million and his losses $4.7 million. A lot of drug dealers went to the casino to launder money, but Jimmy seemingly went to burn it. A pit boss told me about accompanying Jimmy to his hotel suite one evening and watching him dump out footlockers of cash until he had the $915,000 to cover his losses that night.

As rumors of Jimmy's indictment on multiple drug charges circulated, the management at Caesars ordered him out of the Sinatra suite and told him the casino didn't want his business anymore. By now the only casino willing to gamble for the crazy sums that suited Jimmy was Binion's Horseshoe. Jimmy was there every night, usually with a couple of million on the table. In one short span, Binion's estimated that he had winnings of more than $2 million. One memorable evening, after losing heavily at the poker table, Jimmy peeled off $100,000 and said he wanted to play it all on a single hand of blackjack. Jack Binion approved the bet. Dealers laid out cards, a nine and a six for Chagra, a six showing for the house. Playing by the old Syrian rules, Jimmy stayed with what he had. The dealer had a king in the hole and was obliged by the house rules to hit. He took a seven, which busted him. "Jimmy was amazing," Jack Binion told me when I asked about that famous evening. "He had ice water for blood."

Like a pack of jackals smelling blood, cardsharps and golf hustlers followed Jimmy around the gambling venues of Vegas. Some of them even paid finder's fees for introductions to Chagra. One afternoon a small group of crooks, which included close friends of the notorious hit man named Charles Harrelson, took $580,000 from Jimmy by rigging a golf match. Fanning out around the golf course, they repositioned Jimmy's shots so that his ball ended up behind trees or buried in sand traps. Later that same night, they rigged a card game and took another $500,000.

During the World Series of Poker, a huge weekend at Binion's, Charles Harrelson went out of his way to befriend Jimmy. Over several drinks Harrelson listened politely as Jimmy bitched and moaned about having to face drug charges in the court of Maximum John Wood. Jimmy made some crack about how he'd pay anything to get rid of that pesky judge. As usual, Jimmy was just shooting off his mouth—this time, unfortunately, to the wrong guy. It was like that scene in *Becket* when the distraught king raves, "Will no one rid me of this meddlesome priest?" In the next scene, a mob of thugs is slashing Becket to ribbons. When Jimmy heard about Wood's murder a few weeks later, he almost fainted.

Harrelson had gone about his work with cold efficiency. He waited until a morning when Wood was sure to be isolated in the driveway of his townhouse in Alamo Heights, not far from the spot where a few months earlier Harrelson had attempted to assassinate James Kerr. As soon as Wood dropped, Harrelson disappeared into the heavy flow of morning traffic. Seldom had an assassination shocked and stunned so many people in high places: no one could remember a federal judge being killed, certainly not in the current century.

In the two years it took to research and write the book, I got to know and greatly admire Joe Chagra. He was a genuinely nice guy who couldn't say no, especially to his two older brothers. Lee brought Joe into the law firm to enhance his own self-esteem and treated Joe like property, taking what he wanted—including Joe's first serious girlfriend. Jimmy used Joe as a wedge against Lee in a sibling rivalry that consumed the whole family, and then he made Joe an unwitting liaison in the plot to kill the judge.

As the feds' investigation into Wood's murder entered its third year, Joe found himself trapped in a legal snare. By a twist of fate, he was representing both Jimmy and Charles Harrelson. Jimmy was locked away by now in Leavenworth. Harrelson's legal problems started as a routine gun charge but escalated into a major prosecution after a cocaine-induced gun battle with police near Van Horn in West Texas. For weeks, Joe made regular visits to both clients, unaware that the feds had bugged the visitors rooms at both facilities and that all of his conversations were being recorded.

When Harrelson volunteered the information that he had shot Judge Wood—and that Jimmy had hired him to do the killing—Joe was absolutely stunned. "Harrelson went into great detail about how he fired the shot," Joe told me later, his voice almost breaking, still unable to absorb the terrible truth. "He told how Wood quivered and dropped in his tracks. He was laughing when he told me. He *wanted* to kill Wood. The money was secondary." Harrelson even drew Joe a map, showing where he hid the murder weapon.

When I saw Joe a couple of days after his visit with Harrelson, he was still shaking, though I didn't know why at the time. Joe was strung out on coke by then. The combination of drugs and trying to deal with Jimmy was almost too much for him to handle. Typically, Jimmy was trying to blame all his trouble on Joe. In one conversation, Jimmy tells Joe: "You're the one who said do it, do it, do it." Joe tries to conceal his shock by talking tough, telling Jimmy that he never dreamed his brother would hire some "asshole" like Charles Harrelson.

The FBI used these wiretaps to get a warrant to search Joe's home, where they found not only the map that Harrelson had drawn but a stash of drugs. The map led the feds to the murder weapon and the discovery that it had been purchased by Harrelson's wife, Jo Ann. A short time later, Joe was arrested and held without bail in a tiny cell with no air-conditioning, in the heat of the Texas summer. While Joe simmered in jail, the government devised a way to bring its investigation to a successful conclusion.

The feds knew that as a matter of family honor, Joe would never testify against his brother. So they forced him into a no-win situation: either he could plead guilty to being part of the conspiracy to kill the judge and thus neutralize the attorney-client problem that prevented him from testifying against Harrelson, or the government could stack drug charges against him in a way that would make him an old man before he got out of prison.

Joe agreed to a plea bargain and a ten-year prison sentence. By the terms of the agreement, he was obliged to invent a bald-faced lie: he would tell the court that he had urged Jimmy to have the judge killed, a story so far-fetched that people who heard it rolled their eyes. In return for his cooperation, prosecutors promised to work for his early release and help him to recover his law license once time had been served. In fact, the feds did neither.

Jimmy and his wife, Liz, who was convicted for delivering the payoff money, both died in prison. Joe spent six and a half years behind bars, the maximum allowed at the time. I visited him a couple of times, once with Phyllis during a trip to San Francisco. He had become a model prisoner, staying clean, eating a mostly vegetarian diet, lifting weights, maintaining contact with his family. Even though his wife, Patty, had divorced him, they remained friends and she made certain that their two children saw their daddy regularly and thought well of him. After his release in 1989, Joe returned to El Paso and lived a quiet life. When he applied to have his law license restored, I testified at the hearing in support of him, but the federal government didn't lift a finger to help. The judge ruled that restoring the license would not meet "the ends of justice"—whatever that means. A few days later, Joe was killed in a car wreck. What a waste, what a tragedy.

After the manuscript of *Dirty Dealing* was completed but before the book was published, I continued to discover new details of the shadowy happenings. Early in my investigation, I had been told by one of the prosecutors that the Chagra family had mafia connections, a story I rejected out of hand. Months later, to my astonishment, I was contacted by a lawyer who offered a proposition that greatly surprised me. Joe Bonanno, Sr., the notorious crime boss, was worried that his name would appear in my book and was offering me $40,000 to delete it. This made no sense at the time. Why would I feel any need to use Joe Bonanno's name in the book? Eventually, I discovered the reason, which also explained the mysterious $450,000 that Lee had in his office the day he was killed. It was money that Jimmy owed Bonanno for a busted drug deal.

FLUSH WITH ADVANCE MONEY FROM THE CHAGRA project, Phyllis and I moved to Taos, which is located fairly close to where I needed to be to research the book, though location was not the prime motivator in this case. I had dreamed about living in Taos since I first visited it with Bud in the late 1960s. It had the magic of a time when luminaries of the arts like Mabel Dodge Luhan, Aldous Huxley, D. H. Lawrence, and Thomas Wolfe thrived there, and I felt the pull of history deep in my bones. Phyllis and Doatsy went ahead to scout the place and find us a house to rent. They found a four-room adobe built in the 1600s. It was about two blocks from the main plaza and had a large kitchen that opened onto its own patio, and a fireplace in every room. Later we rented a larger place, on the top of a mesa overlooking an ancient village that was home to the oldest church in America. It was an adobe dwelling with fireplaces in every room, including the kitchen, and separate quarters that I could use as an office. Outside my office window, a flock of woolly sheep grazed for a good part of every day. I never learned where the sheep came from, or who owned them, but they were good company.

We had planned to be in Taos a few months but stayed a year and a half, hiking the trails of Carson National Forest with our Airedales—we had one, two, and sometimes three Airedale terriers most of our married life—and exploring New Mexico and Colorado. I took trips to El Paso to research the book, but mostly we just had fun and savored each other's company.

On my trips to El Paso, I usually stayed with my great friend Malcolm McGregor, whose family once owned thousands of acres near what is now Fort Bliss: the McGregor Range is named for their family. Malcolm lived in a classic Prairie-style house in Sunset Heights, near the university, designed by the famed Southwestern architect Henry C. Trost. His law office on the edge of downtown was another classic building, and on any given day it was a gathering place for writers and other interesting people, including the novelist Cormac McCarthy, who used Malcolm's office as a hideaway and mail drop.

Everything about Malcolm echoed the classics. He was a large man with a shock of graying hair that was usually hanging down into his eyes, and he had a heroic belly that lapped over the waist of the Levi's he always wore. The walls of his home and his office were lined with books, thousands and thousands, and he had read almost all of them. He drove an MG convertible and owned two airplanes—an open, double-cockpit World War II trainer, and a fire-engine-red Stearman Staggerwing that he loved dearly. We flew all over Texas, New Mexico, and parts of Mexico in the Stearman, landing at historical sites, searching for artifacts, discovering lost trails to the past. The history of this wild and desolate country had a great influence on what I wrote over the next thirty years. Malcolm was the perfect guide. When he died in 2003, we buried him in the Texas State Cemetery in Austin, and the mourners included such notables as Cormac McCarthy, Willie Morris, and Larry L. King.

ONE OF THE DISPIRITING THINGS ABOUT MY JOB at *Texas Monthly* was opening letters from people in prison. I got one or two nearly every day, always long and usually handwritten, in pencil, on lined school paper, composed by poor souls who claimed innocence and protested against the injustices of the Texas legal system. Experience had educated me to the sad truth that most people in jail belonged there, but I tried to read each letter with an open mind. Sometime in the mid-1980s I started getting mail from a guy on death row, named Randall Dale Adams. He begged me to at least telephone his lawyer, a Houston attorney named Randy Schaffer, who I knew by reputation. Schaffer welcomed my call and told me: "Just do one thing. Read the trial transcript and the police reports. Then let's talk." So that's what I did. It took nearly a week to pore through all that material, but it was soon apparent that the case was dirty: the Dallas police had arrested the wrong man and were desperate to conceal the truth.

The case was by that time nearly eleven years old and traced back to a bitter-cold November night when Dallas police officer Robert Wood was gunned down by the driver of a car he had stopped for a minor traffic violation. The murder case had gone to the U.S. Supreme Court and back in a futile search for justice, and there were still many unanswered questions.

The only one who got a good look at the killer was Robert Wood, and for all practical purposes he was dead before he hit the ground. Wood's partner that fatal night was Teresa Turko, one of the first females ever assigned to street patrol in Dallas. Turko had apparently waited in the patrol car, drinking a milk shake, while Wood approached the car they had pulled over. Badly shaken by the murder, Turko supplied only a skimpy, mostly inaccurate, description of the killer and his car, which she remembered as a blue Vega.

A few days later a thirty-six-year-old woman named Emily Miller told investigators that she and her husband, Robert, saw the shooting from their own car, on the opposite side of the highway. Robert Miller was hesitant to give a description of the killer, but Emily was positive that he was "a Mexican or a light-skinned black" wearing an Afro and driving "a Ford product"—a Mercury Comet, as it turned out. She recognized Officer Wood because the patrolman had befriended the family when her daughter was arrested for driving without a license. For at least a week police searched for the wrong make of car, and for several weeks they assumed that the killer was Hispanic or black.

The investigation took a surprising and unfortunate turn—one from which it never recovered—when it was learned that a young hoodlum named David Ray Harris, arrested in Vidor, near Beau-

mont, had bragged to friends that he had blown away "a pig in
Dallas." When investigators questioned him, the sixteen-year-old,
who was already on juvenile probation, admitted burglarizing a
home and stealing a car, a blue Mercury Comet, as it turned out.
Then he drove the stolen car to Dallas to dispose of his loot. Part
of the loot was a .22-caliber pistol, which turned out to be the gun
that killed Robert Wood. Harris still had the gun when he returned
to Vidor a day after the murder. He freely admitted the burglaries
and robbery, but told investigators that his boast about killing a
cop was just a story he made up to impress friends. But he proposed a deal: if the Vidor police would drop all charges, he would
tell them who really killed Officer Wood.

If one takes into account all that was known at this point—
Harris's record, his boast about killing a Dallas cop, and the fact
that he had the car and the murder weapon—the story that Harris was spinning was childishly far-fetched. But Dallas police were
more than ready to believe him, especially when he told them the
second part of his story. He had picked up a hitchhiker, an older
man named Dale. They had spent the afternoon together, smoking
pot, drinking beer, and pawning the stolen tools, Harris admitted.
That night as they were returning to Dale's motel from a drive-in
movie, a patrol car stopped them. Dale was driving, or so Harris
wanted police to believe. When the cop approached the car window, Dale grabbed the pistol that Harris had stored under the seat
and pumped five slugs into the startled officer. Harris remembered
being told, "Forget what you saw."

In point of fact, Adams was already back at his motel, dressing
for bed, when Harris killed the cop. Harris had hoped that Adams
would invite him to share his motel room for the night, but Adams
refused and went to bed. He knew nothing about the cop killing
until his arrest, and had assumed he would never see or hear of
David Harris again.

But the Dallas police had lost one of their own and were determined that someone had to pay with his life. Under Texas law,
juveniles cannot receive the death sentence. Here was the situation Dallas authorities faced: Harris was willing to say that Adams

did it. All Adams could say was he didn't even know a murder had taken place.

By the time Adams was arrested a few days before Christmas, 1976—three weeks after the shooting—Wood's murder had become a major embarrassment to Dallas, the longest unsolved cop killing in the city's history. When at last a jury convicted Randall Dale Adams and sentenced him to death, there was a feeling of exhilaration within the law enforcement fraternity, a belief that the painful affair had at last been put to rest.

But it didn't rest. It couldn't as long as Adams remained on death row. A group of attorneys working for little or no fee began collecting new evidence and looking again at old evidence. They were assisted greatly by the work of Errol Morris, a prominent New York filmmaker who met Adams and got interested in his case while researching a project on death row inmates. Much of Morris's evidence was contained in outtakes from his film *The Thin Blue Line*, which at the time was still in development. I arrived on the scene of this gripping story in the last of the ninth inning, when even a blind man could have seen the truth, but it immediately grabbed my attention and I began to dig in.

That Adams was even in Dallas at the time of the killing was a quirk of fate, I soon discovered. Indeed, fate had played a large part in what happened to Adams. He and his brother had arrived two months earlier from their family home in Ohio, intending to continue west to California and warm weather. Instead, Adams quickly found a job with a construction crew and they decided to stay in Dallas.

Adams's fate was sealed early that Saturday morning, the day of the shooting, when he showed up at his job site only to learn that work had been suspended for the long Thanksgiving weekend. Having paid another week's rent on his motel, he was nearly broke. His car was nearly out of gas and coughed to a halt after another block or two. Carrying a plastic water jug, Adams walked a quarter of a mile to a service station. But an attendant told him that putting gasoline in a plastic jug was illegal and turned him away. Adams was standing there in the cold, trying to decide his next move, when a blue Comet stopped. The driver introduced himself as David Ray Harris and offered Adams a lift. It turned out to be the longest ride of his life.

The case that the Dallas police turned over to the district attorney was badly flawed. It depended on the jury's believing the testimony of David Ray Harris, hardly a model witness, and on the testimony of Officer Teresa Turko, who had been wrong on the make of the car and had initially said that its single occupant had dark, medium-length hair and wore a heavy jacket with the collar turned up—not a bad description of David Harris. Harris and Turko were the only major witnesses on the list that chief prosecutor Doug Mulder tendered to the defense. On the other hand, Adams's court-appointed attorney, Dennis White, had at least three, maybe as many as half a dozen, witnesses who had heard Harris brag about killing a Dallas cop.

But lawyers who had gone up against Mulder when he worked as a prosecutor for Dallas's hard-nosed district attorney, Henry Wade, knew that this was the perfect situation for an ambush. In his twelve years as prosecutor, Mulder had never lost a capital murder case. He had sent maybe two dozen men to death row, and it seemed unthinkable that his unblemished record would be broken by a cop killer. For reasons not apparent at the time, Mulder didn't include on the witness list he gave the defense the names of Robert and Emily Miller or yet another potential witness who also claimed to have witnessed the crime. Instead, he ambushed the defense by calling the Millers as *rebuttal witnesses*. Rebuttal witnesses are usually witnesses whose testimony cannot be anticipated, who become relevant only because of something that happens in the course of the trial. Three eyewitnesses to the scene of a murder hardly fit that definition, especially since Emily Miller's tip is what started the cops looking for "a Ford product." That tip led directly to Harris, who implicated Adams.

Whether it was a smart tactic or a dirty trick, it worked. At a key moment of the trial, Emily Miller pointed across the courtroom to Randall Dale Adams and said without the slightest doubt or hesitation: "His hair is different but that's the man." Robert Miller, though less impressive as a witness, was no less certain in identifying Adams. So was a third witness, Michael Randell, who earlier had picked out Adams in a police lineup. Outside the presence of the jury, Emily Miller testified that she too had identified Adams in a police lineup, though in fact there was no record that either of the Millers had ever viewed a lineup. Dennis White, Adams's attorney, should have caught the mistake, but he didn't.

This is one of several times White failed to do his job, partly because Mulder was doing all in his power to hide or disguise evidence. For example, White had never heard of Emily Miller until the trial started. He didn't know she had made a prior statement identifying the killer as a Mexican or light-skinned black. Mulder claimed that he simply "forgot" to hand that particular document to the defense, and added that Emily Miller's prior statement wouldn't have assisted the defense anyway. But Mulder was wrong, as the Texas Court of Criminal Appeals later noted when it affirmed Adams's conviction on the grounds that his attorney failed to make a timely request for that vital piece of exculpatory evidence.

A day after both sides had rested, White at last learned, while he was talking with a reporter, about Mrs. Miller's prior statement. At his first opportunity, he demanded that the court recall Ms. Miller. But Mulder objected, arguing that the Millers had checked out of the Adolphus Hotel, where the state had been keeping them, and that he had been told that they had gone to Illinois. Though Mulder must have known that this wasn't true, he convinced the judge that it would be improper for the jury to hear the prior statement since Mrs. Miller wasn't available to explain the contradiction. But Mrs. Miller *was* available. She appeared live on local television that same evening, standing in front of her room at the Alamo Plaza Motel. And Mulder damn well knew she was there: Schaffer found receipts in Mulder's file showing that the Millers had made 135 local telephone calls from the Alamo Plaza Motel, at the state's expense.

Stunned by this most recent setback, White watched helplessly as the judge sent the case to the jury. Notes from the jury room over the next several hours demonstrated that jurors were having problems with the testimony of rebuttal witnesses, but the judge refused their request for clarification. One note even asked if Mrs. Miller had made a prior statement; apparently at least one juror had read about it in the *Dallas Times Herald*, months before the trial. Not long after Adams was convicted and sent off to death row, Dennis White filed a lawsuit and a grievance with the Dallas Bar Association, accusing Mulder of prosecutorial misconduct. Neither action got him anywhere. The sad truth was, White had blown it. He had believed so strongly in his client's innocence that he forgot his lawyerly objectivity. Crushed by the experience, Dennis White never accepted another major case. Eventually, he phased out his law practice completely and got into real estate.

By now, Adams's mother had exhausted her life savings, and the court appointed several appellate lawyers, including Mel Bruder of Dallas and Randy Schaffer of Houston, to represent Adams. Three years later the Supreme Court overturned his sentence on a technicality having to do with the death sentence part of the trial, meaning that Adams was entitled to a new trial. A confident Dallas district attorney Henry Wade immediately informed the media that Adams would be tried—and convicted—a second time. But Wade was bluffing. This time Adams's team of lawyers had considerable evidence to discredit key state witnesses. They had learned, for example, that Mrs. Miller lied when she testified that she drove past the murder scene minutes after leaving her job at Fas Gas service station: in fact, she had been fired from Fas Gas fifteen days before the murder, after shortages in her account were discovered. Two Fas Gas employees also revealed that Robert Miller had admitted to them that he never saw the driver that night. They had also overheard the Millers talking about reward money: it appeared that reward money, not civic duty, was the motive for their stories. One by one, all the rebuttal witnesses who had given such damning testimony at the trial were discredited.

Before the Court of Criminal Appeals could order a new trial, however, the district attorney found a new way to screw Randall Adams. He persuaded Governor Bill Clements to commute

Adams's sentence to life in prison. Removing the death sentence meant that the conviction was otherwise without error. Though spared execution, Adams was still doomed to life behind bars, unless his lawyers could find other appellate roads to develop.

Schaffer was working on the problem and soon started turning up proof that the prosecution had *knowingly* withheld key evidence. The state had neglected, for example, to tell the defense that Officer Turko had changed her description of the killer's hairstyle only after spending time with a hypnotist. Though the law was explicit on this point, nobody had bothered to tell the defense about Turko's visit to a hypnotist, or the damning results it produced. Mrs. Miller had also denied that her testimony was the result of any kind of "deal" with the state, but the defense discovered that the state had agreed to drop robbery charges against her daughter in return for her testimony.

Meanwhile, I had started developing my own scenario of the time and sequence of events, which convinced me that Adams was telling the truth. The second feature of the drive-in movie that Adams and Harris saw that night ended at 11:49 p.m., fifty minutes before Wood was killed. Adams and Harris both remembered leaving partway through the movie. That would easily have put them back at the motel before 11 p.m. Nowhere in Adams's statement was any mention of what time he got home. Nobody asked him, Adams told me. His brother Ray, who was sharing the room, was no help with the timeline. Adams's failure to pin down the time he arrived back at the motel makes sense only when you understand that he didn't even *know* that murder was the focus of the investigation: Adams was under the impression he was arrested as an accessory to burglary, for helping Harris pawn his stolen tools.

One of the first things I noted when I got to interview Adams at the Dallas County Jail was his extreme naïveté: he was thirty-eight years old, obviously a nice guy but somewhat slow and strangely passive and unaware. Though he had been on death row for more than a decade, he showed no anger or righteous indignation, posited no clever conspiratorial theories, offered no alternatives. All he could think to say in his defense was that he didn't do it.

After talking to Adams, I made a trip to the Ellis Unit outside Huntsville, where I had arranged an interview with David Ray Harris, who was now on death row for a more recent crime, this one right out of the sociopath's handbook. Harris had broken into a Beaumont apartment, dragged a young woman naked and screaming to his car, then pumped five slugs into her boyfriend as he attempted a rescue. Harris was twenty-six and looked even younger: his blue eyes sparkled and there was still a boyish charm backlighting his grin.

I waited until my interview was nearly complete before firing off my key question: "Do you ever think about Adams," I asked, "and how different both your lives would be if he'd just invited you to spend the night at his motel?" It was a loaded question: if he replied in the affirmative, it would be an acknowledgment that Wood was killed *after* Harris left Adams alone at the motel.

"I think about it," Harris said, and the memory seemed to touch something deep and difficult to express. "If he'd just said, 'Come on in . . .'"

"Then what?"

Harris didn't reply, but the answer was obvious.

"Adams didn't kill that cop, did he?"

A thin smile played along his lips, as though he were pleased that I had guessed his little secret. He shook his head, no.

"Did you kill him?"

He thought about the question a while. Then he said, "I can't answer that."

"It can't hurt you now," I told him, though I knew that wasn't necessarily true.

"It can't help me either," he said softly. "But if it ever gets to the point where they're strapping me on that gurney, stand by for a statement."

The most convincing and dramatic proof that Adams was framed showed up in the outtakes from Errol Morris's film *The Thin Blue Line*. The filmmaker's technique is to have his subjects speak directly into the camera, telling their stories and whatever else comes to mind, with few interruptions from the camera crew or director. In such an atmosphere, people can be amazingly revealing. Mrs. Miller got ready for her close-up by selecting a scarlet dress. Instead of the black hair she showed at the trial, she sported a sparkling platinum hairdo. She revealed that her lifelong fantasy was to be a girl Friday to a famous private detective like Charlie Chan or Boston Blackie. Even before Officer Wood's murder, she explained, she had been an eyewitness to an incredible number of murders and acts of violence. "When something like this would happen . . . I would go see if I could solve it before anyone else could," she said. The most significant thing that Mrs. Miller said, however, was that she and her husband, Robert, had indeed viewed a live lineup at the police station. That was an extraordinary revelation, because no police lineup identification forms were in the case file, as is required by law. In the filmed interview, she admitted that not only had she and her husband viewed a lineup, but they also had failed to pick out Randall Adams. Robert Miller couldn't pick anyone, and Emily picked one of the decoys. And that wasn't all. As they were leaving the lineup room, Emily Miller recalled that a policeman pointed out the man she should have picked—Randall Dale Adams. Therefore, to Mrs. Miller's way of thinking, it wasn't a lie when she told the jury at Adams's trial that she had identified him at a police lineup.

At the writ hearing, U.S. magistrate John Tolle permitted the defense to introduce some new evidence and reflect on how old evidence had been twisted, but he limited the screening of *The Thin Blue Line* to a single brief clip. After the lead detective told the court that Adams had never denied the murder, a clip from an interview was shown in which the detective made clear that Adams "kept saying over and over" that he didn't do it.

The magistrate didn't rule on the motion for a new trial for nearly eighteen months, at which point he denied it. Adams's attorneys finally won their long and frustrating fight the following winter when a state judge in Dallas heard the evidence and dismissed the case against Adams. Suddenly, it was over. The ending was almost as stunning as the beginning, and nearly as inexplicable.

Ironically, the reason that Adams was finally set free wasn't the evidence but the political and social climate. Errol Morris's brilliant film had become a box-office hit in the weeks just prior to the hearing and was about to be nominated for an Academy Award. The movie changed the climate in a way that my magazine story never could. "Adams was tried in a climate of hate and animosity," Schaffer reflected. "But the movie showed dramatically that they not only convicted the wrong man, they framed him. The public was convinced. In this new climate, it was okay for the judge to grant Adams relief."

The relief came with no apology, not even an admission of error. Though Adams got to tell his story on the talk show circuit and even testified before the Senate Judiciary Committee, he eventually faded into obscurity back home in Ohio. Neither Dallas nor the State of Texas ever paid him a penny for those twelve years that he lost. Adams didn't even get the usual $200 that the prison system hands out when a prisoner is released. Technically, he wasn't released from prison. His case was simply dismissed.

ADAMS WAS ONE OF TWO INMATES I HELPED FREE from prison. The other was Greg Ott, who killed Texas Ranger Bobby Paul Doherty during a botched drug raid at Ott's house in Denton in 1978. I had written about the shooting at the time and knew the case well. Far from the cold-blooded murder that the Rangers had portrayed for years, it was a tragic accident, a senseless and shameful episode in our ill-fated "war on drugs."

An informant who had just been busted and was trying to save his own ass convinced a team of lawmen that Ott was a major dope dealer. This was a ridiculous lie, as the lawmen would have known if anyone had stopped to check the informant's story. Ott was a graduate student in philosophy at North Texas State, a dedicated ascetic who drove an old Fiat, bought his clothes at the Salvation Army, and bragged about grooving on poverty. He worked five nights a week writing his master's thesis, an effort to compare Heidegger's phenomenology with Zen haiku poetry. He was a brilliant, harmless eccentric who smoked dope and sold or gave small quantities to friends.

Narcotics officers from the Texas Department of Public Safety had never heard of him until a few hours before the raid, when their informant fingered him as a major trafficker. These were professional lawmen and should have known better, but they were on a crusade and were convinced they were onto something big. They put together an impressive raiding party of heavily armed agents, including Texas Ranger Bobby Doherty. The raid was an accident waiting to happen. None of the lawmen was in uniform. Some of them had been drinking beer and smoking dope, as part of their undercover act. Ott was naturally paranoid. He had been robbed on two occasions and had watched a woman friend get badly beaten.

When he heard the noise of the raiding party climbing out of their pickup truck, he mistook it for another robbery attempt. One of the lawmen forced his way inside the house and fired a shot at Ott, who was heading toward the back door. When he heard the shot, Ott grabbed a gun from a shelf. He heard a noise outside the back door, and reflexively raised the gun and fired. Unfortunately, Ranger Bobby Doherty was on the other side of that door and was fatally wounded.

It was all a crazy mistake, real cops playing Keystone Kops or worse. I remain convinced that Ott didn't willingly or knowingly shoot a police officer, and the jury at his trial obviously agreed with my reasoning; otherwise the sentence would have been death and Ott would be long forgotten except by his family and a few close friends.

I continued to stay in touch with Ott as he did his time. As the years went by I wrote about him several times, and testified on his behalf at parole board hearings. He had become the pluperfect inmate, a poster boy for the way a parole system ought to work. For more than two decades, the Texas Department of Criminal Justice (TDCJ) repeatedly took note of his cooperation, work ethic, upbeat attitude, and selflessness. One parole officer noted in a letter to the parole board that Ott "is almost an alien in this environment, portraying characteristics that would qualify him as a model citizen." Ott risked his life to save a guard who was being attacked by another inmate. "He put his life on the line for that officer," I was told by the warden of the Darrington Unit. On another occasion, he probably saved an entire wing of inmates and guards at Darrington. Ott was the boiler room attendant when three prisoners who were attempting a breakout beat him and bound him with tape, then killed the power to the boiler despite Ott's warning that they were about to blow up the whole building. He somehow wormed his way out the door and alerted guards minutes before the boiler would have exploded. His only infraction in all that time was for ordering forms from the Internal Revenue Service to pay tax on money he'd made selling his handcrafted leather goods: the tax forms were considered contraband by the TDCJ. Dozens of guards and wardens and even the Denton County DA who had sent him to prison wrote letters urging his parole.

So why was the parole board resisting? Because the man that he killed was a Texas Ranger, and the Rangers were not about to let the parole board forget it. Twice the board voted to set him free, and twice it changed its vote because of an avalanche of protests orchestrated by retired Texas Ranger captain Bob Prince, who had made it his mission to keep Ott locked up.

Attorney Bill Habern of Huntsville, one of my longtime friends, worked for years trying to get the board's approval. Even though the case was a pro bono project by his law office, Habern never once backed away from the fight. I traveled with him to several parole hearings and to visit Ott at the prison. Ott was doing his time without a trace of bitterness or hatred, following orders, accepting guilt. "I strive to be part of the solution, not the problem," he told us on what turned out to be our final visit. By now he was fifty-three, frailer and grayer than I'd remembered, but still upbeat and positive.

In August 2000, frustrated by the parole board's obstinate refusal to act on the obvious, I published a strongly opinionated piece in *Texas Monthly*, titled "Free Greg Ott!" My column didn't persuade the board, but it did catch the attention of two national television shows, A&E's *American Justice* and *Court TV*, both of which decided to devote coverage to Ott's plight. *Court TV*'s Catherine Crier in particularly began to champion his cause. Crier was a graduate of Southern Methodist University's law school and worked for a time as a prosecutor and judge in Dallas. Her daily crusade on Ott's behalf elicited a flood of letters and e-mails to Governor Rick Perry's office and the parole board, eventually prodding a review of Ott's status. At a hearing in January 2004, Crier told the board the simple truth about the case: "If this crime had happened today, it would probably be prosecuted as manslaughter for which the maximum sentence is twenty years." To my great surprise, the board seemed to understand, at last, that Ott had paid for his crime and no longer belonged behind bars.

Habern, Crier, and I gathered for a small celebration when we got the news that the board had decided to free Greg Ott. Habern told us that his law office had worked eleven years on the case. "In the end," he said, echoing what all of us were feeling, "it was worth every minute."

One condition of his parole was that Ott had to leave the state of Texas, and agree to never return—a stipulation he had no difficulty accepting. He moved to Florida, where his aging parents lived, and got a job as a maintenance man at a shopping center. I hated the thought of this brilliant, talented guy making his living pushing a broom, but he didn't seem to mind. Not long after that, he wrote that he had found a better position with a company called Wind Armour, for which he had designed a hurricane window cover/wind abatement system. Two years after his release he sent a photo of himself and his girlfriend, Sue, who would soon become his wife. "Life is good, craft is busy, hurricane season is coming with lots of expected work," he told me, adding that Sue had accepted that he was "a hard-core workaholic" but had promised to break him of that nasty habit. A year later he wrote: "It has taken me a long time to actually get out of prison, to pull loose from the psychic toehold that kept me part in/part out for so long. I believe this has been my first year of actually being out and engaged in the process of living." The following Christmas, he sent a card with this notation: "The difference with this year is that I have shared it, the good and the bad, with Susan, my wife and partner."

I'll never forget Greg Ott, and I think he would say the same about me. I am comforted knowing that our fates are intertwined. Much of my happiness has to do with knowing that he is happy, too, happy and well and free. Nothing in my career as a writer-journalist has given me more satisfaction.

I ALSO COVERED THE MANHUNT AND ARREST OF THE most vicious killer in the state's history, Kenneth McDuff. This experience changed how I felt about the death penalty, which I came to realize was not only justified but even necessary in a few cases. It also bolstered Ann Richards's campaign promise to reform the parole system.

The McDuff case was the beginning of my friendship with two U.S. Marshals, Parnell and Mike McNamara, who were instrumental in tracking him down. They had known about McDuff since they were teenagers because their father, T. P. McNamara, who was also a U.S. Marshal, had sent McDuff to prison years ago for an unforgettably brutal murder. A born thug with a lust for kidnapping, raping, and murdering women, McDuff had started his rampage of crime by torturing and killing two Fort Worth boys and a girlfriend. He shot the two boys in the face as they kneeled and begged for mercy, and then he raped the girl in the middle of the road. When he was done he put a broomstick across her throat and, as one lawman described the act, "broke her neck just like you'd kill a possum." Sentenced to die in the electric chair, he twice received last-minute stays from the court. In 1972, the U.S. Supreme Court issued a moratorium on capital punishment, a ruling that resulted in McDuff's sentence being commuted to life in prison. By this time the parole system in Texas was in shambles, and McDuff was smart enough to use the legal chaos to his advantage. While in prison, he was caught trying to give a $10,000 bribe to a member of the parole board, but the system was so screwed up he was never punished for this blatant violation. On the contrary, he became something of a model prisoner. When a federal court ruled that the Texas prison system was overcrowded and ordered that low-risk prisoners be released, McDuff somehow qualified.

Three days after his release, the bodies of young women began showing up, just as the McNamaras had predicted. Local police failed to recognize the pattern—kidnapping, torture, unbelievably brutal murders, bodies discarded in wooded areas or ponds—much less connect the crimes to McDuff. But Parnell and Mike McNamara recognized McDuff's trademark. Normally, investigating murders is not the work of U.S. Marshals, but the McNamaras got involved anyway, thanks to some special circumstances. As it happened, the U.S. Marshals Service had just assigned several hundred investigators to what was called Operation Gunsmoke, a nationwide effort to target violent offenders and get them off the streets. Under the mandate of Gunsmoke, the McNamaras were able to form a small task force to track down McDuff. They worked out of a mobile command post called Red October, which was parked behind the Federal Building in Waco, and started putting the pieces together.

They discovered, to everyone's great surprise, that McDuff had a daughter. A woman he had raped and left for dead years earlier had not only lived but had given birth to a girl. When the daughter grew up, she tracked down her father and visited him in prison. At first, she was fascinated and drawn to this strange man. Soon, however, McDuff showed his true colors. He conned her into smuggling some drugs for him, and then he made plans after his parole to take her to Las Vegas and be her pimp. Stunned by this revolting turn of events, the daughter agreed to help investigators find her father. About this same time, investigators got another good lead. McDuff and another man abducted a young accountant named Colleen Reed from an Austin car wash, tortured, raped, and murdered her. The killing made headlines across the state and intensified the hunt for the psychopathic killer.

The McNamaras began sorting through a list of McDuff's cronies and realized that a thirty-four-year-old concrete worker named Hank Worley matched the description of the man who had been with McDuff when Colleen Reed was kidnapped. They found Worley living at a cheap motel in Temple. After repeated interrogations, they got him to make a statement, detailing the abduction in sordid detail, which they released to the national media. It became a feature on *America's Most Wanted*, where it caught the attention of a woman in Kansas City who recognized McDuff as the man who drove the garbage truck in her neighborhood. The task force immediately moved into action. When they surrounded McDuff, he surrendered without a struggle, no more the tough guy.

On the day that he was executed by lethal injection in 1998, I sat in my office, staring out the window, dueling conflicts churning in my gut. While I grew up opposed to the death penalty, I was glad McDuff was going to die, glad that justice would be done. And yet, somehow, it wasn't enough. To my surprise, I realized that I actually missed the electric chair. While I was happy that Old Sparky was gone from our criminal justice system, I couldn't help wishing that for this occasion it could be used one last time.

I HAVEN'T HEARD A PEEP ABOUT SATANIC RITUAL abuse in more than twenty years, which seems strange because back in 1991 it was reported to be infecting the whole country with its wacko, totally bogus threat to take over the world. I got interested in satanic ritual abuse (SRA) when Fran and Dan Keller, an elderly couple who ran a small day-care center in the Austin suburb of Oak Hill, were sent to prison for practicing it. Though SRA was long ago discredited as claptrap, the Kellers were still in prison, victims rather than perpetrators of a crime that never happened, or, indeed, even existed.

As I wrote in a column published in *Texas Monthly*: "The criminal allegations that ruined the lives of the Kellers and a lot of other innocent people were so ridiculous they might have struck Stephen King deaf and dumb—witches, monsters and endless supplies of diabolical conspirators who drugged, raped, mutilated and defecated on the heads of small children, and buried them alive with nests of snakes. Satanic Ritual Abuse or SRA was one of those social nightmares that break loose from time to time, convoluted attempts by society to deal with irrationality and demagoguery: we saw it in the 1690s in the Salem witch trials, and again in the 1950s in the Red Scare and the McCarthy outrages. Like its malevolent predecessors, SRA ran unchecked for a while and then died of its own craziness. Even so, today's landscape remains littered with the evil it spawned."

I have visited the Kellers in prison, written about them, testified for them, and never forgotten. But I thought the world had. Then in January 2013, I learned that an Austin attorney, Keith Hampton, working pro bono, had filed an appeal in state district court, presenting evidence that prosecutors and police botched the investigation by blindly accepting the testimony of a bunch of crackpots over their own common sense. Hampton argued in his brief: "A 21st century court ought to be able to recognize a 20th century witch-hunt and render justice accordingly." I agreed that it *ought* to . . .

I first learned about satanic ritual abuse by reading an article that my friend Larry Wright published in the *New Yorker*. It was an account of how the myth of a satanic conspiracy originated—and then bloomed—into a national obsession. It started in 1980 with the publication of the best seller *Michelle Remembers*, written by a psychiatrist and former priest who reported the recovered memory of his patient (and later wife) Michelle. Treated with hypnotism, exorcism, and a conversion to Catholicism, Michelle eventually remembered being ritually abused by her mother and a huge cast of Satanists. Her story culminates with a detailed—and obviously phony—memory of an eighty-one-day non-stop ceremony where Satan himself appears, only to be beaten back by Jesus, the Virgin Mary, and the archangel Michael.

The first SRA prosecution came a few years later, in Los Angeles County, where a mentally ill mother convinced authorities that her child had been molested at the McMartin preschool. The allegations were lodged during a hotly contested district attorney's race in which child abuse was the primary issue. Four hundred children from the school were interviewed by a clinic that specialized in sexual abuses (such clinics were popping up everywhere) and bombarded with leading questions. The interrogators warned the kids that if they didn't tell the "yucky secrets," people would think they were stupid. Not surprisingly, the clinic staff concluded that almost all of them had been molested. The McMartin trial went on for nearly three years without a conviction, but it caused a rash of SRA reports around the country.

The Keller case was typical of what passed for justice at the time: it originated in a day-care center, as did most of the SRA cases. The elements of these cases followed a common pattern: they started with highly suggestible preschoolers, many in therapy for behavioral problems, and over-protective parents, almost all of them also in therapy. The parents were invariably encouraged by untrained therapists, who in turn claimed that they had experienced their own sexual abuse years earlier. Snarled in this daisy chain of paranoia, therapists urged the parents to browbeat their children until they revealed "secrets" and confessed outrages that fit with SRA propaganda. Most remarkably, lawmen and politically ambitious prosecutors read and believed this propaganda and were more than ready to unload on accused child molesters. The allegations invariably got tangled up with junk science such as "recovered memories" and "multiple personality disorders," bogus mental afflictions that cultists were supposed to have been able to induce in their victims at will.

When skeptics wondered why—with all the alleged rapes, electric shocks, and screwdrivers up the anus and urethra—none of the children showed cuts or bruises, true believers always had answers. According to Cory Hammond, a Utah psychologist and leading theorist on the satanic threat, it wasn't the children themselves who were attacked; it was their alternative personalities or alters. Alters, Hammond insisted, could change the color of their eyes and make scars appear or disappear. Although such assertions were ridiculous, even laughable, they were accepted, or at least not disputed, by the media. On the contrary, the media tended to sensationalize them, endlessly repeating far-fetched theories dreamed up by professionals like Hammond and Dallas psychologist Randy

Noblitt, mentor to the therapists in the Keller case. Many Americans blithely accepted that the nation, indeed the entire world, was under siege by an international cult. So-called cult "survivors" appeared on television shows like *Oprah* and *Geraldo*. Accounts of recovered memory and ritual abuse began to appear in countless articles, books, and made-for-TV movies. By the summer of 1991 when the Keller investigation started, a cottage industry of psychologists and therapists steeped in SRA literature was up and running. Two of the three children in the Keller case were in therapy at the time of the allegations, and so were their mothers.

My firsthand indoctrination into the SRA mess came when I accompanied Larry Wright to a meeting of a group of Austin therapists, at the office of Karen Hutchins, who had treated two of the children in the Keller case. Larry had no interest in writing another story about this bizarre stuff, but he wanted me to think about writing one. The meeting was an eye-opener. Nearly all the therapists in attendance had enlisted in the fight against Satan. These were educated women, but they were trained in social work, not medicine, and certainly not common sense. Most of what they knew about SRA came from Noblitt or from literature supplied by Believe the Children, a group organized by parents in the Mc-Martin case.

Hutchins estimated that about half of her fifty patients had been ritually abused and suffered from multiple personality disorder. At that same meeting, another therapist passed out what she claimed was a secret CIA document listing names of people connected to a satanic-influenced mind-control experiment, supposedly run by the federal government. "This will give you some sense of how big the cover-up is," she declared. Among the names were Albert Einstein, Wernher von Braun, Lyndon Johnson, and Mao Zedong. I left the meeting with my head spinning, but I was determined to get to the bottom of this nonsense.

As I began my own investigation into the Kellers' nightmare journey through the criminal justice system, I discovered that it began in August 1991, when Suzanne Chaviers was driving her four-year-old daughter, Christy, to visit the child's therapist. An interior decorator who worked at home, Suzanne had allowed the child to stay home with her until recently, when she enrolled Christy in Fran's Day Care, one of the few programs that accepted kids with behavioral problems. Fran had worked with children with such problems all her adult life and immediately identified Christy as the liar and manipulator that she was. Christy habitually attacked other children and then accused them of attacking her. She hated not being allowed to stay home with her mother and quickly acted out her hatred by becoming unmanageable, biting, screaming, stabbing the dog with a barbecue fork, walking on all fours like a dog, cursing, licking herself, and urinating or defecating on the living room floor. One of the child's most bizarre games was "Here comes the ice-cream truck," in which Christy pretended to run a toy truck into her vagina. Sometimes she inserted marbles and crayons. Suzanne made almost no attempt to discipline the child, having been advised by her therapist against "setting limits."

Sexual molestation was very much on the mother's mind as she drove Christy to the therapist that morning. She was dealing with her own recovered memory of being sexually abused by a drunken father, and was also struggling with a second divorce in which she had accused her ex of physically and emotionally abusing Christy, charges the husband denied. There had been a lot of talk about "bad daddy" around their home—how he enjoyed pulling down the child's panties and beating her with his belt. On the advice of her therapist, Suzanne took the child to the pediatrician for a vaginal exam, one day before enrolling her at Fran's Day Care. The examination revealed no sign of sexual abuse, but Suzanne remained convinced that her daughter had been molested. That belief explained what happened next. When Christy continued to complain about returning to day care, Suzanne demanded to know why. "Because Danny hurt me," the girl said. How? "Like bad daddy," Christy explained, apparently sensing that this line would please her mother and maybe convince her to give up the idea of day care. Suzanne was shaking all over by the time they reached the therapist.

The therapist quickly reinforced the mother's darkest fears. In her notes she recorded that Christy told her that Dan Keller pulled down her panties, beat her and fondled her, then "pooped and peed on my head." Did someone wash her hair? "Fran did," the girl responded. Pressed for more details, Christy shook her head and said nothing happened. When the therapist produced an anatomically correct doll and asked Christy to demonstrate what Danny did, the child stuck a ballpoint pen into the doll's vagina. The therapist immediately telephoned Child Protective Services, which launched a witch hunt that lasted fifteen months.

The case against the Kellers was pretty much clinched that same night, however—because of a hysterical response by Suzanne and a flawed examination by an emergency room doctor. It started when Suzanne continued firing questions at the child. According to the mother, the girl suddenly blurted out: "Danny put his pee pee in me and got glue in me and it was warm and yucky and Fran washed it out." Nearly overcome with fear and anxiety, Suzanne rushed the girl to the emergency room at Brackenridge Hospital, where a young doctor named Michael Mouw did a vaginal exam and reported two small tears in the hymen. Mouw's testimony was extremely damning to the Kellers' case, particularly since the defense attorneys didn't seriously challenge it. When one of the defense attorneys asked Mouw if the tears could have been caused by the child inserting toys in her vagina, he replied: "Could have." That simple explanation should have done serious damage to the prosecution's case, but the Kellers' court-appointed lawyers didn't pursue it. In a sworn affidavit submitted with the new appeal in 2013, Mouw admitted that at the time of the exam, he had minimal training in pediatric sexual abuse. Years after the trial, while attending a medical seminar, Mouw saw a slide presentation on "normal" hymens that included a photo that was very similar to what he had observed in the girl. "I realized that I had mistakenly identified normal discontinuity as lacerations," he said in the affidavit. "I now realize my conclusion is not scientifically or medically valid, and that I made a mistake."

The case eventually took on a life of its own. A second mother, Carol Staelin, learned about the satanic cult when she happened to telephone Suzanne to invite her to a meeting of her twelve-step group. Carol, who had a degree in law but no longer practiced, was a recovering alcoholic. Like her friend Suzanne, she was dealing with memories of sexual abuse as a child. Following Suzanne's lead, Carol had chosen Fran's Day Care because her adopted son, four-year-old Veejay, had serious emotional problems. After learning about the satanic revelations, Carol began a relentless interrogation of her son. Veejay denied that anything had happened, but the more the boy denied, the more determined Carol became to get to the bottom of things. She ordered an SRA checklist compiled by Believe the Children and convinced Suzanne to order one. In time, every one of the twenty-eight "indicators" on the checklist matched an allegation against the Kellers. Carol contacted another mother who would also level charges, Sandra Nash. Sandra immediately rushed her son to a therapist, who noted that the boy showed "anger" at the "Danny Doll." The Nashes were urged to grill the boy until he told the "secrets" about the cult.

All the parents were middle-class, college-educated professionals who had entrusted their children to Fran's Day Care because it was rural, rustic, away from the bustle of the city. Fran was regarded as a stern but good-hearted woman, someone who knew how to set and enforce limits. Both Fran and Dan had grown children from previous marriages and had never been in trouble before. Dan was soft-spoken, easygoing, and childlike, good at repairing things and creating toys out of scrap material—bows and arrows and Indian drums, for example. In the days after the police closed the day care and filed charges, what had seemed so idyllic came across as evil and malevolent. Sandra remembered a day her son came home with wet hair. Fran explained that the boy got into hair gel, but Sandra came to believe that the sticky stuff was semen. The drums that Danny had fashioned weren't toys at all, but instruments "to call Satan at home." Carol swore that the Kellers put horse manure in her son's nebulizer, and that Fran tortured a bunny in front of the kids and told them it was the Easter Bunny. The tales got more and more absurd. The Kellers broke the wings of a flock of doves—*doves*! the symbol of Christianity!—and buried the wounded birds, together with the children, in a casket in a cemetery. Fran dug them up seconds before they ran out of air and explained that "Satan has spared you."

Most of what the children said—or, more accurately, what the parents reported the children said—was complete nonsense. Did the Kellers really cut off the head of a baby and force the children to drink the blood? How about the time they kidnapped a baby gorilla from the Zilker Park Zoo (there was never a zoo, much less a gorilla, at Zilker) and how about the tigers that licked the children, and the sharks in the kiddie pool that ate cut-up baby parts? The Kellers had apparently turned the day care into a working brothel, lining kids up like cuts of meat for customers who paid $2,000 a go. The kids were sometimes taken to military bases for purpose of prostitution, or loaded on jets and flown to Mexico, invariably to be returned in time for their parents to pick them up after work. All of these wild tales went unquestioned, not only during the investigation but at the trial itself.

By the time prosecutors got the kids on the witness stand, they had been interrogated at least a dozen times, first by the family therapists, then by therapists hired by Travis County, and constantly by their parents. The barrage of leading questions and suggested answers must have planted unspeakable memories that, in a more rational setting, would have been prosecuted as genuine child abuse. Though Christy appeared psychologically unable to answer questions, she was the state's star witness—this pristine little girl, pitted against the evil Kellers. In child abuse cases, the state allows an exception to hearsay, permitting the mother and therapist to testify in lurid detail.

Christy denied that she even knew anyone named Dan or Fran, or that she ever told anyone that someone touched her in a way she didn't like. At one point, the prosecution excused the girl from the stand, apparently for more coaching. But when they asked her later if she'd ever told her therapist that Danny did something to her, she waved her lollipop and chirped, "No way, José." (Which, by the way, was one of Suzanne's favorite expressions.) I kept waiting for one of the defense attorneys—or the judge—to call for a mistrial, but that didn't happen. Nor did anyone seriously question the credentials of Randy Noblitt, the state's so-called expert witness, who was paid a hefty sum to research SRA and testify. He was allowed to ramble on about recovered memories and "dissociative disorders" (multiple personalities) as though these bogus concepts were real science. For that matter, nobody even thought to question Noblitt's contention that there really was such a thing as satanic ritual abuse—or that it was part of a plot to capture the world for Satan.

The police assigned to investigate the Kellers used an assortment of dirty tricks to build their case, including coercing a friend of the Kellers to invent a story about an orgy he had attended with them. The friend, Douglas Wayne Perry, provided a vivid description of the orgy, which he claimed was attended by the Kellers, two Travis County constables, and the children from the day care. Though Perry promptly retracted the confession, he was forced by prosecutors to read it from the stand. Perry later pleaded guilty to indecency with a child and received ten years' probation. Shortly before his term was to end in 2003, he was convicted of failing to register as a sex offender and given a new ten-year prison sentence. Charges against the constables were dropped for lack of evidence.

The jury found the Kellers guilty and sentenced them to forty years each. They did twelve years straight time before being considered for parole, which was then denied. I corresponded with them over the years and wrote letters in support of parole. A few years ago I received permission to visit them. It was a heartbreaking sight. Fran was nearly sixty, but still feisty, defiant, and hopeful—still a sucker for bad advice. In 1993, a jailhouse lawyer convinced her that if she divorced Dan and married him, he'd help get her out of jail. She agreed to the divorce but help never arrived, nor did the proposed marriage. She changed her religion from Baptist to Native American, which allowed her to move to a less brutal prison but didn't help with parole. A couple of years after that, she married a Colorado man she met on the Internet. He helped hire a Houston lawyer who somehow persuaded Fran to write a letter to the parole board, confessing the guilt that she had always denied.

"I cried myself to sleep that night," she told me, tears in her eyes. I told her this was the worst legal advice I'd ever heard. While it was true that parole boards are interested only in expressions of remorse and have zero tolerance for protestations of innocence, the letter was now part of her permanent record and, inadvertently, part of Dan's record, too.

Dan was sixty-five, his hair turned silver, his blue eyes placid as always. He still wore his wedding band and vowed his love for Fran. "Tell her I have no hard feelings," he instructed me. I asked Dan how he was able to maintain hope, knowing his life and Fran's had been wasted by lies? "I try to help others," he replied. "And walk with the Lord."

"There is one more tragedy that has gone unspoken all these years," I told him. "Those children. They still haunt me. They would be about twenty by now. What has happened to them? I've never been able to find out."

Dan nodded that he understood, that he thought about them too. "What's going through their brains?" he said. "Believing all those horrible things really happened."

That's the crime our criminal justice system has never addressed.

In late November 2013, after serving nearly twenty-one years for a crime that never happened, Fran and Dan Keller were transferred back to Travis County—where the whole mess started—and finally released on personal bonds. The state didn't actually admit that it made a mistake—it never does—but it agreed with recently uncovered evidence cited in attorney Keith Hampton's appeal that medical testimony presented at the Kellers' trial was false and probably affected the jury's verdict.

The break in the mostly forgotten case came in an article by *Austin Chronicle* reporter Jordan Smith, who revealed that the emergency room doctor, Mouw, who examined the girl realized years later that what he thought were injuries were in fact "normal variants" of female genitalia. There were many other problems with the Kellers' convictions—the Austin police, for example, failed to turn over exculpatory information from their investigation of the alleged abuse—but Travis County District Attorney

Rosemary Lehmberg, who faced her own problems after an arrest for DWI, ignored them. The flawed ER report itself was more than enough to free the Kellers.

As Fran was being released, Jordan Smith asked what she planned to do now. "Buy a toothbrush," Fran replied. For more than two decades she had been restricted to a prison-issued toothbrush that required that she stick her whole hand into her mouth in order to clean her teeth. Real toothbrushes are considered "weapons" in the Texas prison system.

What happened to the Kellers and many other victims of the satanic ritual abuse craziness is the price we pay for our lock-'em-up-and-throw-away-the-key mentality. I've seen it all my professional life, not only in high-profile cases like those of Greg Ott and Randall Dale Adams, but in dozens of daily police reports I scanned as a young reporter in Fort Worth. I've known and admired law enforcement types most of my life, and I have made a lot of friends in the community, but I learned years ago that my role was as a watchdog. Keep the good guys honest and make the bad guys pay.

People who have never been locked up have no concept what it means to be falsely accused and imprisoned, what it does to individuals and families and society as a whole. If Keith Hampton keeps after them, the state will eventually make some kind of monetary settlement with the Kellers—pennies on the dollar for two lives wasted—but cops and prosecutors can't be trusted to recognize innocence or treat evidence fairly, regardless of their dark hunches. That's why we have the Fourth Estate. Editors at *Texas Monthly*, in particular Mike Hall and Pam Colloff, have a proud legacy of exposing wrongful convictions and freeing innocent people. It's an honor and a privilege to be in their company. And it is comforting to know that while the battle will always be heavily tilted toward the state, the free press is a staunch and reliable ally.

ONE OF MY PROUDEST TRIUMPHS, A STORY THAT I called "The Case of the Smoking Panties," started when several Texas cities were infested with Filipino holy men who claimed that they could cure any ailment with bloodless or "psychic" surgery. Some of my best friends—including Bud Shrake and Susan Walker, Jerry Jeff's wife—had ponied up money in the belief that this psychic surgeon could somehow reach into their liver or heart and remove diseased tissue, without leaving a trace of an entry wound. Since faith healing was fundamentally a religious concept, and since few of my friends were interested in religion, I started asking questions.

Bud and Susan had visited a Filipino faith healer named Angel Domingo, who had been working around Austin, Houston, San Antonio, and Lake Whitney, and was at that moment doing a stint at Willie World, as we called Willie Nelson's Pedernales Country Club retreat west of Austin. I decided to join the crowd for a close-up inspection. Shrake had asked Angel to treat a blocked colon, and he told me that he saw a pool of coffee-colored liquid well up between the healer's fingers as Angel removed what appeared to be pieces of hog tripe from Bud's abdomen. At a second session, Angel extracted what looked like a chicken bone from Shrake's left foot, which had been aching for months. Though neither Bud nor Susan experienced much relief following their psychic surgery, both professed to believe in the concept. "I watched him work on a friend with a liver problem," Susan told me, "and saw his hand go into her liver and watched this pulsating organ going around his finger. Then I saw him take that bone out of Shrake's foot. I frigging *saw* it!" Another friend—a renowned skeptic who believed that the Apollo moon landing was a fraud filmed in a clandestine television studio—had no difficulty whatsoever believing that a surgeon could run his hand through person's body and remove damaged tissue. "That seems perfectly logical," he told me.

Thousands of Texans, I soon discovered, had paid for a variety of psychic services. Indeed, Austin was a hotbed of psychic activity, an "energy vortex" where healers, psychics, and other denizens of the Twilight Zone came to recharge their metaphysical batteries.

The operating room was usually in some off-the-beaten-path motel or private residence. The time and place were not advertised—advertising would be an open invitation to legal action—but were passed along by an informal network of believers.

One Saturday morning I joined a horde of true believers at Willie World's Condo No. 10, bringing with me nothing except a bathrobe, a small reporter's notebook, and of course a completely open mind. As I entered a darkened room, I could hear a voice behind a curtain, singing "How Great Thou Art!" It was the voice of Angel Domingo.

I was greeted by a pudgy woman named Jann, founder and spiritual commander of a group called the Planetary Light Association, which acted as a booking agent for the healer. She informed me that I would need at least two sessions and that a recovery time of at least two hours between treatments was essential. "You'll receive so much energy your body can't take it all at once," Jann explained with a straight face, her tone deadly serious. She directed me to the laundry room and told me to undress and put on a robe. Then she had me sign a disclaimer, stating that I understood that the treatment I was about to receive was religious rather than medical, and that the healer—the "minister"—made no promises. There was no fee, but a "love offering" of thirty dollars was requested for each session.

There were about twenty people waiting when I arrived, and more filtered in and out all morning. More than half were older women who looked as though they had read a lot of books about Edgar Cayce, but some were young holistic New Agers with wholesome faces and startled eyes. A tall Hispanic gentleman wearing a VA hospital robe sat rigidly in a folding chair, his vacant eyes fixed on a fireplace as his wife and daughter comforted him. He was dying of cancer and had been to see Angel more than a dozen times. A bearded, bald-headed man in a Japanese robe was so weak that two women had to assist him to the sofa. He had red blotches on his thighs, from chemotherapy, I speculated. Patients awaiting treatment either avoided eye contact or gave each other knowing smiles, as though they shared the true meaning of some exotic secret. Words like "chakra" and "karma" fell smoothly from their lips.

Angel turned out to be a stocky little man with greasy black hair and a baggy, weathered face. He wore a flowery short-sleeved shirt with the tail out, like a Tijuana cabdriver. While he worked he sang, sometimes religious songs but more often tunes like "Spanish Eyes" or "Beer Barrel Polka." I couldn't tell if the songs were for our benefit or for his. A woman assistant read the card that I had filled out earlier and told Angel: "This brother has some kidney damage as a result of high blood pressure. Do you want me to do a scan?" Angel said that he did, and she passed a small towel over my body. Angel held the towel to the light as though reading an X-ray. "Blockage," he declared. Though I was struck silly by the simple-mindedness of this fraud, I tried not to laugh in his face.

As his assistant rubbed my chest and stomach with aromatic balm, Angel directed me to face the window—"the light"—while he prayed for my recovery. I pretended to turn my head, but continued to watch as he flopped a moist piece of cotton onto my belly and began applying pressure with his fingers. The fingers fidgeted and probed until one of them seemed to disappear into my flesh for a few seconds. Angel had blocked my view so that I couldn't see any blood, even if there had been blood to see, and the next thing I saw was a small, stringy piece of gristle, which he exhibited for my brief inspection and then tossed into a trash can beside the table.

"See?" he said. "Blockage! No more bad blood."

I went back several hours later for the prescribed second treatment, paying another thirty dollars. It was no different from the first. I had seen better sleight-of-hand demonstrations from grocery sackers. I didn't feel energized, I felt used. I knew the operation was a fraud, but the proof was in the trash can next to the healer's table. Somehow, I had to get my hands on a piece of that gristle—"congealed energy," the Twilight Zoners called it—and have it analyzed.

Just to be certain that Angel wasn't an aberration among psychic healers, I decided to fly to Mazatlán, Mexico, the following week to visit another healer who had worked Texas and was a friend of Angel's. As I expected, a number of the Zonies I had met in Austin also made the pilgrimage to Mazatlán, including Jann and some of her associates from the Planetary Light Association.

While waiting to see the healer, who I will call R, I talked to a number of the Zonies, trying to determine if they really believed this mumbo jumbo or if they were part of the scam. Jann's husband, Art, an Austin chiropractor, explained that a healer's ability to penetrate a patient's skin without leaving a mark depended on "the speed of the vibration of the electrons." Oh, I see. Tell me more. "If you speed up the vibrations of the electrons on this tabletop," Art continued, rapping his knuckles on the surface of the table at poolside, "you could stick your hand through it." Zonies, I learned in my three days in Mazatlán, have a theory to explain every doubt, no matter how crazy it sounds. Somehow they are able to convince themselves that metaphysics is superior to literal-minded science, which they believe is a conspiracy fomented by the American Medical Association. The White Crow Theory, for example, was a handy way for Zonies to shift the burden of proof to the nonbelievers. "If you've never seen a white crow," Art challenged, "how do you know that one does not exist?"

As I suspected, Art and Jann had a proprietary interest in a field closely aligned with psychic surgery. She was a professional medium or channel, in constant contact with a spirit named Anoah, who borrowed her voice to advise the sick and weary. Anoah, an old man with white hair and a white robe who floated through time carrying a book titled *Wisdom*, was just one of the spirits who used Jann's voice and body. Jann carried in her briefcase tapes of Anoah, which could be purchased for $4. Or you could hear them live, so to speak, during half-hour personal counseling sessions with Jann, at $40 a pop.

Jann was one of three psychics on R's staff in Mazatlán. All of them—in fact, every Zonie I met—had had experiences with reincarnation or past-life regressions. Jann claimed that in one of her past lives, she was a Mayan priest in the Mexican seaside ruin of Tulum. Another had been an Indian chief and had witnessed his own funeral near Fredericksburg, Texas. Still another had been a young German soldier killed in the early days of World War II.

My mission required arranging a one-on-one with R, but for two days he managed to avoid me. Finally, on the morning I was scheduled to fly home, he agreed to a meeting. He was younger and smaller than his friend Angel. His assistant, Dodo, looked like the bandy-legged, puffy-eyed Filipino bantamweight I saw fight once in San Diego. Dodo offered me a Filipino cigarette, brand-named Hope.

Except for me and a young couple from Houston, all of the patients in the motel room in Mazatlán were New Yorkers. Nick, a pious young man who walked with his hands clasped and talked almost exclusively of faith, was there to comfort his mother, Grace, who was dying of cancer. During orientation, Nick mentioned that "walking on fire" was a popular therapy for Zonies on the East Coast and asked Dodo if he thought the practice increased faith. Dodo looked as though someone had dropped a cobra in his lap. "Walk on *fire*?" he said incredulously. "Me?" Nick explained that he was speaking of his own faith, that he happened to believe that faith had no limit. Waving his hands furiously, Dodo shouted, "No, no! No walk on fire! Burn feet!"

R was quicker and, apparently, smarter than Angel had been. No love offerings here. This was a straight cash deal, $80 U.S. for two sessions, no pesos, please. I asked R to remove a small knot just above my wrist—my doctor in Austin had called it a ganglion. Compared to curing cancer, removing a ganglion seemed fairly simple, though I doubted that R could deal with it. The little healer rubbed oil on the knot, then shook his head. He didn't want any part of an affliction that would still be visible when he was finished with his healing. Instead, he fluttered his hands in the area above my kidneys and produced a piece of gray meat. For the second time in less than a month, my high blood pressure had been cured—by producing some gristle that belonged on the butcher's floor.

Flying home that night, I kept thinking that if R had tried to pass off this silly act on a carnival midway in, say, Wichita Falls, he'd be leaving town on a rail, wearing tar and feathers. How could his clientele be so easily fooled? I was more determined than ever to expose this fraud, to get my hands on some of the gristle and have it analyzed.

Fortunately, Angel was still doing his number in Austin when I returned. I made an appointment to see him, but first I visited a doctor friend who owned Austin Pathology Associates, a laboratory that tested tissue samples for hospitals and law enforcement agencies. I told him my plan, and he gave me a bottle of formaldehyde in which to preserve my evidence.

I wasn't sure how the Zonies would react when I made my play, so when I went to visit Angel the next morning I took along two large friends, Bud Shrake and Fletcher Boone, as backups. I took my place on the operating table and watched as Angel began to work on my naked belly. Humming some mindless tune, he produced small pieces of gunk from the area of my kidneys and began to deposit them on my stomach, not suspecting that he was falling into my trap. I waited until he had turned away for a moment, then I grabbed the tissue and leaped from the table, protecting my privacy with a small hand towel.

Suddenly, all hell broke loose. His assistant tried to wrestle the tissue from my fist. I shoved her away. Angel was dancing about and screaming, "You'll destroy my power!" Racing through the reception area, I stopped just long enough to secure the tissue in the bottle of formaldehyde. Other patients in the waiting area had dropped into fetal positions, or were trying to hide under pieces of furniture. "Cover yourself with the white light," someone cried out. "Surround yourself with white light before it is too late!"

Fletcher was waiting by the back door, keeping it open for my escape. Bud had stepped forward to discourage anyone who wanted to give chase, but nobody did. I could hear Angel shouting, "Bullshit! Bullshit!" (I found out later that as soon as we had gone, he complained of a sudden headache, grabbed the cash box, and caught the next bus out of town.)

I went to the lab the following day, carrying with me a piece of tissue about the size of a pencil eraser. I waited for the results.

Several hours later, I learned that the tests were inconclusive. The meat was connective tissue, but no one could say for sure if it was of human origin. This was not good news. I was sure that psychic surgery was a hoax, but I still couldn't prove it.

I had almost given up hope when I received a call from Lana Nelson, Willie's daughter. When Angel had worked on her, he removed a two-inch piece of gristle; she didn't have the actual tissue, but some of the blood had stained her panties and she was offering them as evidence. The famous "smoking panties" could maybe prove my case. That afternoon Lana's panties were on their way to the Bexar County Regional Crime Lab in San Antonio. The stain turned out to be bovine blood, diluted with water. What a surprise! Bovine blood had been my fourth guess, behind chicken, goat, and cat. Nevertheless, the sample had proved my point: that Angel was running a con.

My story appeared in the December 1986 issue of *Texas Monthly*—titled "Touch Me, Feel Me, Heal Me!"—and won an award from the Texas Medical Association. It is one of my all-time favorites.

4

I CELEBRATED MY FIFTIETH BIRTHDAY IN A complimentary suite at the Fairmont Hotel in San Francisco, which was my favorite American city before it got eaten by a giant computer. The gift was arranged by a friend who worked for the Fairmont in Dallas, Debbie Cartwright (no relation). To make the trip even more complete, our drinking buddy Teeta Walker gave us two first-class tickets on Delta Airlines and traveled with us. My son Mark showed up in his own magic style, arriving in a limousine that he had found idling at the airport. He bribed the chauffeur to drive us around town while the Houston oilman who was paying for it was occupied with a high-priced hooker. We toured the bars and Italian cafés of North Beach, had drinks with some of the female impersonators at Finocchio's, and still returned the limo before the oilman got wise.

The following morning, as we admired the bay from our suite, we noticed a fleet of U.S. naval vessels maneuvering in parade formation. Two of them flanked the formation just below the Golden Gate Bridge, spraying giant water cannons in a spectacular arch, as though awaiting the arrival of a bride. Momentarily, we realized they were celebrating the arrival of one of our great battleships, the USS *New Jersey*. Mark and I waited until the battleship had docked, then caught a cab and went to visit it.

After looking over the ship bow to stern, we stopped at the gift shop and bought ball caps with USS NEW JERSEY BB-62 in gold letters above the bill. (I lost mine eventually, but still wear the one Mark bought; it hangs in a place of honor in my bedroom.) That night we celebrated with dinner at Ernie's, one of the great restaurants, then went to the Top of the Mark for more cocktails. Sitting at the bar, drinking in the view, I found myself staring across the bay at Alcatraz, the fabled "Rock," featured in so many crime films from my youth. Teeta placed a Virginia Slim in her pearl cigarette holder, kissed me on the cheek, and remarked as only she could, with her oh-so-casual bite: "I wonder if the boys at Alcatraz are enjoying the view."

My fifty-fourth birthday, however, was a different story. I celebrated that occasion by pigging out at Jeffrey's, on a heroic meal that included pâté, snails, oysters, chicken livers, steak, many bottles of wine, and finally espresso and Chocolate Intemperance. I left Jeffrey's content but somehow uneasy. A few days later, as I was whistling a happy tune on the hike-and-bike trail with my Airedales, Abby and Bucky, I felt a sharp pain in my chest. I figured it was heartburn, a regular visitor at the time.

When I went to bed that night, the heartburn was still there. I took a couple of Rolaids and tried to sleep, but sleep wouldn't come. Usually it went away after a few hours, but this particular night it lingered: it felt like a bear was squatting on my chest. I tried propping several pillows under my head to make breathing easier, but the pain only intensified. By 4 a.m., I'd finished a whole bottle of Rolaids and was getting worried. Without waking Phyllis, I went quietly to the kitchen and telephoned the doctor who had been treating me for high blood pressure. When I described the chest pains, he told me to get to the emergency room, fast.

Phyllis drove, glancing at me from time to time, worried not only about what might be happening but about how I would deal with it. I don't do well with pain. I sat in the passenger seat, sulking, angry to be inconvenienced, smoking what would turn out to be my last cigarette. The words "heart attack" may have crossed my mind—I don't remember—but if they did, their true meaning failed to register. Minutes later I was flat on my back in the ER, wires and tubes running from my arms and chest, doctors, nurses, and technicians moving about in an impressive rush. I vaguely remember someone telling Phyllis, "He's had a heart attack," but I can't remember feeling afraid or even particularly concerned. It was all so unreal.

Eventually, they wheeled me to the lab and did an angiogram. It showed that one section of relatively small arteries on the right side of my heart was completely blocked. A doctor explained my options and they weren't pretty. Either agree to heart bypass surgery, or a risk a second heart attack, which would probably kill me. I did some serious soul-searching. I seldom read the Bible, but I remembered a passage from the Book of Deuteronomy. "Be strong and of a good courage, fear not, nor be afraid of them, for the Lord thy God, he it is that doth go with thee; he will not fail thee nor forsake thee." I kept saying those words, over and over, trying to believe them. Then I began to understand what God was trying to tell me: trust the doctors. By now it was late Friday night; I signed papers, agreeing to surgery. It was scheduled early Monday.

Several of my newspaper friends wrote about my ordeal. In his column for the *Dallas Times Herald*, Dick Hitt wrote: "Ever since his antic and eloquent days as a *Times Herald* sports columnist, there's been a law on the cosmic books granting immunity and perpetual function to taxes, Volvos and Gary Cartwright. The idea of his being under arrest is not an unprecedented concept among Cartwright buffs, but *cardiac* arrest? How could anything so dreary, calamitous and pompous-sounding as myocardial infarction happen to this droll daredevil, our literary loose cannon who viewed the world from strange and wondrous angles . . . ?"

My room was crowded with friends and family the night before surgery, but by 10 p.m. Phyllis had herded them out and shut the door. It was the first time all weekend we had been alone. This could be our last night together, though I didn't let myself think about that possibility. Tomorrow, who knows, a great love affair might be history, and me with it. I prayed some more. I asked God to spare me, to spare Phyllis, to spare our family—if He was so inclined. Either way, I asked, let me face this with a show of courage. I was trying to act unafraid, but not sure I was getting away with it.

"Try to not think about it," Phyllis said, sitting on the side of my bed, holding my hand. I pulled her close and we kissed. I could feel her breasts brushing my arm.

"I am trying," I said. "There's just one thing."

"Let me guess." She smiled. "You're horny."

"How well you know me."

"Okay, sport," she said sweetly. "We certainly can't have you going to the operating room feeling horny."

"I was hoping you would see it that way."

She excused herself and disappeared into the bathroom. I shut my eyes and tried to picture how this would work. One of my arms was wrapped in a blood pressure cuff and the other was hooked to an intravenous tube connected to a support system above the bed. Another wire ran from my chest to the EKG. Not especially conducive to a romantic interlude. But then I thought, I've probably done it under worse conditions. I felt myself drifting, being carried who knows where by the tide of life. I felt that I was going to be okay.

Then I looked up and saw her. She was standing at the foot of the bed, wearing a lacy black slip, one shoulder strap hanging loose. She struck one of her famous Gina Lollobrigida poses, cocking her hip, thrusting her breasts forward in that saucy Lollobrigida way. "I've always been strong in zee legs," she said, mimicking one of Lollobrigida's lines from the movie *Trapeze*.

In the deep throes of foreplay, we did not hear the beeper when it went off. But an orderly down the hall did. The orderly and one of the floor nurses burst through the door like federal agents raiding a nest of terrorists. A few steps behind was the head nurse on my floor, a tall, pleasant woman with a faintly Swedish accent. Only then did I hear the incessant beep-beep-beeping of the life support system, signaling that my IV solution had run dry and needed replacing.

While the orderly and the other nurse did their job, the head nurse gave me a conspiratorial wink. She placed a finger discreetly to her lips, a signal to wait until the others had gone. Then she stood with her back to the door, barring anyone else from entering. "There is no way to lock it," she told us, "but when I leave, put a chair in front of the door. I'll watch from the nursing station and keep them away." That was a memorable night for love, complete and true and characteristically robust. I had already drifted off to sleep when Phyllis left. In my dreams, I saw the saintly face of the Angel of the Cardiac Ward at Brackenridge Hospital, with a faintly Swedish accent.

The following morning, Phyllis walked beside the gurney on our way to the operating room. At the door, she kissed me and told me not to worry. "I'll probably be hungry when I wake up," I told her, still wallowing in postcoital bliss. "Have some barbecue ribs waiting." Inside, the room was cold as a meat locker: they keep it that way so the surgical team won't sweat on your exposed heart. A technician asked what music I preferred. "Mozart," I told him. He looked through a stack of CDs and informed me there was no Mozart. How about Bach? Bach would work. A nurse smiled as she fitted the anesthesia mask over my nose and told me to take a good whiff. The last thing I remember before awaking in recovery twelve hours later is the life-sustaining drive of Bach's Suite in G minor.

THEY WARNED PHYLLIS THAT MY RECOVERY FROM bypass surgery would be punctuated by wild mood swings, to which she responded: "What else is new?" Women who marry writers, or least those who stay married to them, develop a kind of defensive detachment: they learn to chill out from the center, until they achieve a state of grace where time and events free-float at the margins of perception. They view every crisis with the assurance that nothing is ever as bad (or as good) as it appears, that tantrums, sulks, and snits will hit like summer thunderstorms and pass just as quickly.

Having my chest ripped open encouraged in me two virtues that had never troubled me before—patience and humility. I began learning them the moment I woke in intensive care. Pop! I was back among the living, and the pain was something to behold. My entire upper body felt as if I had been blindsided by Dick Butkus. I felt like a newborn baby, helpless and beyond vanity or pride. I couldn't swallow or even clear my throat without a new slash of pain throttling my senses. I got patience and humility the way some get religion, on the road to Damascus, as it were.

After the first shock, I learned quickly to move very slowly, if at all. A quiet inner voice spoke softly, so only I could hear. It said: Deliberate every act carefully. Weigh it against alternatives. Say, for example, that you need to pee in your bedside pitcher. Rehearse exactly how you will manage it, well in advance of the pissing itself. Remember, there is no shame in peeing in a pitcher, only gratitude that you are actually able to perform such a task. Even after they take you from intensive care to the more comfortable ambience of a private room, think before you act. Make every movement a priority of the will and a marshaling of the sum of your knowledge and experience. You'll get the hang of it after a while.

One of the things they encourage a bypass patient in post-op to do is cough. Coughing clears the lungs and reduces the chance of pneumonia and fever. The problem with this advice, of course, is that every cough feels like you've been hit in the sternum by a .45 slug. There is the additional raw pain where they extracted a vein from your leg to use as a bypass, and the stab of countless needles and the irritation of countless catheters leading off to God knows where, but these are nothing . . . nothing . . . compared to the unspeakable pain in your chest.

By the second day I was able to sit up in bed. The breathing tube that had run to my windpipe was removed, permitting me to at last yell at the nurses, though yelling was no longer an act of any interest. Loud speech no longer suited my personality. Did they mistakenly remove my personality while I was out? I didn't recognize the person occupying my body.

Anyone who has gone through a bypass is bound to have mixed and confused feelings. You feel a separation in time, an aging that can't be explained by the calendar. Something is gone from your life, something that cannot be retrieved. Larry McMurtry, who had also had a heart bypass, exchanged letters with me for a couple of weeks. He felt doomed to live in fragments, he wrote to me. In the weeks after surgery, McMurtry felt himself being sucked by what shrinks call an "anniversary reaction"—a psychic devastation that left him feeling as though he no longer existed. "I think the few hours that you are dead [i.e., on the heart-lung machine] opens a gap that's nearly impossible to close," he explained. He wrote an essay describing the emotional deficit that the operation left, but didn't publish it because his cardiologist warned him it would scare too many people.

McMurtry confided that for a time he stopped reading, writing, operating his bookshops, lecturing, or even traveling. He had ceased to be the person he remembered. "I acted or impersonated him as best I could, for the benefit of loved ones," he wrote. "I managed to retain certain of his abilities, but not all. When I began to write again . . . the book I wrote arrived as if by fax from my former self, ten pages a day, typed about as fast as a fax machine can deliver." He slept only about three hours a night, waking each morning at exactly 3:15, feeling "as if I were holding up the ceiling, or holding at bay a beast, by an act of unrelenting will. I felt that to sleep in darkness would be to die . . ."

During my recovery, I wondered if I'd ever write again. Somehow I associated the act of writing with a person no longer with us, a person who chain-smoked as he typed and pushed hard against the inertia of blank pages. A week or so after surgery, I sat at my word processor and wrote a letter thanking all the friends who had stood by me, and, to my relief, the process of writing seemed familiar and reassuring.

Having heart bypass surgery is, in one sense, a fairly easy way to stop smoking. During my first few weeks out of the hospital, my mind challenged my body on the subject of smoking, conjuring up memories of the pleasures while automatically rejecting the process. I didn't particularly *want* a cigarette, but my mind couldn't avoid the memory, that stimulating rush of nicotine, its calming and reassuring effect. Every time the telephone rang, my hand involuntarily reached for a cigarette pack that wasn't there. Smoking had become second nature. Fortunately, my body won these challenges. Much later, after both the pain and the need for nicotine had gone, my mind came to grips with the stupidity and foulness of the habit. Still, the memory of smoking remained for months. When I saw someone smoking on the movie screen, or sat across the table from my friend Dorothy Browne and watched her inhale with an ecstasy that bordered on the orgasmic, an uneasy tingling went up my backbone.

Then, the incomparably exotic Teeta Walker and another of my oldest running mates, the elegant boulevardier Jim "Lopez" Smithum, died in 1996 of chronic lung diseases. Both of them were roughly my age and had smoked heavily most of their adult lives.

Teeta was a Southern belle from East Texas, a timber heiress, a collector of wonderful antiques and items of clothing that seemed to have escaped from a Busby Berkley production, A chain-smoker who loved knocking back straight shots of vodka over ice, Teeta called everyone "my dear" or "darling," and made it sound light and fresh. On special occasions, she gave magnificent gifts, including a set of hand-carved, ivory chopsticks that I have cherished for years. She dubbed me "Emperor of the Entrails" in tribute to my skill at cooking our favorite dish, liver with onions and bacon. Teeta ordered me a special apron, with my photograph printed on the bib over the words "Hip Young Sage." The photograph and the words came from a feature written about me, published in the *Rag*, an Austin underground newspaper.

Teeta's final few months were spent in a long-term-care hospital in Houston, hooked to a respirator. No Russian vodka on the rocks, no cigarettes in an ivory holder, no entrails with wine sauce, no silly games, just a drab room that she knew she wouldn't leave alive. Phyllis and I stayed with her much of those last few days. Teeta became terrified of having the door to her room closed—even the door to the bathroom. Her fear and anxiety of being shut up, even for a moment, caused her to hyperventilate and suffer two heart attacks. The second one killed her.

Lopez also had the choice of continuing to breathe with the

assistance of a respirator, for how long no one could say. He was clearly dying, but he could have chosen to prolong the end. We sat for several weeks in his hospital room—Bud, Doatsy, Phyllis, Dorothy, Jan Reid, Jody Gent, and a few others—waiting for him to die or, in the alternative, decide to live the remainder of his days with a tube down his throat and a tank of oxygen at his side. His spirits were surprisingly high, probably because there was plenty of morphine to brighten his mood. We tried to amuse him with our gallows humor, grim reaper jokes, that kind of crap. We'd been practicing them for years, under less dire circumstances. After a while, it got to be too much for all of us. So we sat quietly, watching his labored breathing and listening to his favorite CD, an album of Chet Baker singing love songs, recorded in the 1950s when we were still in college. After four days, in a gesture that was typical of the man, Lopez pulled himself up for one final *bon mot*. "Somebody call a cab!" he gasped, then he closed his eyes and died.

Bud and I sat outside his room for a time, talking about something both of us had discovered only recently—the indescribably foul smell of cigarette smoke. Smokers don't notice it. But people who have quit detect it everywhere: on the breath and clothes of friends who still smoke; in the lobbies of public buildings; at airports; even on the sidewalks outside theaters. The putrid odor of tobacco smoke can linger for days.

"Imagine all those mornings at the *Times Herald*," Bud said. "God, we must have smelled like grease traps."

"Worse than that," I said. "Remember how we used to make fun of people who didn't smoke?"

"We'd blow smoke in their direction," Bud recalled.

"We thought we were so damn cool," I said. "Nothing makes you feel as cool as knowing how uncool you used to be."

DESPITE MY HEALTH ISSUES, THE YEARS BETWEEN the late 1980s and 2000 were very good to Phyllis and me. We traveled to Europe three times, made three movie deals, bought a vacant lot, and built a home in Austin. Phyllis got a job selling real estate and discovered she was a natural for the profession. People trusted her and she never once betrayed that trust.

Meanwhile, Willie Nelson helped Bud and me sell an old screenplay to CBS, and Phyllis and I used our share of the money to buy a lot she had been looking at for some time. It was in a neighborhood I'd never actually visited, though it was so close I could have hit it with a rock. It was called Judges Hill, because, we were told, three judges who sat on the state's Supreme Court once resided here. We knew the basic layout of the house we wanted and hired an architect to draw up the plans. Our lot was close to the State Capitol and the University of Texas campus, a five-minute drive from downtown Austin, and close to almost any place we wanted to go. The house itself was constructed in 1991, a wonderfully comfortable three-bedroom (one of which became my office) where I continue to live as I write these words.

As more money became available we added a covered patio and a walled-in courtyard that included a garage and storeroom. We called this area our "compound" and it was where we spent most of our evenings, regardless of the weather. The kitchen and also the master bedroom opened onto the patio. Our bedroom had a high ceiling and plenty of tall windows—and a room-size closet for Phyllis. It also had a dressing room and walk-in shower that we both used, though Phyllis preferred the smaller bath in the hallway and made it hers. What would have been the front bedroom became my office, a large space with lots of bookshelves and natural light, tall windows with a view of the front porch, the front yard and a stretch of 18th Street. Over the top of my word processor I can see the fireplace. Over its mantel hangs a stunning black-and-white photograph of a street scene in Estonia, taken about 1909. We purchased it on our trip to Moscow. The house was the best thing we ever did.

Phyllis had become one of Austin's best realtors by this time and was regularly making six figures a year. I've never seen any salesperson so comfortable with clients. She didn't really have *clients*, she just made new friends. Everyone she worked with loved her, loved being in her company. Such grace, such style, such presence. She knew the names of all their children and grandchildren, their birthdays, their sweater sizes. What she loved more than anything was buying gifts for other people's children. "Shopping is my life," she often joked, though of course it was not really a joke, just a passion. For thirty years she bought all my clothes or went shopping with me, to make sure I didn't follow my instincts and dress like the clown I sometimes imitated. She was really smart about colors, introducing me to colors whose names I'd never heard before. Taupe was one: I'd never heard of it until Phyllis decided it was the color of paint that should be used on our house, interior and exterior. She was right, of course. It was a color—I would have called it "gray," but what do I know?—that complemented everything around it. Her own wardrobe was eclectic, expensive, and in harmony with the cadence and architecture of her life.

Phyllis and I knew from the moment we started our lives together that we would live it to the max. Our view was, anything worth doing is worth overdoing. If we had extra money we dismissed the practical option of a savings account and spent it on something fun, like travel.

Almost every year, usually in the autumn when we celebrated our anniversary and her birthday, we took fantastic trips: to New York to hear our favorite opera, *La Bohème*; to Boston and Martha's Vineyard; to San Francisco to celebrate my fiftieth birthday; to Chicago for a rendezvous with Phyllis's old friend Sherry "Bad Bunny" Broder; to Mexico and Canada, and especially to Europe. Taped inside the door of Phyllis's small home office was a list of our ten European ventures, dating back to our tour of Germany, Paris, and London in October 1987. Paris was always our favorite. In the mid-nineties we rented an apartment in the Marais section, near the ornate Gothic-style Hôtel de Ville (City Hall), in the quarter where the nobles lived in the sixteenth and seventeenth centuries. The apartment was on the third floor, at the top of a narrow, very steep stairway that I somehow managed to climb while carrying two large suitcases and a case of wine. In the two weeks that we lived there, we got to know most of the shopkeepers in that part of town. We walked for hours in all directions and stopped for drinks and dinners at cafés and brasseries we'd read about all our lives — Aux Deux Magots, Café de Flore, Brasserie Lipp. With each trip we fell more passionately in love and grew more attuned to and appreciative of the rare gift that God had given us.

Phyllis was a great traveling companion and whenever I got a really interesting magazine assignment, I convinced the editors to pay her expenses to travel with me. Naturally, she became a character in all these stories, usually funny, always insightful.

In 2001, an editor at *National Geographic Traveler* called and asked if I would be interested in exploring and writing about the Malt Whisky Trail of the Scottish Highlands. I said it sounded okay, but I needed to check with my wife. "Guess what," I told her. "They want us to go to Scotland and drink whisky!" She replied that it would take her at least fifteen minutes to pack.

We flew to Edinburgh, rented a car, and drove deep into the mystery and myth of one of the most isolated parts of the country, passing close to legendary headwaters of the River Spey, near the secluded spot where in 1746 Cluny, chief of the Macpherson clan, hid Bonnie Prince Charlie after the prince's cataclysmic defeat at Culloden — the battle that forever changed Scottish history. Fog poured down from granite mountain ranges. The land was mostly rolling hills, naked except for isolated patches of pines and spreads of wild gorse and heather in its brownish-purple autumn dress. At the juncture of a centuries-old trade route where Highland freebooters once took their herds of shaggy-haired cattle and casks of illicit whisky to lowland markets, we spotted the twin cooper chimneys of Dalwhinnie, the highest distillery in Scotland. This is what I was looking for — a place to show off my newly acquired knowledge of what the Scots call *usage beatha* — water of life.

In the tasting room, a middle-aged woman wearing the green and black tartan of the Wallace clan poured us wee drams of their very best, a fifteen-year-old single malt. Most of the single malts are sold to conglomerates, which use them in less expensive blends, but I'd come to sample the real thing — a good single malt, for which I was quickly developing a taste.

"Aye!" I exclaimed after taking a sip. "It's the fragrance of heather blossoms that I detect."

"It tastes like dirt," Phyllis decided.

"What you're tasting, lassie, is the grassy sweetness of pure water from the snowmelt, the faint burst of peat, and something I can't immediately identify, a sort of earthy wildness whose origins are lost in time."

Rolling her eyes, she shoved her unfinished drink in my direction and said, "Have another, laddie, and you'll be sounding like Mel Gibson."

That night we warmed ourselves by the huge open fireplace in the living room of Balavil, a 7,500-acre hunting estate just outside the village of Kingussie. Our host was Allan Macpherson Fletcher, the laird of the estate, who had dressed for dinner in a kilt in his clan tartan. "Is it true, as I've read," I asked Fletcher, trying to affect a watered-down Scottish brogue, "that the whisky of Scotland is inseparable from not only its cold, wet climate and rocky terrain, but from its culture, history, tradition, and unfathomable myth as well?"

"You could say that," Fletcher agreed, smiling at my poor attempt to sound like an over-informed local. "Whisky is our bond, not so much in the cities anymore but very much among country people." Forty miles south of Inverness, this part of the Highlands was sparsely populated—just a few villages, some ancient ruins, and a number of large estates. Balavil had been in the Macpherson family since the 1790s, when Allan's ancestor, the scholar and writer James Macpherson, purchased it with the proceeds from his sensational and controversial book, *Fragments of Ancient Poetry*, purported to be the work of the third-century Gaelic bard, Ossian. Ossian's book was woven through the tangled history and inexplicable mystery of this strange land. It led indirectly to the crushed rebellion at Culloden and the infamous Highland Clearance, which in turn prompted Highlanders to either migrate to the United States or take up the illicit trade of whisky making.

Highlanders love to hunt and fish, almost as much as they love to drink. When they aren't hunting and fishing, they are drinking and talking about hunting and fishing. At a pub in Dufftown we listened as five men, dogs at their feet, talked about an exclusive club whose membership required them to shoot a stag, bag a grouse, and land a salmon in the same twenty-four-hour period. "We thought 'a toughen it so ye also had to make love to a virgin from Inverness," said one, a snaggle-toothed gamekeeper. "But then they's nae such thing." Five Frenchmen were registered at Balavil, and one afternoon after they had returned from the shoot I asked about the "hunt" and was promptly corrected by Arthur Duffus, the estate's feisty little gamekeeper. "We dinna hunt here, sir," he informed me. "We staaalk." I didn't fully appreciate the distinction until a few hours later, after I had climbed to the top of a moor and had a good view of the countryside: there wasn't a tree or even a large rock in sight, nothing to hide behind except the omnipresent sheep. Countless springs bubbled out of the rocks, flowing in a network of streams beneath the ground cover of heather. What appeared from a distance to be solid ground was often a peat bog, deeper than a man's head. In this terrain the red stag would have an insurmountable advantage over any mere hunter. "Except for Arthur," Fletcher told me. "Arthur is half animal himself. He knows how to think like a stag."

The Speyside Region is the heart of whisky country, home to more than half the distilleries in Scotland. Every few miles we spotted the pagoda roof of another malting chimney, and the weathered gray stones of the distillery's cluster of buildings and warehouses. The names of the whiskys were mouthwateringly familiar—Glenfarclas, Glenfiddich, Glen Grant, The Glenlivet, Cardhu, and many more. The grounds of these great estates are immaculate and often nestled against spectacular backdrops, hills alive with heather and gorse, and rushing rivers brimming with trout and salmon. Distillery managers pride themselves in being stewards, as well as historians, of the land. A fifteenth-century cemetery sits near the banks of the Spey on The Macallan Estate. The ruins of Balvenie Castle, a thirteenth-century stronghold that once sheltered Mary Queen of Scots, looks down on the mashhouse of Glenfiddich.

Life in all the small villages in this part of Scotland revolves around the rhythms and traditions of distilling—the time-honored task of growing and harvesting barley; the skill of cooperage; the laying aside of whisky to age. When a boy finishes the equivalent of junior high, he is expected by tradition and circumstance to apply for an apprenticeship in some phase of the industry. Gordon Innes, a sixty-four-year-old with a thick working-class brogue and hands the size of catcher's mitts, told us that he toiled more than three decades as a cooper, building and repairing thirty casks a day, six days a week, because that was the job available when he was young. When he got too old to manhandle the barrels, he worked another eighteen years as a warehouseman. "And then they made me *redoondent*," he said, biting down hard on the word management had used to tell him he was too old to go on working. Innes was finishing out his life as a part-time tour guide, at the Speyside Cooperage.

With a population of only about 400, the tiny village of Craigellachie (cray-GELL-ackie) boasts two competing distilleries, the Speyside Cooperage, and the finest hotel in the Highlands—the Craigellachie, generally referred to as just the Craig. The hotel sits on a hilltop above the handsome Spey Bridge, across the river from The Macallan Estate. The Craig caters to golfers, sportsmen, and especially to whisky connoisseurs. When guests sign the register, they are treated to a dram, from a bar stocked with more than 600 malts. Prices for a dram ranged from two pounds-fifty (about $3.60 at the time) up to 100 pounds ($144) for the really fine stuff.

At the tiny Fiddichside Inn, just down the road from the Craig, we met the owner, Dorothy Brandie, who turned out to be the granddaughter of a famous old bootlegger named James Smith, whose illicit still was on display in the museum of one of the big distillers. She poured us two whiskys and charged us just one pound-fifty for each. When I mentioned that some of the whiskys at the Craig go for more than a hundred pounds a shot, Dorothy's weathered face twisted into a Judgment Day scowl. "Nothin's worth that!" she declared. "After th' first whisky, it all tastes th' same."

We completed our ten-day journey on the Speyside coast at the tiny village of Pennan, near where the river empties into the North Sea. Pennan was made famous by the classic underground movie *Local Hero*. People came here from all over the world just to pose in front of the little red phone booth that was prominent in the film. The barkeeper in the local pub, a twenty-one-year-old New Zealander named Nathan Doel, poured us two drams of twelve-year-old Glenglassaugh, from a distiller near the ancient port of Portsoy that had closed in 1986.

"There's something almost holy about drinking whisky from a place that no longer exists," I remarked.

Phyllis sipped the golden nectar and allowed it to linger on her tongue. "Tastes like newly made beds," she decided. "Let's hav' unother."

FOR OUR TRIP TO MOSCOW, ANOTHER ASSIGNMENT from my friends at *National Geographic Traveler*, Phyllis whimsically chose to call herself Natalya, a name that naturally rings off the tongue. She named me Ivan, to which I added the family name Dangerosky. So we traveled all over Moscow as Natalya and Ivan Dangerosky, igniting curious stares from people in bars and restaurants.

The reasoning behind this assignment was Moscow's famous economic miracle, a renewal that had the city rocking and tourists flocking. We soon discovered that the place was indeed rocking, but in many respects hadn't changed and was still rife with corruption and political violence. These were not our concerns, however, and we determined to make the best of whatever we discovered.

Our Western eyes were instantly assaulted by the profusion of tiny, brightly colored and ornate prerevolutionary churches spread all over the city. They were like something out of *The Arabian Nights*. One near Gorky Park called St. John the Warrior had us gaping like newborn tourists at the psychedelic checkerboard of reds, blacks, yellows, and greens that adorned its dome.

"What do you make of that?" Natalya asked, pointing to the gaudy dome.

"Marx believed that religion is the opium of the masses," I mumbled.

"Marx didn't know the half of it," she observed coolly. "The Bolsheviks never had a prayer."

"I never knew the Russian people were so soulful," I said. "The irony is, their soul is non-negotiable. Whoever convinced the czar that a people so soulful and steeped in mysticism could be subdued with political dogma ought to get a medal for stupidity."

We saw examples of Soviet dumbness all over Moscow and were constantly amazed to observe how easily the people took it in stride and neutralized it with their stubborn will to enjoy life away from Soviet rule. Photographer Macduff Everton, who had been to Moscow twenty years earlier, told us that it used to be one of the most boring cities in the world. Now it was exciting, exotic and changing almost before our eyes. We began to seek out examples of Soviet knuckleheadedness for our own amusement. There were, for instance, a theater designed in the shape of a star, an apartment created to look like a hammer and sickle, and a cultural affairs center shaped like a tractor. The Moscow Hotel appeared weirdly lopsided because Stalin's stooges were simply too cowardly to point out that he had absentmindedly approved two competing sets of blueprints. "Stalin apparently failed to notice that form always follows function," Natalya observed dryly.

Moscow was often compared to Chicago in the 1920s, a city sinister and out of control yet always exciting. International oilmen cut deals at the lobby bar of the Radisson Slavyanskaya and arms dealers whispered in dark corners of Casino Moscow. Their eyes darted around the room as though they were sweating the last train out of town. The term "mafia" has a different meaning here than it would in Chicago. Anyone with a lot of money and political clout is considered mafia. Despite all this, we felt safer walking the streets of this city than we would the streets of, say, Dallas.

The streets pulsated with the sweep of history. Strolling Old Arbat, a fifteen-minute walk west of the Kremlin, I was struck by the loggias, balconies, and Baroque grandeur. This street could be in Rome or Paris, except almost all the buildings have a unique

Russian twist, including trimmings of cherry red, mint green, and ocher. The nineteenth-century villas along the Boulevard Ring, a greenbelt that circles central Moscow, are simpler and more severely Russian because they were constructed after Napoleon's invasion in 1812, a time of financial austerity. Tolstoy lived near here, in a modest wooden cottage on a narrow street that bears his name. Throughout the city, buildings tended to be either the monotonous shoebox apartments that infest the suburbs (built during the rules of Khrushchev and Brezhnev) or gigantic let's-hear-it-for-socialism Gothic towers, such as the "wedding cakes" built around 1947, at the end of World War II. The wedding cakes, located throughout Moscow, house government offices, apartments, and sometimes hotel rooms. They stand out like mutant giraffes, lending a ghostly charm to the city's skyline.

We thought the most interesting street was Old Arbat, which was now a pedestrian-only area inhabited by artists, fortune-tellers, sidewalk cafés and kiosks—Moscow's Greenwich Village. Street vendors hawked a variety of ethnic foods, along with such novelties as T-shirts that ridiculed Lenin and the KGB and, of course, those ubiquitous *matryoshkas*, traditional wooden dolls-within-dolls-within-dolls.

For lunch, we found our way to the famous Actor's Club, where Russian artists, writers, directors, and conductors gathered to discuss business. Over a meal of caviar-stuffed salmon, augmented by repeated toasts of ice-cold vodka, we learned of Moscow's enduring infatuation with Mikhail Bulgakov, whose satirical masterpiece *The Master and Margarita* made such ferocious fun of Soviet life that it couldn't be published until the late 1960s—and even then only in censored editions. For many years, however, copies of the banned manuscript passed from hand to hand, making Bulgakov a literary icon, especially with older Russians. The book is a phantasmagorical tale of two lovers who join up with the devil and a retinue of weirdos at a spot called Patriarch's Pond. The group includes a beautiful naked witch and a huge talking black cat with a taste for chess and vodka, and together they wreak havoc on a city that believes in neither God nor Satan, but somehow manages to bring peace to the tortured lovers.

The next morning, we went in search of Patriarch's Pond and the house where Bulgakov lived. The legendary pond is well known among locals. It is a beautiful spot, shaded by stately elms, under which people gather to talk, read poetry, play cards, nap, or dream. Two lovers about the age of the Master and Margarita drifted past, oblivious of our presence. Bulgakov died in 1940, but people who lived during Soviet times speak of him in the present tense. "In this courtyard," our guide, Tatiana, told us, opening a window so we could better appreciate the scene, "Margarita flies on her magic broomstick." With help from three students, we located Bulgakov's apartment, three blocks away and up four flights of dark, moldy stairs. Walls and ceilings were covered with graffiti celebrating Bulgakov—messages, slogans, drawings of devils, naked witches, and jaunty cats. The adjoining apartment, also featured in the book, was now a gallery. Among a display of black-and-white nudes taken in the 1920s, the proprietor pointed out a sullen, dark-haired woman who is said to look exactly like Stalin's second wife. "Who knows?" he said with a wink.

We had lunch at the tiny Café Margarita across from the park, identifiable by a demonic mural at the entrance. Inside, walls were lined with books, paintings, and tiny figurines of black jazz artists. We ordered the kind of simple Russian fare favored by writers and nobility—blinis with red caviar and sour cream, washed down with glasses of cold vodka. Lena, a pretty waitress with flashing black eyes and lips like ripe cherries—Phyllis decided that she must be Margarita's granddaughter—told us that most pilgrims who find their way to this place are foreigners. "Young Russians either haven't heard of Bulgakov or don't care," she said ruefully.

Reminders of the old Soviet order were everywhere, and often tweaked with irony. In what was formerly October Square there remained a seventy-foot bronze statue of Lenin—and just across the street was the neon-roofed Starlite Diner, its motif right out of the 1950s American heartland, Buddy Holly jamming from the jukebox and waitresses in bobby sox serving frosted Cokes. The lobbies of the good hotels were thick with former KGB agents, only now they worked as private security guards. In parks and plazas you spotted old men in ragged coats, their chests covered with medals and campaign ribbons. The stations of Moscow's metro system were virtual Soviet museums, great chandeliered archways with busts of Lenin and elaborate mosaics of happy peasants, foundry workers, and beribboned commissars. One night as we were taking photographs inside the Kievskaya metro station, a pudgy, ill-tempered guard toting a machine gun ran from far down the hall to warn us that picture-taking was not allowed. "Old habits die hard," Natalya said, shaking her head.

Near the great red-walled Kremlin was Resurrection Gate, the entrance to Red Square and the zero-kilometer mark by which all distances in Russia are measured. The enormous gate and its tiny chapel that looks like a child's playhouse were recent restorations: Stalin ordered the originals destroyed, so he could drive his tanks into the square for parades. The chapel housed an icon that Muscovites believe protected their city from evil. Crowded on the chapel steps were the great unwashed of Moscow life—a crippled babushka in a faded shawl, a gnarled Asian without shoes, and a fiery-eyed, gray-bearded priest from the provinces, all of them soliciting rubles from a steady procession lined up, waiting to kiss the icon.

Like many her age, Tatiana despised and feared communism. She was badly shaken one morning when we happened on a small communist rally in front of the Kremlin and urged us to hurry along. "This can be very dangerous," she warned. "Look at their faces, how angry and agitated!" Her grandparents lost their land and everything they owned to the Bolsheviks. Before founding her own travel company, she served her country as a loyal guide and interpreter, parroting Soviet propaganda about a worker paradise she now realized never existed. Awakened in the 1980s by her travels for Intourist, she had opportunities to defect—including a marriage proposal from an American—but remained loyal, partly because she was the sole support for her mother and son, but also because she was Russian and loved her country.

I had expressed interest in seeing how a Muscovite family fared in a home setting, so on our final night in the city Tatiana invited us for dinner at the apartment she shared with her twenty-year-old son, Gleb, and her mother, Olga. A third-floor walkup near Victory Park, the apartment was small by Western standards—three bedrooms, a tiny kitchen, a bath—but during the Soviet era four or five families would have shared this space. Olga greeted us at the front door with bread and salt, the traditional Russian welcome, and Gleb waited with a tray of cold vodka. Olga's brother, Arkady, joined us for dinner. The dining room/sitting room was also Tatiana's bedroom.

Dinner lasted nearly three hours. We were served almost every product this vast country produced—a variety of cold meats, cheeses, fruits, and raw vegetables from Georgia and Armenia, salmon and sturgeon from the Caspian Sea, red and black caviar served with Olga's homemade blinis, several kinds of meat pies with dumplings. In addition to vodka there was beer and champagne, and we made repeated toasts to our two countries and freedom. "In the old days," Olga told us, "we would have been arrested for having Americans in our home."

We walked back to our hotel, more than a tad drunk, enjoying the blue and green lights from the wedding-cake tower of the Ukraina Hotel dancing across the Moscow River. It was the week of the summer solstice—"White Nights"—and although it was nearly midnight there was still enough daylight to read a newspaper. Natalya nudged me and whispered, "A simple people." Simple, humble, soulful. Like the Master and Margarita, people tortured by their convictions. I put my arm around Phyllis, I mean, Natalya, and said: "You're right. The Bolshies never had a prayer."

THE OTHER THING I REMEMBER MOST ABOUT MY SIX months at Paisano was reuniting with my son Mark, who came and stayed for several weeks. Starting with my stay at Paisano and continuing until his death thirty years later, we became best friends.

Because he grew up a thousand miles from where I lived—in Los Angeles, then Chicago, and finally Atlanta—I saw him only a few times a year. All that changed in May 1975, when he graduated from high school. A week after that, he packed up and moved to Austin to attend the University of Texas. For a while Mark and his girlfriend, Christian, slept in my big walk-in closet. After a short time, Christian returned to Atlanta. I wasn't married at the time, so I found a larger apartment and Mark and I set up housekeeping. We did everything together—shopping, cooking, eating, listening to music, having adventures.

My dad had passed on to me an appreciation for cooking and eating, and I passed it on to Mark. Before long he was cooking gourmet meals that took three days to prepare and five hours to eat. I nicknamed him Maurice, a name that sounded appropriate for a first-rate chef.

Later, after he married Helen and took a job as publisher of a monthly magazine in Little Rock, Arkansas, Maurice graduated to seated dinners for ten or twelve, which became the talk of the town. Journalists and politicians—including Bill and Hillary Clinton, who were just becoming well known in political circles—gratefully accepted invitations. For one of my birthdays, he whipped up a five-course meal that included rack of lamb, dove breasts wrapped in bacon and sautéed in wine sauce, roasted ancho peppers with goat cheese and salmon, and an unbelievable dome-shaped dessert with layers of crushed Heath bars, fudge cake, and ice cream, with a toasted butterscotch crust. Naturally, Maurice selected the appropriate wine for each course.

Sometimes we wrote songs together, Mark strumming his guitar and me jotting down the words. We could compose an entire opera in an afternoon. When my friend Sue Sharlot graduated from UT Law School (where her husband, Mike, was a professor, and later, dean), Mark and I wrote a number for her graduation party, titled "All You Gotta Do Is Know the Law, Then Boogie 'Til You Puke." Another all-time favorite was "Beat Me Like the Bitch

I Am." We wrote alternate lines, laughing so hard we could barely get the words out: "Reel and Rod Me/Marquis de Sade me/Make me feel so fine/But beat me like the bitch I am/And tell the world you're mine."

We were never like father and son—more like brothers, or best friends. He called me by my nickname, Jap, never Dad or Daddy. He found it easier to express his love than I did, and in his effortless manner taught me to express my love, too. He also taught me to appreciate his favorite expression: *"Nothing to it."* The easy way that he said it made the phrase a manifesto of his indomitable spirit, an attitude that recognized no limits. He had always been a bright, resourceful, resilient, uncommonly stubborn kid. I remember when he was about ten, him bugging me to take him along on a business trip to New York. I tried to explain that I didn't have time to show him the sights, but he wanted to tag along and I couldn't say no.

We stayed in the guest room at Dan and June's apartment near Central Park; they were out of town, so we had the whole place to ourselves. Our first night in the Big Apple, in a hurry to keep an appointment, I gave him $20 and a key to the apartment, and dropped him off in Times Square. "Are you sure you'll be okay?" I asked him. "Sure," he said. "Nothing to it." My cab hadn't gone half a block when the stupidity of what I had just done slapped me upside the head: I had deposited my ten-year-old boy in the geographical center of the evilest, most sinister square mile in America. I threw the cab door open and raced back against oncoming traffic, but by that time he had been swallowed up in the crowd. For the next few hours I was nearly sick with fear, imagining what might happen. But when I got back to the apartment, there he was, propped up in the king-size bed, a cat on his lap, eating a bowl of ice cream and watching a John Wayne movie on TV. "Are you *okay*?" I asked, badly shaken. "Sure," he said, grinning at me as though we were co-conspirators in a plot to overthrow the world. "Nothing to it . . ."

I just naturally assumed Mark could do anything he put his mind to, and I guess he felt the same about me. Together, we thought of ourselves as unconquerable. And for many years we were. Then in July 1996, our family was shocked to learn that Mark had been diagnosed with the most severe type of acute myelogenous leukemia. It was a condition called M-5, in which white blood cells (called blasts) take over bone marrow and prevent it from making normal cells, gradually weakening the victim until life completely shuts down. The only cure was a bone marrow transplant, a long, dangerous, and enormously expensive process which requires massive doses of chemotherapy to force the cancer into temporary remission, followed by a search for a matching donor. The chemo wouldn't destroy the cancer cells, but it would hopefully put them in remission long enough to allow a bone marrow transplant. The trick was finding someone with matching bone marrow.

Unfortunately, no one in our family was a match. Together with family and friends, we organized drives to find matching donors in Austin, Little Rock, and Atlanta—*Texas Monthly* publisher Mike Levy donated a full page for us to advertise the search. And although we added 1,500 new names to the National Bone Marrow Registry, we never found a match. People called from all over the country, volunteering to be tested, extending support, contributing money to the Leukemia Society of America. One doctor speculated that finding a match for Mark was extra difficult because our family had traces of Native American blood. Rosalind Wright, a sister of Austin writer Larry Wright, telephoned from Lexington, Massachusetts, where she had rallied thirteen tribes of Native Americans and personnel from a military base to get tested. My friend Marvin Schwartz, the Buddhist monk, sent a seed blessed by the Dalai Lama, with instruction on how Mark was to ingest it. The clock was ticking and I was desperate, ready to try anything. I pored through dozens of letters searching for a solution, or at least a clue, and one that caught my attention was from a guy in federal prison, doing twenty years on a drug charge. This guy claimed to be a Mexican *curandero* and advised me to find some new top leaves from a creosote bush and brew them into a tea. I showed his letter to Mark and told him, "We might as well give it a try." He replied in his typically nonchalant fashion: "Why not?"

Our search for fresh creosote plants took us on a very long and arduous journey to the Chihuahuan Desert, east of Van Horn. The letters instructed us to travel together, and to leave "a gift of water" for the plant from which we borrowed leaves. We flew from Austin to Dallas to Midland, where we rented a car and drove 125 miles to a desolate spot within sight of the Davis Mountains. We carried with us two bottles of Evian, figuring that spirits strong enough to cure cancer wouldn't settle for tap water. Mark slept almost all the way, wracked with fever, chills, and nausea. The trip was sapping what little energy he had remaining. We had just celebrated his fortieth birthday a couple of weeks earlier, but he was thin and fragile as a leaf. After I collected a sack of leaves, we spent the night in a motel in Midland, the kid so sick that I wondered if he would last the night. I was awake until two in the morning, talking long distance to friends and family, trying to figure out our next move. We agreed that as soon as he arrived back in Atlanta, they would take him directly to the hospital. I wanted to travel with him, but Mark told me he wanted to fly alone. He was so weak that I had to load him into a wheelchair and deliver him to the gate. He had eaten almost nothing for a week, so I stopped at a coffee bar and bought him a banana and a Coke, which he was barely able to keep down. Looking at him at that moment, as pale and weak as a newborn pup, I couldn't help but remember that a year earlier the two of us had worked out at my gym in Austin, both of us fit and seemingly invincible. As recently as Christmas, he had looked reasonably strong and cheerful. But now I could almost see his life leaking away. I think that was the worst day of my life, worse even than when he died.

I know now that even had we found a match for Mark, a transplant would have been useless. All that horrible chemotherapy had destroyed his immune system and done great damage to his organs. Mark's doctor in Atlanta, Daniel Dubovsky, compared cancer cells to cockroaches. "You might kill ninety-five percent of them," he told me, "but the remaining five percent emerge stronger and more resistant." Two and a half weeks after our trip to the Chihuahuan Desert, Mark was again in the hospital. A few days later,

Dubovsky informed us that there was nothing more he could do. Mark said that he'd like to go home, meaning his mother's house, not far from the hospital.

Phyllis and I flew to Atlanta for the death watch, not sure how we would handle it but trusting that Mark would set the style. Getting reacquainted with his longtime group of pals, we realized that he'd set the style years before. In high school he had put together a combination rock band and chili cookoff team called the Chain Gang, and they were with him until the end, respecting his wish that nobody feel sorry for him, or for themselves. Tom "Meat" Smith sat at the foot of his bed and regaled us with stories about "the Great Cartwright." It seems that the women of Atlanta were not one hundred percent unanimous in their devotion. Meat told us that one woman Mark jilted when they both worked for Turner Broadcasting System was unable to speak his name without pausing to spit on the floor. Meat demonstrated, feigning a high-pitched voice: "Oh, you must be referring to Mark—*hoc, spitooowe*—Cartwright." Sick as he was, Mark doubled over with laughter. All the guys who had played with the Chain Gang were there, too, including Sammy Rawlins, an especially close friend, who, like Tom Smith, had gone all the way through high school with Mark. Sammy inherited Mark's guitar and added it to his own growing collection.

Also on hand was the latest and last of Mark's many girlfriends, Susan Shaw. She was as tough and tenacious as they come. Almost single-handedly she had organized a drive that put 500 new names on the bone marrow registry. She could have bailed out at any time and no one would have blamed her, but Susan wasn't the kind to bail. The only time she lost it was the day Dubovsky told us it was over. "It wasn't supposed to be that way," Susan told me later, her eyes red and swollen from a day of crying. "I had imagined our twilight years, sitting on the porch watching our grandchildren. Suddenly I just went to pieces. I was crying and calling out to God, saying, "Why Mark? Why me?" Soon after, Susan got a call from the National Bone Marrow Registry, telling her that she was a partial match for a fifty-four-year-old man from the Midwest. "God works in mysterious ways," she concluded sadly.

What got us through those last few weeks was Mark's remarkable courage, the grace, dignity, and measured good humor with which he faced death. He resolved to put his affairs in order, dictating a will and making it clear that when the end came he didn't want any paramedics resuscitating him. He asked that his body be cremated and his ashes scattered in the Gulf of Mexico. (One exception: Some of the ashes would be handed over to the Chain Gang, whose members would find an appropriate container—most likely a cowboy boot—and take them each year to the chili cookoff in Athens, Georgia. As his replacement in the Chain Gang, he selected a Cajun friend, Jonathan "Gator" Ordoyne.)

I asked if he was scared and he said, "No, strangely enough I'm not. I've been sick for so long that what I really want is a few good days." That wish became my prayer, and God must have heard it. For a few days Mark was almost his old self. He got out of bed and spent several hours sitting in the sun. He was able to eat solid food for the first time in a week and even drank a cup of foul-tasting creosote tea. He went to a couple of movies with Susan and the three of us spent an afternoon at the Atlanta Botanical Garden. We drove the rural back roads, where spectacular explosions of azaleas, redbuds, and dogwoods seemed to be blossoming specifically on his behalf, and we had dinner at his favorite Mexican restaurant.

With Meat at his side, he spent a day at the Master's Golf Tournament, then flew to Little Rock on Friday, April 11, to visit his children, nine-year-old Katelyn and seven-year-old Malcolm. It was an act of pure willpower, his last. By the time he returned to Atlanta, his fever was back, signaling that the brief reprieve had ended.

On the patio that last day, Mark kissed me and said he loved me. I said I loved him, too. "I can't bring myself to say good-bye," I said, choking back tears. "So, until I see you again." He gave me his big smile and said, "Until I see you again." Then he turned and went to his bed. He died on Sunday afternoon. His last words were to Susan. "I think this is it," he said softly. "I'm packing 'em in."

SIXTEEN YEARS LATER, IN THE SPRING OF 2013, I relived all these memories, and created a bunch more, at a reunion in Atlanta that brought together four generations of our family. The occasion started as a wedding shower for my fabulous granddaughter, Katelyn Cartwright, who would be married the following October, but it soon blossomed into much more. It became a gathering in which I was reintroduced not only to my grandchildren but to *two great-grandchildren*. Suddenly, without having much time to reflect on what was happening, I found myself the patriarch of a family that had grown much larger and far more interesting than I had taken time to calculate.

My daughter, Lea, and her husband, Ed, picked me up at the Atlanta airport and I spent the first night at their home in the mountain village of Big Canoe, in the high pine country south of Atlanta. To my great surprise, I learned that my sister Gail was also in town, visiting her daughter, Cindy, and her grandson, Brandon, both of whom live in the Atlanta metro area. Brandon and his wife, Heather, had given birth to a baby named Jackson less than a month before my visit, and the following day, still trying to adjust to the whirl of activity, I sat on their couch holding this four-week-old baby named Jackson, trying to make sense of the reality that he was my (I could hardly bring myself to use the term) *great-grandson*.

A few hours later, I was reunited with two more grandchildren, Katelyn and Malcolm, who are Mark's and Helen's children. I had seen them only a few times since the death of their mother, who died of brain cancer about a year after Mark's death. Katy was a gawky teenager when I saw her last, but now she was a beautiful and very talented 26-year-old, working on a graduate degree in art history and teaching a class of disabled students at a private school in Little Rock. I was pleased to find that she had inherited her mother's striking beauty, as well as Mark's charm. With both of their parents gone, I was Katy's and Malcolm's only link with our line of the family—our family's patron, the final living male connection to our past.

But the cascade of family connections and unexpected links to the past didn't end there. I spent the next two nights with Laura and Sammy Rawlins—Sammy had been a member of the Chain Gang and one of Mark's longtime school buddies. Katy was staying there, too, as were Malcolm and his girlfriend, Kathleen. Before I knew it, I found myself cuddling yet another great-grandson, four-month-old Kellan Cartwright, Malcolm and Kathleen's baby. Kellan had amazingly bright eyes and a smile that made me weak in the knees: it was love at first sight. Though I was now in my late seventies, I realized once again that life's surprises just keep coming.

WE WERE SITTING ALONE IN HIS BUS, ME AND Willie Nelson, drinking coffee and sharing a smoke, two geezers talking about how it feels to approach age sixty-five, commiserating about the predictable decline of kidneys, eyesight, knee joints, rotator cuffs, and sexual appetites. We agreed that when dealing with life's vagaries—the hits, misses, insights, and sorrows—attitude is everything. "However you want things to be," Willie reminded me, "create them in your own mind, and they'll be that way."

The rules were mapped on his face and crusted in his voice, which has always seemed less melodic by daylight. Willie had traveled the day before, Thanksgiving Day, 1997, arriving in Las Vegas from the Bahamas just before show time. When he had visited the Bahamas back in 1978, I reminded him, they threw him in jail for smoking pot and then banished him from the island for life. So they did, Willie recalled with a good-natured nod. He was so happy to be free from that damned jail he jumped off a curb and broke his foot. The following night, his foot in a cast, he celebrated again by firing up an Austin Torpedo on the roof of President Jimmy Carter's White House. "That was an incredible moment," he admitted, "sitting there watching all the lights. I wasn't aware until then that all roads led to the Capitol, that it was the center of the world." Also, the safest spot in America to smoke dope, he added. Willie credited God and the hemp plant for much of his good fortune and advocated both at every opportunity. Without encouragement, he began listing all the consumer items produced by the lowly plant—shirts, shorts, granola bars, paper products, and motor fuel, not to mention extremely enlightening smoke. "Did you realize the first draft of our Constitution was written on hemp paper?" he marveled.

From the window of the bus we could see the front entrance of the Orleans Hotel and Casino, where he would be performing for the next few nights. Though management had reserved a suite for Willie at the hotel, by long habit he slept aboard the bus, venturing out only to play golf or make it onstage in time for the first note of "Whiskey River," his traditional opening number. Willie told me that inside his head there is a network of communication outlets, that he has a mental tape recorder that starts with "Whiskey River" and lasts two and a half hours—the time needed to complete a concert. He also receives messages from angels, archangels, and several bands of broadcast signal, some in languages unknown to the human race.

This bus, the Honeysuckle Rose, is Willie's home, office, and sanctuary, not only on the road but also at Willie World, his compound outside of Austin, which includes a house, a recording studio, a golf course, and a western film set. The bus is the one place he truly feels comfortable. It is well equipped, with multiple TV sets, a state-of-the-art stereo and sound system, a kitchen, a toilet, showers, and beds. Willie's private compartment at the rear is as cozy and as densely packed as a Gypsy's knapsack. One of Willie's old aunts once confided to writer-producer Bill Wittliff: "That Willie, he can pack a trailer faster than anyone I ever saw." On his king-size bed rest three guitars. Surrounding it are Native American paintings, beaded necklaces, and breastplates; a giant American flag; photographs of his two youngest sons, Lukas and Micah (by his fourth and current wife, Annie); a jump rope; some dumbbells; and a speed bag anchored to a swivel above the door. Willie's elder sister, Bobbie Nelson, and his daughter, Lana, also travel on the Honeysuckle Rose. Members of his band and road crew ride in two additional buses and a truck that make up Willie's relentless caravan.

"I don't like to be a hermit, but I'm better off staying out here by myself," Willie explained, taking a drag and passing the smoke across the table. "Too many temptations. In the old days we'd stay in town after a gig and start drinking and chasing women, and some of the band would end up in jail or divorced. That's when I started leaving right after a gig, driving all night just to get out of town. If it wasn't for the bus and this weed, I'd be at the bar right now, doing serious harm to myself."

For a man who would be soon be eligible for Medicare, Willie appeared fit, trim, content, and comfortably weathered, a man who had not only transcended his wounds and scars but also made them part of his act. In his unique American Gothic way, he appeared semi-elegant, a country squire in an orange sweatshirt, jeans, and running shoes, his hair neatly braided, his eyes crackling with good humor. He looked ready to run with the hounds. Willie exercised daily, jogging, stretching, jumping rope. He could make the speed bag rattle like a snare drum. Just three weeks ago he went three rounds with former heavyweight Tex Cobb, and he was about to get his brown belt in tae kwon do. Onstage the previous night, without warning, Willie kicked a microphone off a stand higher than his head. This was a regular part of the show and the audience roared its approval. How many geezers can high-kick like a majorette?

As we talked, Willie squeezed a rubber ball, releasing nervous energy. "I have so much energy that it gets to be a problem," he told me. "I don't smoke weed to get high, I smoke it to take the edge off, to level out, so I'm not out there like a turkey sticking his head into everything." Though this natural energy is part of his creative process, it must obey the laws of physics: the action of whiskey, women, music, and life on the road eventually produces the reaction of self-destruction. Anyone who has spent time with Willie knows that he is as tightly wound as he is mellow. Bud Shrake, who helped Willie put together his autobiography, told me: "Willie has a violent temper. He gets so furious his eyes turn black, and he has to leave the room or kill somebody." In the book, Willie tells about a bloody brawl in a parking lot in Phoenix after a concert—some irate husband swinging a Crescent wrench and Willie defending himself with a two-by-four. "Having a temper is like being an alcoholic," he said. "You always know it's there." He has learned to control his temper, or at least modify it. His mantra in the nineties was positive thinking. As he counsels in one of his songs:

> Remember the good times
> They're smaller in number, and easier to recall.

Willie has battled his share of ailments—pneumonia four or five times; a collapsed lung that required surgery (he wrote the album *Tougher Than Leather* in the hospital); followed by a relapse when he ripped out the stitches while on a movie set in Finland; chronic back pain that dates from stacking hay bales as a boy; the usual prostate and bladder problems. But an uncanny survival instinct has enabled him to weather the ravages of time. "I've never been healthier," he assured me. "I'm at the top of my game."

Watching from the theater wings at the Orleans Hotel, I was reminded once again that Willie and his music are inseparable, that his songs are more than mere footprints of life, that they are fields of cosmic energy that direct, shape, and reveal everything that he is or has been. Dressed in his stage outfit—black T-shirt with sleeves and neck cut away, jeans, sneakers, a straw cowboy hat that he quickly exchanges for a headband—Willie was singing one of his legendary cheating songs, "Funny How Time Slips Away." His tone was generous but accusatory, reflecting the mixed emotions that he was feeling when he wrote it back in the late fifties. Though I couldn't see her face from where I was standing, I knew that he was focused on some knockout blonde with large breasts seated in the fourth row, singing directly to her. It's a trick he uses to help his onstage concentration.

Willie was just twenty-six when he wrote "Funny How Time Slips Away," during an incredibly hungry and productive period of his life. He wrote that song and two other equally memorable classics—"Crazy" and "Night Life"—in the same week, driving in the early-morning hours from the Esquire Club on the east side of Houston, where he was playing six nights a week, to the apartment in Pasadena where he lived with his first wife, Martha Jewel Matthews, and their three kids, Lana, Susie, and Billy.

These were his pre-Nashville days and he was poor as a Sudanese cat. Living in Houston, Fort Worth, San Diego, and a lot of other places, Willie worked by day selling vacuum cleaners or encyclopedias door-to-door and playing by night in honky-tonks. He worked as a deejay when he could. Whatever it took to survive, Willie did. He sold not only the rights but all claim of authorship to "Night Life" for a measly $150. "Night Life" is one of the great blues numbers of all time and has been recorded by everyone from B. B. King to Aretha Franklin, but Willie gave it away for the equivalent of a month's rent. He had to use the alias Huge Nelson the first time he recorded it. He sold "Family Bible" for $50 and tried to sell "Mr. Record Man" for $10. Writers were like painters, Willie believed. An artist sells a creation as soon as it is finished, so he will have enough money to create again.

"A lot of times when I'm driving alone," Willie told me, "and my mind is open and receptive, it will pick up radio waves from somewhere in the universe and a song will start. A line, a phrase. You don't call up creativity, it's just there. Like the Bible says, 'Be still and know that I am.'"

"Do you pull over and make notes?" I asked.

"I never write it down until the whole thing is in my mind," he said. "If I forget a song, it wasn't worth remembering.

"I don't like to think too much. It's better coming off the top of your head. Leon Russell had this idea of going into a studio with no songs, just turn on the machine and start writing and singing. Don't you remember the night you winged 'Main Squeeze Blues?'"

Sure I remembered, but I was surprised Willie did. It was the night Phyllis and I got married in the backroom of the Texas Chili Parlor and eventually found ourselves at Soap Creek Saloon, where Willie was playing. On an impulse I jumped onstage with Willie and began improvising a song that I called "Main Squeeze Blues."

I don't remember any of the words, but the audience seemed to enjoy it.

"I see what you mean," I said. "When you're sailing high, or when you're in a hard place worrying about rent or food for the kids, something kicks in and words start gushing."

"That's right." Willie smiled. "And the air is full of melodies. You just snatch one out of the air."

I first heard of Willie Nelson back in 1966, when I was covering the Dallas Cowboys. Don Meredith was always talking about Willie or singing a line or two from one of his songs, and when I started asking questions—who *is* this guy?—Meredith handed me a copy of an album that Willie recorded live at Panther Hall in Fort Worth. Listening to it over and over that night was one of the most profound experiences of my life. Whoever this man was, he was extraordinary. Nobody had written such perfect words since Cole Porter.

I didn't actually meet him until 1972, when he played his first gig at Armadillo World Headquarters. Both of us were in our late thirties at the time, long comfortable with drugs and long hair. Bud Shrake and I had helped with the founding of Armadillo and we were in the small office that Armadillo founder Eddie Wilson had set aside for Mad Dog, Inc., when Willie smelled the aroma of marijuana down the hall and stuck his head in our door. "Mind if I join you?" he asked. That was a real eye-opener for me, not just smoking dope with Willie but discovering that his audience was the same one that got turned on by B. B. King and Jerry Garcia. This humble cotton picker from Abbott, Texas, had somehow blended blues, rock, and country into an altogether original and evocative form of music.

There is such a powerful presence about Willie that some people believe he's a mystic or even a messenger from God, a misinterpretation that Willie hasn't always tried to correct. His road manager, Billy Cooper, nearly convinced me that Willie had a magical ability to commune with snakes and birds, and that he can, with a wave of his hand, convert negative energy to positive. Other members of his road crew told me about a ferocious gunfight in a parking lot after a concert in Birmingham. With cops squatting for cover in doorways and civilians diving under pickup trucks, Willie stepped calmly from his bus, wearing tennis shoes and cutoffs with two Colt .45 revolvers stuck in his waistband. "Is there a problem?" he inquired coolly. In an instant, all guns were holstered and Willie was signing autographs.

Willie believes that his life is a series of circles in which he is continually reincarnated, each version a little better than its predecessor. There is some theological support for this belief. One of the magician-priests who live on the island of Maui where Willie has a vacation home, a chap by the name of Kimo Alo, claims that Willie is "an Old King," reincarnated to draw the native races together. When I asked Willie about the Old King theory, he dismissed it—though I suspect he secretly thinks it's reasonable. In his autobiography, he wrote: "Even as a child, I believed I had been born for a purpose. I had never heard the words reincarnation or Karma, but I already believed them and I believed in the spirit world." Raised as a staunch Methodist, Willie was teaching Sunday school when the pastor gave him an ultimatum: stop playing in beer joints or stop teaching Sunday school. Willie left the church, went to the library, and began reading about religion. "Soon as I read about reincarnation," he said, "it struck me just the same as if God had sent me a lightning bolt. This was the truth and I realized I had always known it." He understood that it would take many reincarnations to triumph over his lustful urges, but at least he was on the right track.

He often jokes that he is "imperfect man," sent here as an example of how not to live your life. This was the theme of *Yesterday's Wine*, his most personal and spiritual album, and arguably his best. Written in the early seventies after a series of personal disasters—including a fire that burned his home in Nashville, in which he lost many possessions but managed to save his marijuana stash—the album follows a man from birth to death, ending with him at his own funeral.

"Maybe I was imperfect man, writing my own obituary," he told me at the end of our conversation on his bus. Unexpectedly, he broke into song:

> There'll be a mixture of tear drops and flowers
> Crying and talking for hours
> About how wild that I was
> And if I'd listened to them I wouldn't be there.

The song ends with God telling imperfect man that there is no explanation for the apparent random cruelty of life:

> After all, you're just a man
> And it's not for you to understand.

I didn't understand his meaning at first, but after a few years I discovered that Willie told me a profound truth: once you chose the night life, all roads are pretty much the same.

Willie also taught me the value of patience, and the importance of believing in yourself and trusting your own instincts. While Willie was working with Bud on his autobiography, he happened to pick up and read a copy of a screenplay Bud and I had written years earlier, titled *Rip*. Willie liked the script, and his interest convinced the bosses at CBS Television to finance the project as a Movie of the Week.

It was the story of a no-nonsense Texas Ranger, Captain Rip Metcalf, who finds himself literally handcuffed to a well-known safe burglar, Billy Roy Barker, during what amounts to a prolonged prisoner transfer. The plot drew on a practice we had observed as reporters in Fort Worth, police using a Texas Ranger to either beat a confession out of a crook or make him disappear long enough that the cops could manufacture enough evidence for a conviction.

Willie played Billy Roy as a charming rogue with a caustic sense of humor and the hands of a master magician. The audience loved him enough to accept the flimsy storyline: as the burglar and the Ranger travel the back roads of Texas, they discover how much they have in common and work together to solve a real crime, a series of murders of young women the same age as the Ranger's daughter. Willie brought along his pal Kris Kristofferson to play Ranger Rip Metcalf, and convinced the very talented actor Rip Torn to fill the role of a retired Ranger and lifelong psycho named Jack Parson. CBS changed the title to *A Pair of Aces*. It drew a sizable audience and convinced the deep-thinkers at CBS to commission a sequel. Shrake and I weren't interested in writing a sequel, but we accepted the title of co-executive producers and hired veteran screenwriter Rob Gilmer to write a follow-up version. It was called, of course, *Another Pair of Aces*. Together, the two made-for-television movies provided us a handsome payday. I used my half of the money to buy my house. I think of it as The House Willie Built.

Working with Willie on those two movies helped me appreciate his big heart and generous nature. Wherever he goes, and whatever he does, Willie finds himself surrounded with people he has helped. He helps in such a low-key, unobtrusive way that the recipient hardly notices the hand up. It's a saintly quality, softly stated and nearly obscured by the trappings of fame and wealth. But it is the core of a most remarkable man it has been my privilege to know.

PHYLLIS AND I NEVER GOT TIRED OF NEW ADVENTURES, travel in particular. We sought out spots we had grown up reading about or seeing in movies, romantic getaways famous for being famous. One memorable journey was an overnight trip aboard the Orient Express, from London to Venice.

Boarding the British Pullman at Victoria Station, Phyllis and I were greeted by a porter, who escorted us to our compartment, down an Art Deco passageway of gleaming brass luggage racks and overstuffed seats. Soon as he had opened our cabin door and stored our luggage, he poured us two glasses of champagne. Phyllis gave me a conspiratorial wink, meaning: *We are in our element*. The cabin was snug but comfortable, and like everything else on this train, elegantly appointed in wood paneling and antique fixtures. After a long, leisurely dinner in a dining car decorated in Chinese-style lacquer and glass panels, we took snifters of brandy back to the cabin, where, like a couple of trained acrobats, we figured out a way to negotiate the angles of love in a bunk bed barely wide enough for a child.

In the morning, fully refreshed, we woke to the astonishing grandeur of the Swiss Alps, swallowing the sky and overpowering the earth as far as the eye could see. We passed through vineyards and newly plowed fields and pretty villages with cobbled streets where people in front of small bars or cafés or on their way to church paused to wave at us. We felt like citizens of the world and, for the moment, we could claim that distinction.

Our grandest trip, however, was the two weeks we disappeared in the village of Positano, on the fabulous Amalfi Coast of Italy, south of Naples. Dan Jenkins had been to Positano the previous year and had warned us against trying to drive the narrow, winding road that skirts the Amalfi peninsula. So we hired a driver at the airport and sat back in comfort in his minibus, marveling at this insanely beautiful land that defied gravity and shamed description. Jenkins's advice was dead on. The highway was impossibly narrow and clogged with huge trucks driven by dark men who were crazy or angry, or both. The highway passed through Sorrento, Ravello, and other vertiginous villages that clung to the sides of mountains like strands of brightly colored beads, sloping down to the sea in drunken angles. The coast's largest town, Amalfi, was a maritime power until 1131 when it was subdued by King Roger of Naples, and eventually emerged as a playground for the rich and famous. At the time of our trip, Ravello, just down the road from Amalfi, was the preferred hangout for folks like Gore Vidal and Jackie Kennedy.

Looming above us and dominating all the known earth was the legendary despoiler of countryside, Mount Vesuvius, which in A.D. 79 erupted with a roar heard for hundreds of miles, burying the villages of Pompeii and Herculaneum under twenty feet of pumice and ash. Vesuvius last erupted in 1944, but occasional rumbles cause small earthquakes and remind that where the Next Big One is concerned, it's not if but when.

At the crest of a hill, we caught our first breathtaking view of Positano, which from a distance seemed to be a scattering of colorful villas arranged up and down the banks of a road that in its previous life had been a snake trail. Our villa perched on a gradual incline, halfway up the mountain. To reach it required climbing 183 steps. The steps were carved out of solid rock and augmented by an occasional handrail. Halfway up was a bench where you could rest your legs or await a heart attack. Everything in Positano is either up or down, and after a few days' practice, negotiating a mere 183 steps seemed routine. Anyway, we were too excited to feel fatigue.

The villa had three bedrooms and a large, open kitchen and living area. Like all villas in this part of Italy, it was white with lots of red tile and open windows. A wide patio ran along two sides of it, giving us an uncluttered view of Capri and two other islands. Tiny minibuses cruised on the road below, and also the road above, like restless insects. They ran all day, every day, and cost almost nothing to ride. There was a good grocery and market just down the road, in easy walking distance. Downtown Positano, just minutes away by bus or even by foot, had a hardware store, a market, a bakery, several sidewalk cafés and bars, and a small number of shops that sold stuff you didn't want to be caught dead with, much less carry home. The town backed up to a long beach of black volcanic sand and rock, which swept off in two directions before disappearing around steep curves. The water was too cold for our Texas-conditioned bodies but was popular with local swimmers. Sunglasses were required apparel. Bathing suits appeared to be optional.

There were three or four good restaurants in town, but mostly we grilled fish or ate pasta with butter and garlic or kale that we cooked at the villa. Fruits and vegetables grown in this rich volcanic soil were the best I've ever tasted. Tomatoes were so sweet and so juicy that you wanted to eat them in the shower. Crusty bread was baked fresh two times a day, and the local wines were cheap and of excellent quality. Life was about as good as it could get.

We took day trips by bus, train, and ferry (sometimes all three) to Pompeii, Herculaneum, Capri, and of course Naples, the capital of the region called Campania. Founded by the Greeks and refined by the Romans, Naples became a prize for foreign invaders like the Normans, the Hohenstaufen, the French, and the Spanish. A chaotic, spectacular city, it sits on the edge of the Bay of Naples, with Mount Vesuvius on one side and the islands of Capri, Ischia, and Procida just offshore. Naples is one of the few European cities of the ancient world that was never completely extinguished. It's infamous as the world headquarters of the Camorra (Mafia), which controls all aspects of its commerce and keeps the streets fairly safe and lively.

WHILE OUR COMBINED MARITAL RECORDS HARDLY inspired confidence, Phyllis and I were more in love than ever and making plans to celebrate our thirtieth anniversary with a trip to Istanbul with our friends Jan Reid and Dorothy Browne. We were the envy of all who knew us. Bill Broyles remarked, "Could any two people have had so much fun, shared so much heartache, lived so fully, loved so much?" When he saw us together, Bill said, he thought of a scene in the movie *When Harry Met Sally*, after Meg Ryan simulates an orgasm in the middle of a crowded diner. As the last moan dies down, an old woman at the next table turns to the waitress and says, "I'll have what she's having." But it all came crashing down that spring.

The first hint of mortality came in early March when Phyllis was unexpectedly short of breath during a tour of a house with some realtor colleagues from her company, AvenueOne Properties. A day or two later, she complained of a sharp pain in her chest. I immediately thought it was a heart attack. I took her to the emergency room at Seton Medical Center, where a CAT scan revealed a mass in the left side of her chest, a tumor that was pressing against the veins of the heart and causing pain and shortness of breath.

Our primary care physician, Dr. Belle Hoverman, met us at the ER and after a quick look, told us bluntly: "It's cancer." I was stunned. Phyllis began to cry. She was a crier by nature—crying was her safety valve, her way of dealing with extremes of emotion. She sometimes burst into tears during sad movies or while reading gripping novels or when someone did something nice and unexpected—for example, when I brought her a bouquet of lavender tulips that time in Paris—or even, on occasion, over something as inelegant as my remembering to pick up my towel after showering. Doing nice things for people was second nature for Phyllis, but when someone did something for her, it touched that deep well where her tears were stored. But this was different. These were dark, smoldering tears that came in hot bolts. She was terrified. We both were. Nothing in our lives would ever be the same—that much I knew already.

The diagnosis was "a poorly differentiated tumor of unknown primary," which meant that the primary source was unknown and would likely remain unknown. It also meant, I found out later, that a cure was unlikely. Belle Hoverman's husband, Russell Hoverman, was an oncologist at Texas Oncology Cancer Center in Austin, and she recommended a doctor from his group, John Sandbach, to take charge of Phyllis's treatment. Although a mammogram the previous fall had revealed no problems, Sandbach thought he felt some lumps in her left breast and ordered a biopsy. There were several small tumors. Sandbach ordered chemotherapy. The first round took about three hours but was so easy that we decided to join some friends that night for a book signing and cocktail party for Stephen Harrigan. Phyllis was her usual self: beautiful, warm, sexy, funny, an alluring and spontaneous presence who lit up the room.

A nurse warned that after her second chemo treatment, scheduled in three weeks, her hair would begin falling out. Predictably, Phyllis took matters into her own hands and had her regular hairstylist give her an attractive buzz cut. Then she went shopping for a wig. Help poured in from all corners. Our next-door neighbor, Ken Shine, who was executive vice chancellor for health affairs for the University of Texas System, called the staff at M. D. Anderson, the university's famed cancer center in Houston, and arranged for us to get a second opinion. For the moment, we felt good about the future.

But the pain in her chest got progressively worse. Realizing that the tumor was particularly aggressive and spreading fast, Sandbach decided not to wait for a second round of chemo and started her immediately on a full-bore course of radiation treatments—five days a week for six weeks. The radiation beam was trained on the tumor in her chest and was much worse than the chemo: it blistered her throat and esophagus until she could barely swallow. I assigned myself the task of measuring out her medications, which included not only la-la land doses (Sandbach's term) of morphine and codeine but also pills for anxiety, nausea, depression, and constipation (constipation is a common side effect of large amounts of narcotics). A radiation specialist prescribed a local anesthetic solution called triple mix, which when gargled and swallowed numbed her throat and permitted her to eat small servings of soft food. Even so, eating or sipping water was almost more than she could bear, and dehydration was a serious concern. And no matter how many laxatives she took, constipation was a daily problem. As the drugs accumulated in her body, the pain began to subside, but the constipation only got worse.

Doatsy volunteered to drive Phyllis to Houston so that the doctors at M. D. Anderson could give us a second opinion, at which time Phyllis got it in her head that she no longer needed the pain meds. Once she stopped taking the pain meds, she reasoned, the constipation would take care of itself. Unfortunately, it wasn't that simple. By this time she had been on large doses of narcotics for nearly a month and, without knowing it, was addicted. The next day she went into severe narcotics withdrawal and had to be rushed to the emergency room. And then came the second opinion: a breast cancer specialist at M. D. Anderson determined that the primary cancer was not in the breast, as Sandbach had believed, but in her lungs. Whatever this portended, I knew it wasn't good.

Four days after returning from Houston, Phyllis was back at Seton, suffering from severe dehydration and malnutrition, the staff pumping her full of fluids and nutrients. They were simultaneously trying to adjust her meds so she would be both alert and pain free, something that was proving increasingly difficult. Phyllis pretended it was business as usual. She kept her cell phone on her bedside table and personally answered every call. Long after she was gone, Doatsy and I continued to recall a certain afternoon when, awakened from a deep, drug-induced sleep by the ring of her cell, she bolted upright, went into her husky businesswoman register, and began rattling off prices and square footage from memory. Another time I heard her promise to meet a client at a Town Lake townhouse that afternoon at three. She couldn't make it to the bathroom without help and here she was promising to meet a client; the narcotics were doing the talking. "Phyllis Ann!" I said in my best scolding voice. "Doing business is *not* a good idea just now." She looked hurt. Tears welled in her eyes. It hadn't occurred to her that something as trivial as cancer could get in the way of work.

Real estate had been a huge part of her life, and she was very good at it. "Realtor to the stars," one journalist had labeled her. Her clients had included the actors Dennis Hopper and Diane Ladd, as well as a number of well-known writers, artists, and musicians. With no apparent effort she became friends for life with nearly every person she worked with, or just met for a drink and a laugh. In short order she knew the names of their children, grandchildren, and pets and was ringing their doorbells with gifts of toys, children's clothes, or Milk Bones. People knew that she would be there for them.

Phyllis's mom, the unsinkable Lucy Mae McCallie, came from her home in Wetumka, Oklahoma, and the two of us camped at her bedside from early morning until late at night. Doatsy, Dorothy Browne, and Michelle Keahey, a young realtor whom Phyllis had taken under her wing and had come to love like a younger sister, became part of our core group of caregivers. Michelle showed up at Phyllis's room one day with an enormous stuffed dog, nearly as big as our male Airedale terrier, Willie. Phyllis called him Rufus and slept cuddled against him.

I sensed that the cancer was spreading. What appeared to be a small tumor started swelling beneath her naked scalp. The wigs she had selected were too hot and uncomfortable, so she switched to a series of scarves and headdresses. A mysterious pain afflicted one of her knees, and, on top of everything else, a racking cough developed into pneumonia. Phyllis had already lost twenty pounds. Her skin sagged and her muscle mass flattened; she was virtually skin and bone, a sad relic of the stunning and curvaceous high-kicker who had once twirled flaming batons for the Wetumka High band. I watched her sleep one afternoon, relieved on the one hand that she was resting peacefully but aware, too, that she was literally vanishing before my eyes.

It got worse. Toward the end of her twelve-day hospital stay, doctors ran a fiber-optic bronchoscope into her bronchial tubes and took photographs. The pictures made Doatsy and me cringe: in brilliant color, they showed splotches of blood covering one quadrant of her lungs and masses of ugly white cancer cells clumped along the base. We tried to keep the photos from her, but Phyllis insisted on looking for herself. The sight was too much: she had a full meltdown and had to be sedated.

On a routine visit to Belle Hoverman's office a day before she was supposed to go home, I learned the terrible truth: her cancer was terminal. *Terminal!* It was a word I hadn't dared use, but here it was, bigger than life. The cancer cells were spreading essentially unchecked, and the chemo and radiation were only making her sicker. The battle was hopeless. It was time to concede the inevitable: she would be dead in a few months. Belle mentioned hospice care and the importance of keeping her as comfortable as possible. I thanked her and walked out to the parking lot, shaking all over.

At the time I thought this was the worst day of my life, but even worse days were to follow. I drove around town for a long time that afternoon, thinking, praying, wondering why this had to be. Later,

I broke the news to Doatsy and Dorothy and a few close friends. In the meantime, the staff at Seton had given Phyllis a blood transfusion, and when I next visited her room, I could hardly believe the change. She was sitting up, laughing and jabbering on her cell phone. She blew me a kiss and gave me one of those smiles that always buckled my knees. I knew that I had to tell her the truth, but not just yet. She was due to be discharged the next day, a Saturday, and Doatsy and I decided to wait until at least Sunday night to tell her the news. Let her enjoy a day at home with her family and our beloved Airedales.

She didn't break down the night we told her, as I had feared. Tears filled her eyes, but she looked away to another part of our bedroom and said in a dry voice, "So it wasn't just my imagination." She knew. But in a strange way, hearing the terrible news from me somehow made it easier. Belle had told me that victims of terminal diseases often feel a sense of relief when they hear the truth. I felt relief, too. For five awful weeks I had struggled with enormous frustration, desperate to do something to help her but never knowing exactly what. Now I knew: Help her with the end. Care for her. Make her comfortable. Protect her from pain.

Doatsy went with us to Dr. Sandbach's office the next morning. We had already decided that additional chemo and radiation would only prolong her agony. He agreed. He was one of the founders of Hospice Austin, which offered a wide range of home medical and nursing care and emotional support for people who were dying. He offered to arrange everything. "How long?" Phyllis asked him. At the outside, he said softly, six months. On the way home, she told me, "I don't want to wait six months."

When you've lived life to the max, dying seems especially slow and clumsy and mean. For a time I kept praying for a miracle, knowing that God wasn't disposed to honor this particular miracle. Watching her suffer was the hardest thing I'd ever done, but it would have been infinitely harder without the caregivers at Hospice Austin. They stocked our bedroom with oxygen equipment, a hospital bed with adjustable rails, a wheelchair, and a walker. Nurses were on call twenty-four hours a day. Anything Phyllis asked for, they found. They made house calls weekly, or more often if Phyllis needed them, making sure that not only Phyllis but everyone in our family was okay. They checked regularly to see that we had a good supply of medications. My instinct was to overmedicate, to aggressively fight the pain, but our head nurse, Barbara Winchell, made sure I knew when and how to use each medication in our kit. The most important thing she did was listen to Phyllis and talk to her, letting all of us know that we were not alone. Knowing what to expect in the normal process of dying helps alleviate some of the fear; we came to understand that these final days were a celebration of what Phyllis's entire life had meant.

I had gotten a glimpse of the hospice experience when my mom died years earlier, but this was the first time I understood what hospices are really about. They're about helping families deal with death. Patients who have an incurable disease and less than six months to live are eligible for hospice home care, which is usually paid for by private insurance or Medicare. Ability to pay is not a consideration at Hospice Austin, one of only two nonprofit hospices in Central Texas. The hospice depends on donations from individuals, corporations, and foundations, as well as a group of about four hundred volunteers who augment the two hundred on the professional staff. Each patient is assigned a team of caregivers.

Over the years Phyllis's boundless generosity and infectious good humor had helped or supported or made life easier for countless people, and now they overwhelmed us with love and offers to help. Dozens of cards and letters arrived daily, and Phyllis read every one of them, some several times. She compiled meticulous lists of people she needed to write and thank. One letter in particular caught my eye. It was from a former Austin hospice nurse named Lorri Hatfield, who Phyllis had befriended some years earlier while Lorri and her husband were looking to buy a house. Lorri suffered from bipolar disorder, a manic-depressive netherworld where all things are dark and fearsome and where sufferers are forever alone. Naturally, Phyllis had adopted her on the spot. I didn't understand the significance of their friendship or its depth until I read Lorri's letter. It said in part: "When my life was hanging by a thread, my illness raging, you never once passed judgment or met me with anything but genuine compassion and respect. You listened to me through the darkness and the light . . . loved me when I could not love myself. . . . Thank you for every visit to the hospital, every cup of coffee, every letter and phone call . . . every smile and laugh that we shared, every hug. Thank you for believing in me . . ."

As Phyllis's disease took control, there were mostly bad days, but there were some good days, too. One of the best was a Saturday when Michelle and her colleagues from AvenueOne showed up at our house with a pickup load of plants, dirt, paving stones, and crushed granite. Phyllis had always taken pleasure in a semiannual ritual in which she redid the landscape of our backyard, but her illness now made the chore impossible. So Michelle and the others came to do it for her. Over the next twelve hours they transformed patches of weeds and hard-packed dirt into a magical open space of flowers, leafy things, casual boulders, stone pathways, and terraced beds—a job that would have cost thousands of dollars if professionals had done it. It was a gift of astonishing generosity and love.

When there was a medical crisis that couldn't be handled at home, Hospice Austin sent patients to Christopher House, a hospital-style facility in East Austin. More like a resort than a hospital, Christopher House was surrounded by shaded pathways and a lush garden with chirping birds, a gazebo, and a bubbling fountain. Fifteen large private rooms were spread along a hallway, each equipped with a TV, VCR, refrigerator, microwave, lounge chair, and couch that unfolded into a bed so that family members could catch a few hours' sleep. Each room had a rear entrance opening onto a patio and garden, which was especially designed so that families could bring their pets for a visit. "Pets are part of the family, part of the therapy," one nurse told us. I brought our dog Willie to the room, where he kept watch until the end.

Phyllis went to Christopher House twice but only came home one time. That's the usual routine, I gathered. Terminal patients frequently appear to be improving ten or twelve days before the end, what they call "the rally stage." Appetites suddenly return. They feel energized, alert, and alive. Then they crash and die. So it was that, after our first emergency at Christopher House, Phyllis began to rally. She was sitting up, laughing, joking, and telling me what she really wanted right then was a big, fat hamburger, with extra mustard.

Those final two weeks are still a blur. It was now early summer of 2006. Somewhere in there she fell and fractured her ankle in two places. The days were long and often difficult, but for one brief interlude she seemed to be her old self again; though much weaker and less graceful, my peerless, unconquerable angel had returned. She read, sewed, wrote dozens of thank-you notes, and reorganized her files, all the while talking on the phone or visiting with old friends. She found chores to keep me occupied and out of trouble. One or two times each night, she woke in pain. I'd give her some morphine or some triple mix to numb her throat and help her swallow. Then I would assist her to the toilet and get her back to sleep again. She woke up every morning at 6:30, as she had for years. Half-asleep, I'd help her to her wheelchair and take her to the living room, dragging fifty yards of oxygen hose behind me. Lucy Mae would have already started the coffee. I'd fetch her book and her sewing basket, and then Phyllis and her mom would spend the morning chatting and enjoying this last time together. In the evening Phyllis and I would sit on our patio, drinking in the explosion of colors and textures of our newly refurbished backyard, listening to jazz, sipping wine, laughing at silly things the dogs did. Phyllis asked me to bring her BB gun and began taking potshots at a marauding squirrel that had overturned a potted plant. However infirm, she was still a crack marksman.

The last chapter took me by surprise. We had spent a pleasant evening on the patio, when Phyllis began to complain about being very tired. I gave her some meds and put her to bed, but she woke with terrible pain in her left breast and side a few hours later. Obviously, the drugs were no longer effective. I woke Lucy Mae and together we tried to comfort her. By now Phyllis was crying and calling out, over and over, "Oh, God, please stop this pain. Please.

God. Stop it!" I telephoned the hospice, which sent out a nurse, who quickly assessed the situation and called for an ambulance to take her to Christopher House.

Lorraine Maslin, a nurse with a thick Scottish accent and a strong, almost saintly demeanor, met us in the reception area and took us to Room 11, which they called the Willie Nelson Suite in recognition of the time Willie played a benefit concert at Christopher House. "Look, darling," I said as nurses helped her into bed, "we're in the Willie Nelson Suite!" By now she was hurting too much to care, but I was somehow comforted by the familiar connection. The doctor on duty that night, Sarah Leggett, a palliative care physician, ordered a morphine drip and a battery of other painkillers and tranquilizers. Then she hugged me and said, "We're going to take care of her. We'll keep increasing the level of drugs until she's out of pain." Making her comfortable was by now my only concern. Death was no longer the enemy.

All the following day, friends and family arrived—Doatsy, Bud, Jan, Dorothy, Michelle, Lucy Mae, Phyllis's brother Jim McCallie and his wife, Melinda, who had just driven in from Oklahoma. By now Phyllis was deeply sedated. We took turns sitting beside her, holding her hand, talking to her, not really sure she could hear us. We talked among ourselves, laughing at things we'd done or said over the years. "Remember that time you guys were coming home from a late party," someone recalled, "and you had to pee and stopped on a country road. And Phyllis woke up and didn't realize you weren't in the car and drove off without you?" Hours crept by. We sent out for food. We played a Dave Brubeck album. I paced the pathway to the garden and back, dozens of times, and for a long time sat alone on a bench by the fountain, listening to the music of waking songbirds. Lorraine had told us that Christopher House was a happy place where sad things happened, and now I understood what she was telling me.

After the others had gone home, I moved the heavy lounge chair next to the bed so that Lucy Mae could sit close to her daughter and clutch her hand. I unfolded the couch into a bed for myself, but didn't sleep. In the dark, we could hear Phyllis's breathing, getting more and more labored. Around three that Sunday morning, the night nurse came to check on her, and we understand the end was here. We positioned ourselves on either side of the bed, each stroking one of her hands. Her eyes were half-open, but I knew she didn't see us. A small rattling sound escaped from her mouth, and an instant later I felt her spirit lift and float away. I kissed her and said, "Now you're at peace, my angel." Lucy Mae repeated, "Now she's at peace." In all those weeks that Phyllis was dying, that was the only time I saw Lucy Mae break down. She cried for a long time, me sitting with my arm around her. An hour later, just before the crew from the funeral home took her away, I went back to the Willie Nelson suite to say one last good-bye. I kissed her lightly on the lips and stood over the body, realizing that Phyllis wasn't there anymore. She died June 15, 2006.

At her memorial, Bud spoke these lines: "In my life there are a few very special people that I refuse to let death have. Instead of thinking of them as what we call dead, I prefer to believe they have moved to France to some beautiful small town way up in the Alps where the phones don't work very well and there's no Internet. So that way I'll be seeing them again somewhere down the road. Phyllis is one of those special people. She's probably wearing ski boots by Chanel this afternoon in her chalet in the mountains in France. So I am saying, 'Au revoir, Phyllis. I love you. I'll see you in Paris in the spring.'"

People asked me how I endured each day without her, how I could live in that house with all those terrible memories. Well, I told them, the house had been here for eighteen years and only recently had it been host to bad things. Phyllis was everywhere. She was there in her huge walk-in closet, amid the stylish in-your-face clothes, heavy on black, leopard and zebra print, every rack coordinated, every shoebox carefully labeled. She was puttering in her office, old photographs of me and her kids and our grandkids pasted to the wall, next to a priceless newspaper photo of Phyllis herself as a Wetumka high-kicker. Those carnival masks we bought in Venice? They still mock me from atop the bookshelf, make me think of her and smile. And the framed photograph of a 1909 Estonian street after an early-morning rain that we discovered in a gallery in Moscow. And that photo of Phyllis and Doatsy in front of Les Deux Magots in Paris. Was that just last November? God, both of them are so beautiful. Every drawer and closet and crawl space has her fresh prints. Every painting, plant, lamp, and piece of furniture is where she willed it, in its perfect place. When I turn out the lights at night, I hear her whisper. And when sadness threatens to swallow me, I feel her kiss.

After her death, I invited four or five of her best friends to come together inside her huge closet, and to divide her wardrobe among them as best they could. That was an unforgettable sight, those women, squealing and laughing and being part of Phyllis's life to the very end. From time to time, I still look across a crowded room and recognize a blouse or sweater that she made famous.

For a long time I felt as though I was coming apart. But then I would catch myself and realize that our dogs were staging a vicious fight at my feet, hoping to amuse me. The dogs knew. They gave me funny glances, as though I was hiding her somewhere in plain sight. I laughed and reassured them: "She's here. Can't you feel her?" And they begin to romp and frolic and tug on a section of knotted red cloth that she sewed for them. I didn't know if she was in Paris or up there organizing God's first rank of angels. I just wanted to be there with her.

As I had promised, I scattered her ashes in the Gulf of Mexico, between Galveston Island and the Bolivar Peninsula, near where we had scattered Mark's ashes a few years before. One of these days my remains will join them there.

OUR CORE GROUP OF COMPANIONS, WHICH MET every Friday at either Scholz Garten or at one of our homes, included most especially David and Ann Richards. David was one of Austin's most progressive attorneys and represented, along with his law partner Sam Houston Clinton, such liberal organizations as the American Civil Liberties Union of Texas and the *Texas Observer* (as well as those of us who fell into the clutches of the law because of our use of prohibited herbs). Ann was his live-wire wife and our designated social chair. Bud and I knew them back in Dallas, before we moved to Austin, and had long considered them our extended family as well as key members of Mad Dog.

During the warm weekends of spring and fall, we took overnight camping trips to the Hill Country, or a meadow near the San Gabriel River owned by the Richards family. Sometimes we traveled all the way to the Big Bend and camped on the banks of the Rio Grande, just across from Mexico. On such occasions David usually wore a huge black cowboy hat—I nicknamed him "The Sheriff"—and took command of the campsite. Ann entertained with stories about her childhood growing up in Waco and led sing-alongs and political discussions centered around our grand design to someday seize political power in Texas. Good luck with that, right?

Ann was more than a good friend. She was a major influence on my life, and allowed me to influence her in some ways. She was the one person I felt comfortable confiding in, the one who listened and assured me that however bad things seemed at the moment they would turn out okay. She was strong and vulnerable and smart and funny, and she was always there when I needed her.

One Friday night while we were holding forth under the trees in the beer garden, Ann started lecturing the men at our table, demanding to know when we intended to get off our butts and involve ourselves in politics. Later that same night, while several of us were sharing a joint on the footbridge over the creek behind the beer garden, I interrupted and asked Ann: "What about *you*? Why don't you quit weeding your garden and go run for office?" It was too dark to see the look in her eyes, though I sensed that the question hit home. A few weeks later, she surprised us all by announcing her candidacy for the office of Travis County commissioner. She was a natural and won the election without much trouble. She was one of the best commissioners we ever had. Her subsequent decision to run for the office of governor of Texas shouldn't have come as a surprise—but it did. Like all of her other friends, I constantly underestimated Ann Richards, sold short her talents, her stubborn resolve, her ability against all odds to get things done.

Except for an occasional puff of grass, Ann never used any illegal drugs. She did have a problem with alcohol (vodka, as I recall) and the combination of booze and diet pills made her reckless and a menace to herself and others. Finally, a collection of family and friends convinced Ann to get help at a chemical dependency facility in Minneapolis. By this time her marriage to David was pretty much on the rocks, headed for separation and finally divorce. Once she quit drinking, Ann threw herself into her career and helping friends deal with their own problems. During one of my low periods she cheered me up with a fan letter, writing that "maybe age is upon us, but I think back on some truly insane adventures with real fondness. We may have slowed down a bit or redirected our energies but you can't keep a mad dog down."

She and Bud began corresponding, and a casual friendship that dated back to our days in Dallas became much more. Bud had also given up hard drink, because of a liver problem, and they began "going steady" (as Bud described it to me), meeting regularly for movies, or dinner, or weekend trips. Phyllis and I watched with pleasure as their flirtation developed into a full-flowering love affair. They admitted that they were planning to "grow old together" and maybe open a retirement home for all of us—which they called "Curtains."

By this time Ann was such a star on the political stage that she was invited to give the keynote speech at the 1988 Democratic National Convention. Bud wrote to her, offering the Flying Punzars as an opening act for her address. We would rush out from the wings and perform our famous double-pyramid flip, the act that broke a table and three chairs at the University Club. Not that Ann needed any help. This was the famous speech in which she made great fun of George Bush, remarking, "He was born with a silver foot in his mouth." Ann demonstrated her toughness by weathering a vile political attack that painted her as a lesbian drug addict who hated God and was probably pals with the famous atheist Madalyn Murray O'Hair. Such libelous nonsense failed to slow her. Ann Richards was on a path to become the state's first woman governor in half a century.

Those were the best of times, but they ended too soon. Ann and Phyllis were both diagnosed with terminal cancer about the same time. They shared a determination to fight to the end, which they did, with grace and courage. Texas lost two of its best daughters the same year, from the same terrible disease.

THE LONELY WEEKS THAT FOLLOWED PHYLLIS'S DEATH were made less painful by the arrival of what I came to call the "Casserole Ladies"—in retrospect, their arrival was pretty much what a widower of a certain age might expect. They came several times a week, offering condolences and bearing covered dishes of eggplant, tuna, leeks, Gruyère, peppers, and cream. I ate a few spoonfuls of their concoctions and stored the leftovers in the refrigerator until they turned green and were ready for the disposal. Sometimes I invited one of the Casserole Ladies to join me in a glass of wine or for dinner. But mostly I stayed by myself, preferring the solitude to whatever might be out there for me. Then one evening in August, things changed. The doorbell rang and I received a vaguely familiar, slender, attractive woman whose name I couldn't immediately recall.

"I'm Tam Rogers," she said, smiling at my confusion. "I met you ten or twelve years ago when I was engaged to Bud Shrake."

Slowly, I began piecing it together. After her brief fling with Bud, I remembered, Tam married John Rogers, a retired British Army officer and graduate of the Royal Military Academy Sandhurst, Surrey. John died in 2002. Tam was something of a social butterfly, a fixture among Austin's music, dance, and gardening crowd and an accomplished cook who operated a successful party-planning business. At various times she had worked as development director for the historic Paramount Theatre, Ballet Austin, and KLRU public television, and she seemed to know every interesting person in town. She had two grown children and four grandchildren. I was overwhelmed by her warmth, intelligence, and boundless energy and began spending evenings at her house on Vista Lane, which was always spotless, perfectly organized, and filled with fresh flowers or fruit, some of which she had grown from a bottom-less supply of seed that she collected everywhere she went. Tam had a natural talent for life, a joie de vivre that washed over every-thing she touched. Eventually, she moved into my house on 18th Street, with her faithful dog and constant companion, Cyrus, who became fast friends with my Airedale, Willie.

I didn't think I'd ever fall again, but Tam was so easy to love that I was a goner in no time. After a few months, I knew that I wanted her as a permanent part of my life. We were married in April 2008, in a ceremony that Tam personally choreographed, in the gazebo and garden of the home of her great friend, Meta Butler Hunt, in West Lake Hills. As our two groups of friends came together, we discovered that they were pretty much the same crowd we had been hanging with all along. Some of the names were new, but faces and lifestyles were part of our beings. Ours was merely an-other happy encounter in a long series of happy encounters, but it was happening now: we were glad to be alive and to have found each other. It was marriage No. 4 for both of us, and I composed an invitation around the slogan "Who Says There Is No Act Four?"

HAPPINESS AND CONTENTMENT HAD ONCE MORE settled over my life, but I was jarred back to the harsh reality of death in September 2008, when I received a mass e-mail from Bud, informing us that he had stage four lung cancer. It had spread into his abdomen and things did not look good. In the seven years since his kidney surgery, he had lived a fairly disciplined life, taking walks with his dog every day, working out at the gym two or three times a week, eating properly. He no longer smoked cigarettes and drank very little. He continued his lifelong habit of daily work: he had published three books since his kidney surgery. His most re-cent lab report indicated he was in good health. But a routine chest X-ray, almost an afterthought by the medics, showed a lump in his chest. Dr. Jack Whitaker, an old friend and an oncologist, exam-ined the X-rays and gave Bud the hard news: it was inoperable and undoubtedly malignant. "I do not regard this as a Sudden Death sentence like being stood against the wall at dawn," Bud wrote in the e-mail that he sent to good friends. "I am looking at this as an adventure." He was working on two projects at the time, a play about Jack Ruby and a new novel that he called *Monster on the Mountain.* He quipped that he intended to finish both and use any remaining time to "redesign the elephant." In the meantime, he asked people to respect his solitude: if they really wanted to help, people could send him a carrot cake and a tub of Amy's ice cream. In a postscript, he advised everyone to get a chest X-ray.

His first chemo treatment looked positive, but a second treatment blasted his white blood cells and made it nearly impossible for him to fight infection. A few days later, his longtime assistant Jody Gent found him semiconscious in his bedroom and called an ambulance. Friends rushed to his hospital room, knowing the end was near, but there was nothing anyone could do. I felt an urgent need to be there with him, to say good-bye or whatever there was time to say, but I had been in bed for several days with pneumonia and listened to Tam's advice to stay put for at least one more day. But there wasn't another day. He died just after midnight. Ben was with his father at the end. He kissed his cheek and removed a necklace that Bud had worn for years. On a leather strap, Bud had hung a cluster of medals: a St. Christopher, a St. Jude, a silver cross, and a silver arrowhead that Bill Wittliff had given him. Ben put it around his own neck, where it has remained.

FOR SEVERAL WEEKS AFTER BUD DIED, I FOUND IT impossible to write or even read with any concentration. Tam sensed that we needed to get away for a few weeks. We both loved to travel, and she arranged a trip to Rome, Amsterdam, and, finally, Athens, which was one of her favorite cities. She was eager for me to see Athens, her special place, and we threw ourselves into the local scene. I loved the city from my first glance, which, as it happened, was a fantastic view of the Parthenon from our hotel balcony. I literally cried out in astonishment, which greatly pleased Tam. Just moments later we watched a street riot in the square below. Athens was alive with possibilities. We drank the wine, walked the streets, visited the many ruins, made love to the sounds of honking horns and people singing and yelling. Tam was a great travel companion, always ready to try new adventures.

Back home in Austin, Tam began to build a life for us, first by rearranging my house to suit her own tastes, which, to my surprise, pleased and comforted me. She didn't so much change the furnishings as make them feel new, fresh, and alive.

With the dogs yapping at our feet, we took long walks almost every morning, usually on the hike-and-bike trail at Town Lake. Tam hired five or six Mexican laborers, bought a wide variety of plants and flowering shrubs, and personally landscaped our front yard, making it a showpiece for the Judges Hill neighborhood.

It says in the Book of Ecclesiastes that life is short and veined with futility, but it also instructs us to celebrate it while we can. Tam had a well-honed sense of humor and the good breeding to take what life offered, to either make it better or, failing that, adapt to its possibilities. "There's an old Jewish joke about a local restaurant," she told me once. "They say the food is awful—and in such small portions."

We enjoyed laughing at ourselves, at our lifelong habit of taking ourselves too seriously, and at our failures to welcome compromise when compromise was clearly the only option. "But we're only human," I reminded her, and we had a good laugh. We both had old, deep scars, marks of our brushes with mortality. I was in my seventies and constantly worried about my bad heart; ten years my junior, Tam was a survivor of breast cancer, which had nearly killed her in 1995 and had necessitated a double mastectomy. I had remembered her as a strikingly shapely and full-breasted beauty, but time had eroded her perfect breasts, leaving just a maze of red scar tissue. I won't pretend it didn't matter, but after a time it didn't. She was who she was, and I loved her dearly. We felt lucky to have made it this far.

Tam sensed that the cancer would eventually return. I dismissed her fear as silly superstition, but in the fall of 2012, in the sixth year of our marriage, she began experiencing sharp pains in her chest and side, much as Phyllis had. The cancer reappeared as a mass of cells in her lungs and liver. We both knew that this time it was terminal.

Even before the cancer returned, it was a particularly difficult time for us. We had quarreled and temporarily separated. I can't remember what the quarrel was about, only that it was something ridiculous, something of no importance until it unexpectedly got out of hand. As I recall, she cursed me, at which I point I shoved her. She fell backward and hit her head against a chair back, then against the floor. She was crying as I stormed out. I was back home after a short cooling-off period, but by then she had gone to the home of her daughter, Melissa. I apologized and it might have ended there except that her children, Melissa and Matt, were actively encouraging her to leave me, to move into her own apartment and start a new life. They helped her find and furnish an apartment on Lake Austin Boulevard.

At first, Tam found that living alone made her life seem secure and comfortable. We saw each other almost every day and she eventually forgave me, but the separation was a strain that damaged the bond we had created. After a few weeks, she telephoned and told me, "I'm miserable. I don't like being alone." I confessed feeling the same. "Why don't you come home?" I told her. "Let's try again." She agreed and moved back with me to the house on 18th Street, but after one night together changed her mind: living with me, she explained, would be to betray her children. "But I love you," I protested. "I love you, too," she replied, "but this is how it has to be." So we struck an agreement: we would stay married and carry on, but keep the affair secret from her children. All of our friends welcomed our decision to stay together—i.e., maintain our marriage and love, but live apart—but we were determined to hide the truth from her children.

I should have known it wouldn't work. As the cancer spread, she was hospitalized and finally admitted to Christopher House. When I arrived for a visit, she sent everyone else out of the room, pulled me close, and whispered her instructions: "Please don't try to visit again. My children don't understand." Very reluctantly, I agreed to keep my distance. A nurse at Christopher House gave me updates on her condition, which continued to worsen, and once when no one was watching I snuck into her room and kissed her on the forehead, without waking her. But I respected her wishes and stayed away. On February 12, 2013, I got word that she had died. While her family and friends gathered for a memorial service at Mayfield Park and Preserve in Austin, I went to my gym and worked out alone.

I continue to think of Tam. We never got closure. At least I didn't. I haven't seen or talked to her family, which I greatly regret but feel obligated to leave in peace. All I can do is write this book and confess that, all things considered, I've been a very lucky guy.

I COULDN'T HAVE PLANNED OR EVEN DREAMED THE way it all fell into place—the jobs, the books, the successes. While composing an acceptance speech on the occasion of winning a lifetime achievement award from the Texas Institute of Letters in April 2012, I found myself reflecting on the improbability of all that has happened. The Lon Tinkle Award is the most prestigious honor bestowed by the TIL: previous winners included Tom Lea, John Graves, Larry McMurtry, Horton Foote, Cormac McCarthy, Larry L. King, Bud Shrake, Bill Wittliff—writers of that high caliber. Just reading that list of illustrious names brought me once again eyeball to eyeball with the recurring fear that sooner or later I was sure to be exposed as a fraud. I tried to second-guess the mood of the audience, wondering if anybody out there had even heard of me until now, but all that materialized was a ghostly voice whispering, "I thought that old fart died years ago!" To my everlasting surprise, I find that I'm still here.

Over many years I've discovered that the process of writing is agonizingly slow and painful, that for every high there are dozens of soul-searing lows. The writing life is a series of crushing failures, or it can seem to be. Writers learn the hard way that success always sits on a deep pile of failure. I have a need to warn would-be writers how it is when you hit the wall—and you *will* hit the wall! Sooner or later it happens to all of us. The discipline of writing demands that every one of us experience the unspeakable panic when the words simply refuse to dance. Worse still, as writers get older and ostensibly wiser, their storehouses of facts—commonly called memory—become frosted with cobwebs. Writers must accept and understand this simple truth: only a crazy person would try to write for a living. And yet, and yet . . . against all logic we go on tinkering with words, moving them about, listening to their cadence, standing them on their heads, turning them inside out, waiting, hoping, praying . . . that the magic will return, as it always has. So far, so *bueno*. So I ended up telling the gathering of writers that night at the Texas Institute of Letters banquet something that most of them already knew: "The trick, if there is one, is this: Don't lose your nerve. Don't let the bastards know that you're not in control."

I intend to savor retirement with a daily cocktail or two, some good reading material, and the company of friends and loved ones. I especially hope to spend a lot of time with my newest girlfriend, Jane Hall, a non-practicing lawyer who, with her daughter, runs an adoption agency and who keeps me happy with her wit and charm. And I'll most likely accept an occasional writing assignment, just to remind folks to watch out. Wave if you see me on your street. I'm probably just out baying at the moon.

NAME INDEX

The abbreviation PS indicates that an individual is pictured in the unnumbered photo section.

Schramm, Marty, 82

Schramm, Tex, 48–49, 50, 59, 82

Schwartz, A. R. "Babe," 75–76

Schwartz, Marvin, 93–97, 100–102, 106–108, 214

Scott (Candy Barr's paramour), 130–131, 136

Scruggs, Earl, 118

Sedlmayr, Doatsy. *See* Shrake, Doatsy Sedlmayr

Shafter, Texas, 90

Shankar, Ravi, 118

Sharlot, Mike, 88, 212

Sharlot, Sue, 88, 212

Shaw, Izora, 5–7

Shaw, Susan, 216, 217

Sherrod, Blackie: at *Dallas Times Herald*, 25, 35, 37, 38, 63–64, PS; as Flying Punzar member, 82, PS; at *Fort Worth Press*, 26, 28; at Midwinter, 32

Shine, Ken, 232

Shrake, Ben, 29, 246

Shrake, Bud. *See* Shrake, Edwin "Bud"

Shrake, Creagan, 29

Shrake, Doatsy Sedlmayr: in Acapulco, 81; in Austin, 85–86; and author's third wedding, 119; in Durango, 92, 103; and Phyllis, 232–235, 239, 241; and Jim "Lopez" Smithum, 199; at *Sports Illustrated*, 68; in Taos, 153; in Zihuatanejo, 79

Shrake, Edwin "Bud," PS; and Armadillo World Headquarters, 224; in Austin, 68; and cancer, 245–246; in Dallas, 32–33; at *Dallas Morning News*, 41; at *Dallas Times Herald*, 35–36, 38–39, as Flying Punzar member, 82–83; at *Fort Worth Press*, 16,

22, 25, 26–28, PS; and Kennedy assassination, 52–53; and Lon Tinkle Award, 249; at Lopez's deathbed, 199; and Mad Dog, Inc., 88–91; and Don Meredith, 102; and Willie Nelson, 221; in New York City (mid-1960s), 55–57; as novelist, 31, 45–46, 84; and Oswald assassination, 55; and Phyllis, 239, 240; and "psychic" surgery, 181, 186; and religion, 30; and Ann and David Richards, 242; and Ann Richards, 243, PS; and Joyce Rogers, 29; and Tam Rogers, 244; as roommate, 19, 42–44, 50, 51; as screenwriter, 86–87, 92, 100–101, 103, 105, 106, 226–227; in Taos, 153; at TCU, 15; as Town Drunk in *Dime Box*, 94–95; as wedding officiator, 119; in Zihuatanejo, 79

Shrake, Joyce Rogers, 28–29, 30, 31, 32–33

Sickles, Mike, 137, PS

Sickles, Phyllis (author's third wife), PS; after death of, 244; and author's cardiac arrest, 192–195; and Candy Barr, 137; and cancer, 230–239; funeral of, 240; in late 1980s to 2000, 199–202; and Mark's death, 216; mementos of, 240–241; and Willie Nelson, 118–119; and Ann Richards, 243, PS; in Taos, 153; traveling with, 202, 203–211, 227–230; and Teeta Walker, 198; wedding of, 223–224

Sinatra, Frank, 132

Slammer, Crew, 25–26, 36

Slusher, Doc, 125, 135

Slusher, Juanita Dale, 125. *See also* Barr, Candy